2.75

VICTORIAN COMFORT

The Railway Station, painted by William Powell Frith in 1863. This shows the interior of Paddington; but to avoid excessive reduction the right-hand part of the picture has been omitted. *Reproduced from the original painting in the possession of Holloway College.*

VICTORIAN COMFORT

A Social History of Design from
1830—1900

BY

JOHN GLOAG

DAVID & CHARLES
NEWTON ABBOT

0 7153 6329 8

First published by A. and C. Black Ltd 1961

This new impression published by David & Charles 1973

Printed in Great Britain by
Redwood Press Limited Trowbridge Wiltshire
for David & Charles (Holdings) Limited
South Devon House Newton Abbot Devon

Dedicated to
AUDREY AND JACK COHEN

CONTENTS

ILLUSTRATIONS IN THE TEXT

LIST OF PLATES

The Railway Station, by W. P. Frith   *Frontispiece*

The Plates

REFERENCES

References to authorities, sources of quotations and so forth, are numbered consecutively, 1 to 168, and are set out under their appropriate chapters at the end of the book, beginning on page 235. Sources of illustrations and the names of artists are included in the captions, so are the references to any quotations relating to drawings or engravings. Robert Peacock Gloag, who is mentioned on page 190, is not related to the author.

THE PHILOSOPHY OF COMFORT

UNLIKE many people who write about the Victorian period, I happen to have lived in it, and was brought up in the suburban civilisation that reached its resplendent maturity in the 1870's and '80's, though when I was born, in 1896, it was past its prime. The period did not die with the Queen in 1901: it rumbled on with its copious vulgarities and expansive comfort, its formal clothes and precise manners, until 1914: thereafter, so many changes and shocks were packed into four years, that when the Great War was over, everything pre-war seemed dubious or out of date, certainly everything with a Victorian air: ideas, morality, clothes, furniture, architecture—even some of the eminent Victorians looked slightly bogus after Lytton Strachey had attended to them. The Albert Memorial was mocked, though not so cruelly as it had been by some of its contemporary critics like John T. Emmett; the achievements of the Gothic Revival and Ruskin's inspired prejudices were exposed to ridicule; and Victorian faith in the sanctity of science and the inevitability of progress was openly doubted. At the turn of the century such views would have been regarded as almost indecent heresies, to be rejected by ordinary people as disruptive threats to comfort, for the Victorians loved comfort without shame, as the Georgians before them had loved pleasure without apology. In time, the love of comfort debilitated the critical faculties, and the decline of taste in the 1820's and '30's coincided with the rise of an insensitive plutocracy whose leaders unconsciously cultivated a philosophy of comfort, which was adopted by the middle classes, expounded in its material aspects by Dickens—who liked writing about cosy rooms and cosy inns and food and drink and good fellowship—and embraced by everybody who enjoyed modest, easy, or affluent circumstances. Like Mr. Pickwick when Mr. Pott entertained him by reading extracts from the *Eatanswill Gazette*, they closed their eyes, "as if with excess of pleasure," and, revelling in comfort, lost their sense of sight so far as the form and colour of their cities and homes were concerned. The decline of educated taste and appreciation of good design began in the 1820's, sinking lower and lower until the Great Exhibition of 1851, when Victorian comfort and Victorian taste were stabilised respectively at high and low levels, which remained, with minor exceptions and variations, generally acceptable to all classes for the rest of the nineteenth century.

Owners of homes, large or small, would have liked Mr. Pickwick's place of retirement at Dulwich, which was, as he observed, "fitted up with every attention to substantial comfort, perhaps to a little elegance besides. . . ." They would have approved of the glowing inventory of its attractions. "Everything was so beautiful! The lawn in front, the garden behind, the miniature conservatory, the dining-room, the drawing-room the bed-rooms, the smoking-room, and above all the study, with its pictures and easy-chairs, and odd cabinets, and queer tables, and books out of number, with a large cheerful window opening upon a pleasant lawn and commanding a pretty landscape, just dotted here and there with little houses almost hidden by the trees; and then the curtains, and the carpets, and the chairs, and the sofas! Everything was so beautiful, so compact, so neat, and in such exquisite taste, said everybody, that there really was no deciding what to admire most."

The key words in these quotations from the last chapter of *Pickwick* are: "every attention to substantial comfort. . . ." They became the theme song of the Victorian age.

This study of Victorian comfort is *not* impartial; few books worth reading or writing are; and those lovers of the period who have been misled by nostalgia into condoning ugliness and bad design will certainly conclude that it was *not* worth writing; but it attempts to illustrate some aspects of social history through the design and character of many things that ministered to the comfort, physical and moral, of the Victorians. A companion volume is in preparation on Victorian taste, as it was manifested by architecture and industrial design, and influenced by men like Pugin, Ruskin, Morris, and the great engineers. These two books, together with their predecessor, *Georgian Grace*,* which covered the period of 170 years between 1660 and 1830, are intended to reincarnate some of the habits, pleasures, and beliefs of our forefathers, by scrutinising the things they used, admired, or ignored.

NOTE TO SECOND EDITION

Some minor corrections and revisions have been made, but otherwise the text, illustrations and captions are the same as the original edition. The companion volume, *Victorian Taste*, was published in 1962 and reprinted by David and Charles in 1972. Since the book was written the subject of Chapter IX, "Memorials and Monuments", has been dealt with in far greater detail and with scholarly care by Mr. James Stevens Curl in his admirable study: *The Victorian Celebration of Death*.**

* Published in 1956. London: A. & C. Black. New York: The Macmillan Company.
** Published in 1972 by David and Charles.

CHAPTER I

THE VICTORIAN SCENE

W HEN Queen Victoria began her reign, London still looked like a Georgian city; so did other towns in the United Kingdom and the Eastern States of North America. Indeed, New York retained much of its eighteenth-century likeness as late as the 1880's, for its skyline was still dominated by church spires, as yet unquenched by the shapes and shadows of tall buildings. (See plates 1 and 2.) Long before the new skyscraper construction had been introduced in New York, the Georgian serenity of London had been disturbed by the intrusion of various revived styles, applied to façades to create Gothic, Byzantine or even Saracenic effects. The idea of a street as a series of horizontal units was destroyed by aggressive individualism. Ruskin had urged people not to "think of unities of effect," and they cheerfully complied. Pre-Victorian London streets were unified in character more by the proportions and disposition of the windows in their façades than by continuous horizontal features; but generally there was an orderly effect, arising from the use of classic moulded detail for cornices, string courses, door and window architraves and the fascias and glazing bars of shop fronts. In 1838–39 a detailed record was published of the elevations of buildings on several of the main thoroughfares; it was known as *Tallis's London Street Views*, and six sections from it, showing the Strand and Fleet Street, are reproduced on pages 2 to 7. Some of the buildings illustrated remained until the '90's and even later; but they were mostly shouldered aside by bigger but not better structures, which denied sunlight to streets that had not been widened to correspond with the higher building line, so many hitherto sunny shopping areas were filled with shadows.

In no previous age had so much building been done. Between 1831 and 1901, the population of England and Wales rose from 13,896,797 to 32,527,843: in a comparable period, 1830 to 1900, that of the United States increased from 10,240,232 to 33,533,630. This huge expansion stimulated the spread of industrial slums and suburbs in England. There was more room in America; a good many towns in the United States were still in a sketchy stage of development, while established cities like Philadelphia and Pittsburg and Boston had plenty of space for spreading out, and after the '70's American cities began to grow vertically, beginning with Chicago and New York.

I

Here, and on the five pages that follow, both sides of the Strand are shown, as they appeared in *Tallis's London Street Views*, published in 1838–39. The tradesmen whose names are printed presumably paid the publishers: those who objected to advertising were omitted.

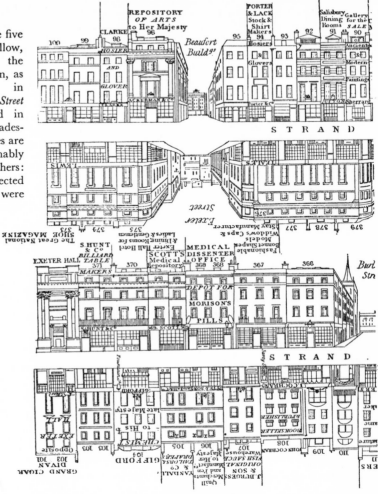

The contrast between the growth of American towns and the enlargement of English cities during the nineteenth century was not entirely due to the limited area of an island like Britain, for the Victorians spent their wealth of land recklessly, and allowed their cities, hampered by mediaeval street plans and seldom capable of growth within those ancient limits, to over-flow into the countryside. New suburbs everywhere met and joined old villages, engulfed them, reached out still farther and surrounded market towns, so that London seemed destined to stretch from Reading to Southend and from St. Albans to Brighton. Since the Middle Ages, the capital had grown beyond its walls, pleasantly enough, along the Thames; but by the end of the eighteenth century

Continuation of buildings in the Strand. Although exact horizontal unity was not achieved, and the lines of cornices and fascias were often broken, there was an orderliness about the grouping of the buildings, partly derived from the proportions of the sash windows, and the size of panes and arrangement of glazing bars in shop windows.

(See opposite page.)

the riverside scene was smudged here and there by industry. Until then the Surrey bank of the Thames, from Vauxhall to Richmond, remained serenely rural. Upstream from Vauxhall was the small village of Nine Elms; then Battersea Fields, and the mansion of Lord Bolingbroke, who died there in 1751. The house, bought for Earl Spencer in 1763, was largely demolished in 1778, and its site occupied by a mill and a malt distillery. The market gardens of Battersea were famous for cabbages and asparagus. Between those gardens and Putney the Wandle entered the Thames at Wandsworth, a residential locality favoured by the gentry, that was changed during the first half of the

The Strand side of
the Adelphi develop-
ment, showing the
entrance to Adam
Street. The continua-
tion eastwards to
Fleet Street is on the
opposite page.

nineteenth century into a flourishing industrial area. There were some old,
discreetly limited industries at Wandsworth, and Huguenot refugees late in
the seventeenth century had set up cloth works there. That popular guide
book to London, *The Ambulator*, which had reached its eleventh edition by
1811, recorded the extensive growth of industrial Wandsworth, mentioning
many "considerable manufactures," including iron furnaces and foundries for
casting shot, shells and cannon. There were also calico-printing works, linseed
oil and white lead mills, and a large vinegar works. The first public railway,
the Surrey Iron Railway completed in 1803, ran from Croydon to Wandsworth,
where goods were unloaded. Such development was unquestioned. Before and
during the Victorian period it was accepted as evidence of the progressive

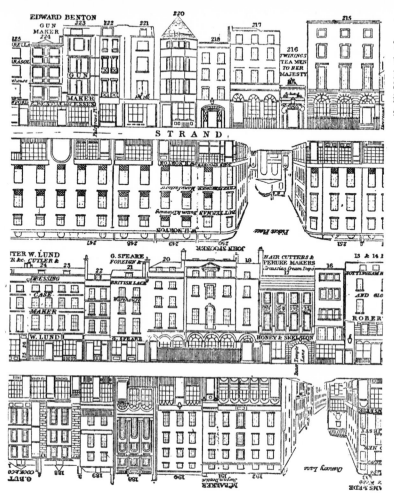

The illustration at the upper part of this page shows the Strand: Fleet Street is below. (See pages 2 to 4, also 6 and 7.)

tendencies of the age; and John Fisher Murray, whose *Picturesque Tour of the River Thames in its Western Course* was published in 1859, ignored the disruptive growth altogether, contentedly quoting Pope's reference to the Wandle, "the blue, transparent Vandalis," mentioning the pursuit of manufactures "with spirit and success" by the Huguenot refugees, and concluding his remarks on Wandsworth by stating that the first Presbyterian congregation in England was established there. Industrial development was gradual: mills and foundries, factories, breweries and distilleries, wharves and warehouses, advanced along the river banks, fouling the air, polluting the water, and replacing parks and gardens, fields and orchards.

The north and south sides of the Strand above: Fleet Street below, with Wren's Gateway to the Middle Temple.

Nobody apparently observed the creeping devastation, and few people criticised it.[1]

In 1851 a forerunner of the air photograph was published, called *A Balloon View of London, as seen from the North*: it was a large folding sheet mounted on linen, showing every street in the City and West End, and extending westwards to Kensington and southwards to Lambeth and Battersea. (A companion view, taken from the South, was also published.) Eight sections of this detailed view are reproduced on pages 8 to 15, and on the latter page the group of factory buildings on the south bank, east of Battersea Bridge, shows that Battersea, still rural and residential, was going the way of Wandsworth, a

The eastern end of the Strand at Temple Bar is shown below, with Fleet Street, and the church of St. Dunstan's in the West, above. Reproduced, like the illustrations on the five previous pages, from *Tallis's London Street Views,* 1838–39.

mile or so upstream. Writing in 1902, H. G. Wells said: "Great Towns before this century presented rounded contours and grew as a puff-ball swells; the modern Great City looks like something that has burst an intolerable envelope and splashed."[2]

Most of the Victorian cities expanded with restless disorder: they thrust out jagged points deep into rural areas, their direction often determined by that of a railway line. Apart from the enormous increase of comfort in travelling, described in Chapters V and VI, the chief economic and social contribution of railways was the expansion of existing and the development of new industrial areas, the linking of manufacturing centres with ports, and

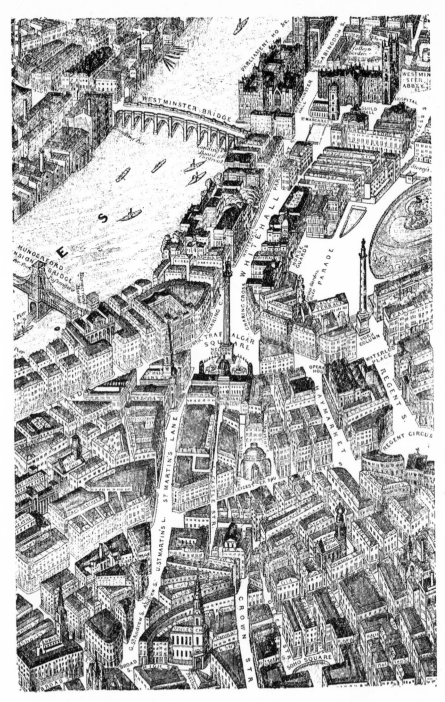

I. Westminster to Kensington in 1851. On this page, and the three that follow, the streets
and buildings are shown, from St. Martin's Lane westwards to Kensington Gardens.
Reproduced from *A Balloon View of London, as seen from the North*, published on May 1st, 1851,
by Banks & Co., 4 Little Queen Street, Holborn.

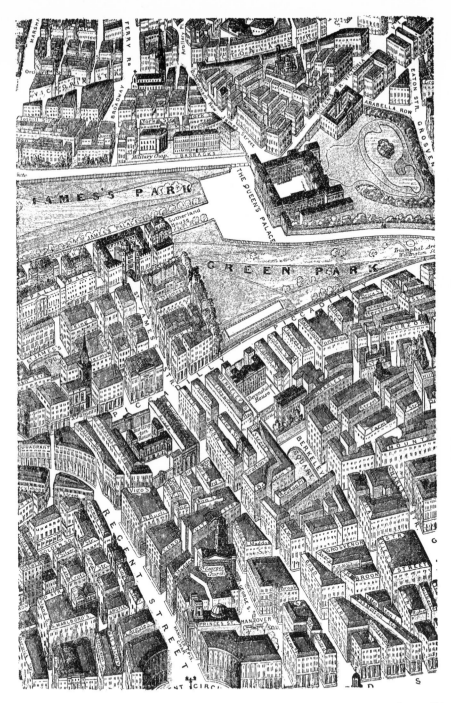

II. The Georgian lay-out of Mayfair persisted: great mansions, like Lansdowne House and Devonshire House still stood in their own grounds: Regent Street was comparatively new, though its colonnades had been removed in 1848. (See opposite page for continuation eastwards, and pages 10 and 11 for continuation westwards. From *A Balloon View of London*.)

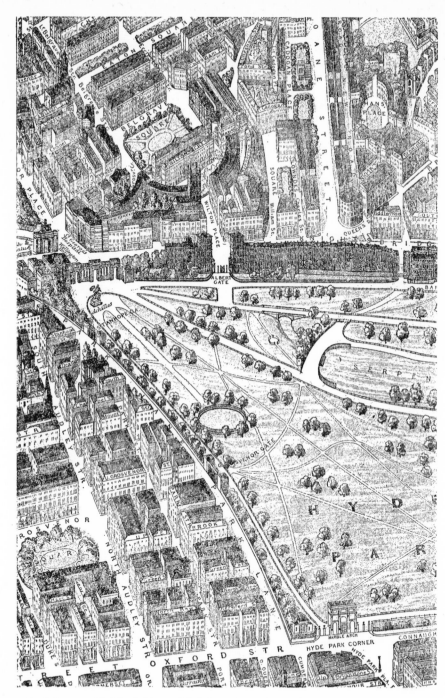

III. From Park Lane to Knightsbridge, with Belgravia to the south, which had been planned and developed by Thomas Cubitt in the 1820's, and "Hans Town," consisting of Sloane Street, Cadogan Place, and Hans Place, which had been planned in the late eighteenth century by Henry Holland, who named his scheme after Sir Hans Sloane. (See pages 14 and 15 and opposite. From *A Balloon View of London.*)

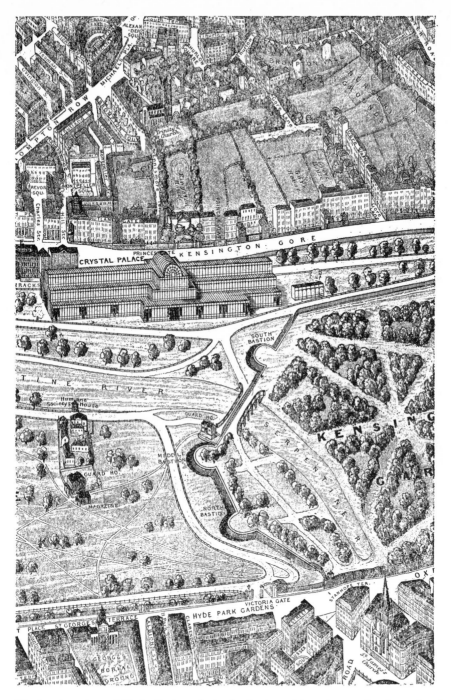

IV. Continuation of Hyde Park and the beginning of Kensington Gardens, showing the Crystal Palace on its original site, the gardens and open spaces behind Kensington Gore and the still rural area of Brompton Vale. (See page opposite, and pages 8 and 9. The southward extension, from Lambeth to Battersea, appears on the next four pages. From *A Balloon View of London*.)

V. The Thames from Lambeth to Battersea, 1851. This is the southward continuation of the view of Westminster on page 8, with Lambeth Palace in the foreground, and the London and South Western Railway line, which had been extended from its original terminus at Nine Elms, running almost parallel with the river. Vauxhall Gardens still existed, but with an impaired reputation, and they were closed in 1859. Beyond Kennington Common and south-east of the Clapham Road there was open country, "ripe for development," as the speculative builders would say at a later date. A century earlier, Vauxhall Gardens were adjacent to open country on three sides. Albert Embankment, between Westminster Bridge and Vauxhall, was begun in 1863 and completed in 1866: in this view, wharves and warehouses line the riverside on the south side. (See opposite and pages 14 and 15 for continuation westwards. From *A Balloon View of London*.)

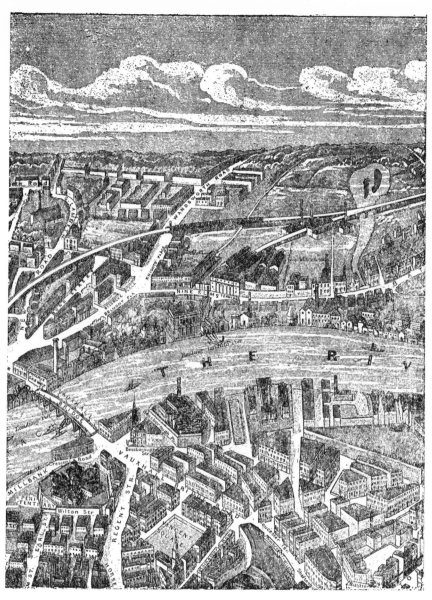

VI. Vauxhall Bridge was opened to traffic in 1816, and was the first iron bridge built across the Thames. It was originally known as Regent's Bridge, and was demolished at the end of the century, being replaced by a new bridge which was opened in 1906. Pimlico, the district in the foreground, was almost uninhabited before the nineteenth century, though the name in the form of Pimlico dates back to 1626. On the south bank, the original terminus of the London and South Western Railway is at Nine Elms. (See page 164.) Victoria Station, on the north side, was not built until 1862, as a terminus for the London, Chatham and Dover Railway. (See opposite page for continuation eastwards, and page 9 for continuation northwards. From *A Balloon View of London*.)

13

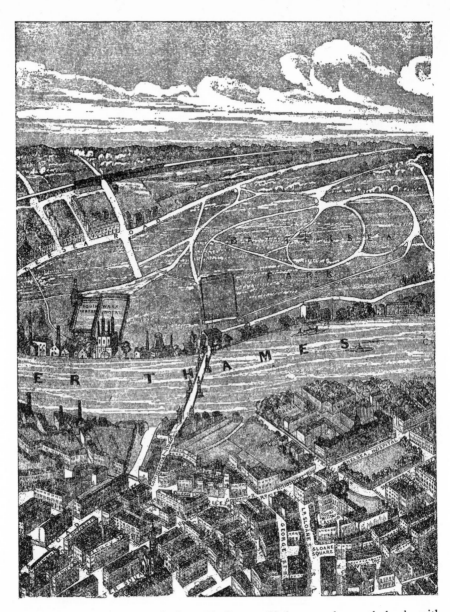

VII. The view continued westwards from Pimlico to Chelsea on the north bank, with Battersea Park and fields on the south side. Although Chelsea Bridge is shown, work had only begun on it in September, 1851, and it was not opened to the public until March, 1858. Chelsea Embankment, extending from Chelsea Bridge to Battersea Bridge, on the north side, was built between 1871 and 1874. Pimlico and Chelsea were largely residential, and the open space of Battersea Park, indicated in the view, checked industrial development on that part of the south bank which lay between Chelsea and Albert bridges. The Park was opened to the public in 1858. (See opposite page for continuation westwards, and page 10 for continuation northwards. From *A Balloon View of London*.)

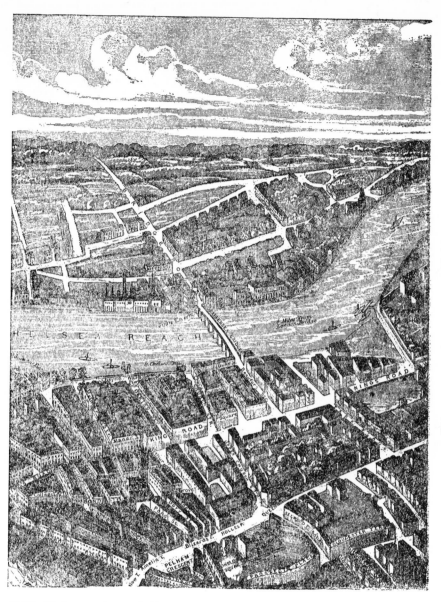

VIII. Chelsea on the north, Battersea on the south of the Thames. The first bridge, a wooden structure built in 1771–72, was still standing. Battersea, despite the industrial buildings east of the bridge, was still largely rural, with a few great houses, a Georgian church, with fields stretching to Battersea Rise and Lavender Hill. In all the views that have occupied the previous pages, a Georgian spaciousness has survived: gardens and squares, crescents and parks have kept green places and trees within the built-up areas, and the prospect of open country is never far away. This was London midway in the nineteenth century: during the next fifty years it became unrecognisable, its old graces were obliterated, and the Gothic Revival, as interpreted by speculative builders, everywhere gave substance to the phrase, "cheap and nasty." (See pages 8 to 13 and opposite. From *A Balloon View of London*, 1851.)

LAST FEW DAYS OF ST. PAUL'S.

Now then, make haste, make haste, and pay a visit to Ludgate Hill, and behold, for nearly the last time you will have the opportunity, the vast and celebrated Cathedral of St. Paul, erected by that famous architect SIR CHRISTOPHER WREN, in the reigns of their Majesties the last of the Stuarts. Be in time, be in time. In a very short time this remarkable edifice will become invisible, owing to the great improvements which the march of intellect and the progress of commerce, providentially force upon this Great Metropolis. Therefore, be in time before the view is shut out for ever and ever by the highly ornamented tank in preparation by the Railway Company. The architecture will well repay inspection, the *façade*, henceforth to be seen no more, is regarded as one of the finest things in the world, and the majestic appearance of the west front defies at once competition and description. There is no charge, so long as you keep out of the building, and in short this is an opportunity which can never occur again in the history of London. Be in time, be in time.

RAILWAYS INVADE THE CITY OF LONDON

When the London, Chatham and Dover Railway proposed to extend its lines from Blackfriars to Holborn, the idea of a railway bridge across the bottom of Ludgate Hill was distasteful to the City Corporation, who delayed approval of the Company's plans. *Punch* feared the worst, and on August 8th, 1863, published this depressing prediction of the horrors to come. The reality was far more agreeable than anybody anticipated; the view of St. Paul's was not wholly obliterated; and the bridge itself was an ornate iron structure, painted, gilded, and embellished with the arms of the City and the Railway Company. Reproduced by permission of *Punch*. (See page 19.)

the extension of residential suburbs all over the country. Suburban villas, standing in their own grounds, and semi-detached houses and terraces, spread along the railways, their back gardens bordering the tracks; a form of ribbon development that was unnoticed by the public, though anything more unsuitable than a railway running beyond the fence of a back garden could hardly be imagined; but by the time main and suburban lines were established, the nation had become deaf as well as blind. Mechanical noises were accepted as part of life and progress. "The country made the railways," said George Stephenson, "and in return the railways made the country." One of those shrewd half-truths that Victorians readily believed. The gains were so richly apparent; the disadvantages, of which old-fashioned people peevishly complained, so relatively unimportant. Cities had always been noisy, declared the champions of the new scientific industrial age; another half-truth, for previously they had been loud with human noise, the chatter and bustle of crowds, street cries and songs, the voices of tradesmen selling their wares in shops and markets, the jingle and rumble of horse-drawn traffic, and, before the Reformation, cities all over Christian Europe had been melodious with the sound of bells, day and night. Railway trains performed day and night too, whistling, puffing, and speeding along the permanent way with a rattle and a roar. Only when railways entered a city through tunnels was their noise subdued; but often they ran on high-level viaducts, and sometimes altered the character of a famous or almost sacred view. This happened when the London, Chatham and Dover Railway extended its lines from Blackfriars to Holborn in 1865, and built a bridge across the foot of Ludgate Hill. There were many protests when the proposal was made; *Punch* published a depressing prediction of the horrors in store two years before the bridge was erected; but the structure was far more agreeable than most people had anticipated—gay, ornamental, painted and gilded, and embellished with the arms of the City and the Railway Company. (See opposite and page 19.)

In England, Scotland and Wales, the railways built in the '40's and '50's passed through areas that had not been developed, either residentially or industrially, and although controls were enforced to protect the public from the dangers of the permanent way, which was fenced and guarded against people and cattle, no controls existed over the use of adjacent land. The railways acquired land for their stations and marshalling yards, and manufacturers and speculative builders then did exactly what they liked in the vicinity of the line, without hindrance from civic or local authorities, anywhere. Only the existence of many wealthy landed proprietors preserved for a few generations the rural character of large tracts of country.

While railways in Britain stimulated the expansion of existing towns, in the United States the railroad often created new towns. English towns and cities had grown up gradually at road junctions, around or near some fortified or sacred edifice. America started with a limited inheritance from the past.

The Colonists even abandoned their first permanent settlement, at Jamestown, Virginia, when they moved the government of that province to Williamsburg in 1699. Four years after the thirteen Colonies became the United States, the capital of Virginia was transferred to Richmond, and Williamsburg declined in importance, fell into partial decay during the nineteenth century, and has, since 1927, been restored and reconstructed with such skill, that today its urbane buildings must closely resemble those adorning the Georgian city which was chartered in 1722.

Many American towns owe their origin to the establishment of some industry. Grand Rapids, in Kent County, Michigan, for example, was founded on the site of a large Indian village. A Baptist Mission, established there in 1824, was supplemented two years later by a trading post, and a saw-mill was built in 1833. From such small beginnings, Grand Rapids grew into the largest furniture manufacturing centre in the United States. A waterway or a railway nearly always brought the American town into existence. The latter was the new and often the only road; it was invariably called the rail-*road*, and was the backbone of many a village, determining the line of its main street, while the establishment of a railroad depot often started the expansion of a village, so that it grew into a town and ultimately became a large city. "On either side of the track, houses would spring up, a saloon, an hotel, a store, and within a generation there would be streets branching off at right angles to main street, while down main street itself trains would be steaming through pedestrian and horse traffic, the bells of their locomotives tolling to keep the track clear. As the town grew, building lots were acquired by speculators or far-sighted citizens and quickly developed. This growth was temporarily checked in the '60's by the Civil War, which ruined the old-established towns of the South, and afterwards accelerated the expansion of cities in the Middle and Far West."[3]

Great cities like Chicago grew from the most inconspicuous beginnings. In 1804 the place was established as a post by the Federal Government, and called Fort Dearborn. A few years after, it was surrounded by a settlement of fourteen houses: in 1830 the population was below 100, by 1840 it rose to 4,479, and in 1870 it was 306,000. This expansion was due largely to the fact that Chicago became the biggest railroad junction in the country. In October, 1871, the city was devastated by a disastrous fire. Two-thirds of the buildings were of wood, and the whole built-up area was practically wiped out. Thousands of people were made homeless by the disaster, a relief fund of $4,996,782 was raised, nearly $1,000,000 being contributed by foreign countries, of which Britain's contribution was $500,000. Chicago was rebuilt rapidly, unfortunately at a time when American architectural taste was even more lusciously ambiguous than Victorian.

"Until nearly the end of the nineteenth century, American architectural fashions followed those of England, particularly in New York. The flood of

The Railway Bridge across Ludgate Hill was built in 1865, two years after *Punch*'s protest. In this drawing, made from a photograph taken in the 1890's, the traffic has been omitted. The signals mounted on the bridge interrupted the view of St. Paul's far more than the actual bridge, which was a gay, ornamental structure. Like many other new things, it was deplored by old-fashioned people and ignored by the majority, but it appealed to that uncharacteristic Victorian, Samuel Butler, who wrote about it in the introductory chapter of *Alps and Sanctuaries* (1881) and said: "I know of nothing in any foreign city equal to the view down Fleet Street, walking along the north side from the corner of Fetter Lane. It is often said that this has been spoiled by the London, Chatham and Dover Railway bridge over Ludgate Hill; I think, however, the effect is more imposing now than it was before the bridge was built. Time has already softened it; it does not obtrude itself; it adds greatly to the sense of size, and makes us doubly aware of the movement of life, the colossal circulation to which London owes so much of its impressiveness." *Drawn by Marcelle Barton.* At some subsequent date, certainly later than the '90's, advertisements appeared on the sides of the bridge, for in 1903 Frank Dicksee, R.A., said: "although I do not think the view damaged by the bridge, yet I do object to the advertisements, there as elsewhere in London." (Article on what artists thought was "The Finest View in London." *The Strand Magazine*, Volume XXVI, No. 153, September, 1903, page 325.)

Head office of the United Telephone Company, Coleman Street, London. A web of overhead telephone wires was a feature of late Victorian London. (See view of the Strand on opposite page.) From *The Graphic*, September 1st, 1883, page 232.

The Strand looking east in the early '90's. Reproduced from the cover of the first issue
of *The Strand Magazine* by permission of George Newnes Limited.

bad taste in design that had inundated Europe and England in the middle years of the century also reached America, though the regional variations of bad taste in American building were less distinctive than the regional variations that had given to colonial Georgian architecture and to American design generally such agreeable character during the eighteenth century. New York continued to grow at a speed that far outstripped contemporary English cities; and it had this considerable advantage over most English cities—it was confined to an island, and a street plan had been made and followed. Horizontal development was therefore under some kind of control. That control was orderly rather than imaginative, but at least it saved the city on Manhattan Island from becoming an untidy cat's-cradle of streets. Some open spaces were preserved and, as in London, a few were adorned with inferior statuary, for despite their independence of spirit, the American nation cherished many English ceremonial habits and ideas, and, throughout the nineteenth century, displayed a comparable incapacity for artistic perception."[4]

As the city invaded the countryside in England, so did industrialism invade the city. Factory chimneys competed with church spires. In the '80's and '90's, telegraph and telephone wires were slung over streets from poles on the roofs of buildings. The original cover of *The Strand Magazine*, started by George Newnes in January, 1891, gives a view of the Strand looking east, with the title of the magazine hanging from cables that crossed the street. There were hundreds of such cables, and they were a once familiar feature, criss-crossing the London sky. (See pages 20 and 21.) But although London and other cities changed architecturally, and a few street-widening schemes led to the abolition of some overcrowded areas, the greatest change, and one that affected the whole concept of civilisation during the period, was the growth of suburbs which housed the respectable middle classes, with their delicately adjusted social levels, and their sincere support for the rigid edifice of snobbery, erected and maintained by their betters. United by a sense of superiority to "the lower orders," segregated from the congestion of the slums, they were proud of being householders. They had respectability, comfort, and a considerable, though unevenly distributed, share of the country's fluctuating prosperity.

Typical examples of terrace and semi-detached houses, dating from the '60's, '70's and '80's are shown opposite and on pages 24 and 25. Houses like that reflected the comfortable, solid worth of their owners and tenants; but suburban development, which was in the hands of speculative builders, did not always exhibit such comparative restraint. Ruskin had an unfortunate effect upon the uneducated, and fresh generations of speculative builders were always ready enough to adopt his advice about pointed window-heads and Gothic porches. The same mixture of ideas that disrupted city streets was used in the suburbs. Roofs of purple slate rose steeply, their lines complicated by gables, turrets, dormer windows and mass-produced cast-iron cresting on

Terrace houses on St. John's Hill, Battersea, *circa* 1860–70, commodious and designed with some respect for the street, unlike the semi-detached, chaotic individualism exhibited by Vardens Road on page 24. At the end of the terrace St. Paul's Church stands, a Chapel of Ease to St. Mary's, Battersea, designed by H. E. Coe, and completed and consecrated in 1868. Built at a cost of about £6,300, it is a stone structure with a tall spire.

Thirty years earlier the classical tradition still had affinities with the Georgian period. The terrace shown to the left was built about 1835. These small houses of red brick, with moulded plaster door and window architraves, and slate roofs, stood on the Lower Richmond Road at the north side of Mortlake Green, and were demolished in 1960. *Both drawings by David Owen.*

Typical suburban development, with semi-detached houses, still retaining traces of a classical tradition, and showing the influence of copy-books like Loudon's *Encyclopaedia*. This is the west side of Vardens Road, Battersea, which was developed between 1860 and 1868, when Battersea was changing from a rural area to a residential suburb. Originally called Garden Road, the name Vardens was first used in 1860 and may have been connected with Thomas Varden, a wealthy resident of Battersea who died in 1809 and was buried in St. Mary's cemetery. He was evidently a man of some property, though whether he owned the site of Vardens Road is conjectural. The spire of St. Paul's Church on St. John's Hill (see page 23) appears above the roof tops. The public house on the left, built in 1863, was originally called the Freemason's Hotel, and was renamed The Roundhouse in 1962.

the ridges. Ornamental tiling was popular; horizontal bands of brickwork in various colours gave disquieting emphasis to the imperfect proportions of the houses they were supposed to beautify; while Victorian indifference to texture was everywhere apparent, and most noticeably so in the use of cheap bricks, hard red, yellow, or pale grey, the latter changing to a repellent hue after a few years of exposure to the sooty air. Usually they were set in dark mortar,

The east side of Vardens Road, which was developed with two terraces of houses during the 1880's. Until then the semi-detached villas on the west side had open ground between them and the railway with a view across a strip of Wandsworth Common. The later development of Vardens Road was the speculative builder's interpretation of Ruskin's ideas of ornament, suitably modified, with a touch of Gothic carving on keystones and the capping of door and window piers. The terrace at the south end of the road had three storeys over a sub-basement, the ground floor above street level, and the front door approached by a flight of steps. The bays ascended from the sub-basement to the string course that marked the first-floor level. The terrace that occupied rather more than half of the northern end of the road had three stories and no basement, with bay windows ascending through two floors, with panels of ornamental brickwork set below the first-floor window sills. This was probably built a few years after the terrace at the south end, which was more ambitious in scale, and more in keeping with the earlier development on the west side. (See opposite page.) *Drawn by A. S. Cook.*

The architect was regarded as a purveyor of styles, and this illustration, from *The Englishman's House from a Cottage to a Mansion*, supports that commercial quality of the architectural profession. The author, C. J. Richardson, himself an architect, highly approved of it and praised the responsiveness of the public. "However much the occupations of our countrymen may partake of the commercial character," he wrote, "the mental qualities requisite to such pursuits have not been so displayed as to exclude a taste for art. Where, for example, can be found superior specimens of art-choice than exist in their mansions, villas, or cottage-ornées. . . ." (Introduction, pages 6 and 7.)

Described as "a double suburban villa," this mixture, in "the domestic style of the reign of Henry VII," was "intended for erection on a leasehold estate at a little distance out of London." It was Design No. 17, in *The Englishman's House from a Cottage to a Mansion*, by C. J. Richardson, published in 1870. (See page 30.)

which increased the dinginess of wall surfaces, and for the clumsy bay windows, sand-coloured Bath stone was used to frame the double hung sashes, which were no longer cut up into small panes by glazing bars, but consisted of two large expanses of sheet or plate glass, for the manufacture of glass had been progressively improved during the nineteenth century. Materials were abundant and cheap; builders were no longer dependent on local supplies; in 1850 the tax on bricks was repealed, and the window tax went too, the year after. North, south, east and west of London, mile after mile of streets were lined with these drab houses, each with cast-iron railings and front gates of identical pattern, bay windows and porches with fussy Gothic trimmings, and drain-pipes carrying water from gutters and bathrooms disfiguring the façade, for the external evidence of plumbing was never made part of the design.

Above the roof line, half a dozen chimney pots of various patterns, like dirty
fingers making some abortive gesture of defiance, poured smoke into the air,
many of them crowned by metal cowls to correct the defects of the flues they
served. Each house had a small garden in front, a mere excuse for a privet
hedge, with a larger piece of ground at the back with a neat lawn and a few
flower beds and borders. A wire basket lined with moss and filled with soil in
which ferns and geraniums grew, often hung in the porch.

In London, the population of the city continued to fall, dropping from
123,563 in 1841 to 25,932 sixty years later, while that of Greater London rose
in the same period from 2,235,344 to 6,581,402. These figures showed the
scale of the new suburban civilisation that had been established, and what
happened to London and the home counties happened elsewhere. Every city
began to devour the surrounding country; woods and fields were replaced by
row after row of the ugliest homes people have ever lived in; their inhabitants
cut off from rural life, but forming no part of the life of a city. A slender link
with the soil was preserved by amateur gardeners, for all vehicles were horse
drawn, and those innumerable little back gardens were manured with dung,
shovelled up into buckets by street arabs and sold from door to door. (Every
city and suburb smelt of the stables.)

Although a high proportion of suburban householders worked in city offices,
they were remote from civic life, and devoid of even a casual sense of civic
responsibility. Villages that were submerged by the new suburbs sometimes
retained a semblance of local patriotism, kept alive, perhaps, by the vicar or
rector of the parish church, and by one or two innkeepers. But suburban life,
with its exclusive privacy, the desire of householders "to keep themselves to
themselves," and the raw newness of the recently developed areas they
inhabited, minimised their interest in local affairs. Few people aspired to enter
local government except tradesmen with an axe to grind or reformers with a
theory to inflict, and householders tended to vote for anybody who promised
to keep down the rates.

Commercial development in the new suburbs often changed main streets
from residential to shopping areas. Landlords who had built terraces of houses
on an eligible site could be tempted by the higher rents offered to convert
them to shops. This was done by gutting the ground floor and building the
shop over the former front garden, so that it projected from the original line
of the elevation. Year after year this process of conversion took place, and the
thoroughfares of London suburbs like Battersea and Wandsworth exchanged
their spacious, semi-rural air for the bustle of thriving shopping centres. In
Battersea, Lavender Hill—a name of magical beauty—was transformed in
this way during the '90's; and all along the continuous road that runs from
Vauxhall to Richmond, of which Lavender Hill is a short part, shops began
to eat their way into houses, and this happened to all the big roads radiating
from London, which, on their way out, became the main street of some old

IN PROSPECTIVE.

Architect (to Rich Manufacturer, whose rival, Smith, having built himself a Country House, determines to have one also).—"WELL, MR. NES, WHAT PROSPECT WOULD YOU LIKE YOUR NEW HOUSE TO HAVE?"
Mr. Jones.—"PROSPECT! PROSPECT! WHAT SORT OF PROSPECT HAS MR. SMITH'S GOT?"
Architect.—"OH! HIS HAS A SOUTH PROSPECT."   *Jones.*—"AH! WELL, GIVE ME TWO OF THEM."

This example of Victorian patronage for architecture is reproduced from *Fun*, May 27th, 1885.

village that had grown into a large suburb. The result was an irregular patchwork of shops and dwellings, which finally destroyed all traces of rural character.

Some of the more prosperous members of the middle class began to settle in the countryside, hoping to buy their way into county society, and occasionally succeeding. After breaking through that snob barrier, they were patronised or treated with amused tolerance by people whose great-grandfathers were in many instances tradesmen or brewers who had broken through comparable barriers into Georgian society, becoming, after a generation or two, identified with the nobility and gentry. The Victorian countryside was thickly and richly and decoratively wooded: Georgian landlords had planted for posterity, and their avenues and groves, and those clumps of trees dotted about by Capability Brown and sometimes called "Brown's Buttons," gave to the face of the land the likeness of some nobleman's park, interpersed with cornfields and the gardens of great houses. The old regional traditions of building were in decay; the houses of the well-to-do were afflicted by all the tawdry elaboration of town houses; and the new middle-class householder who settled in the country, or in one of the more spacious and expensive suburbs, was not satisfied by the simple and convenient plan of the modest Georgian house, with its few large and well-proportioned rooms; instead his love of ostentation insisted on a house with lots of rooms, and his ignorant demands often embarrassed the architect who had to satisfy them. (A drawing from *Fun* in 1885, reproduced on page 29, ridicules that form of purse-proud patronage.) The demand for houses with far too many rooms, and the ever-rising cost of land, compelled builders to crowd these suburban mansions into the same space as that occupied by older and better houses, thus reducing the size and spoiling the proportions of individual rooms and increasing the use of basements, sub-basements and attics. An example of this absurd ostentation and the compression of space that went with it, is illustrated on page 27, where "a double suburban villa" is reproduced from C. J. Richardson's book, *The Englishman's House from a Cottage to a Mansion.* In such suburban Gothic mansions the rooms were not only mean in size, but unrelated to each other: odd spaces and awkward corners appeared, and if they occurred on a landing or in a passage, they were fitted with a door and turned into inconvenient cupboards. Larger houses were so ill-planned that any amount of space was wasted by dark, rambling passages; while the service quarters in the basement were even darker. In design, they were full of disconnected after-thoughts, and the enormous amount of housework they demanded could have been met only by that acceptable Victorian labour-saving device—a large staff of underpaid servants. Even the small and equally inconvenient suburban homes had their maid-of-all-work, and reproduced on a much reduced scale and in cheaper materials the furnishing and equipment of wealthier worshippers of comfort and respectability. No previous civilisation had ever honoured such uninspiring gods; but no previous civilisation had ever had so many citizens who combined high moral standards with deplorable taste.

CHAPTER II

HOME

EW documents disclose more about the social aspects of architecture
and furnishing than an auctioneer's sale catalogue, particularly when
the subject is a large, well-appointed country house. For example, the
scale and character of Victorian country life is revealed by a catalogue
issued in 1889 for the sale of the Hurst House estate in Lancashire after the
death of the owner.(5) Many Victorian country houses were remodelled or
greatly expanded Georgian mansions, the original house often forming the
core of the new one, and Hurst House, "situate in the townships of Huyton
and Knowsley, seven miles from Liverpool," incorporated a much older, and
far smaller building, which had occupied the site and is shown on Greenwood's
map of 1818. The house described in the catalogue was built at some time
during the 1880's, for it was stated that "The Mansion, Homestead, Lodges,
Stabling, Glass-houses and other Offices, are all of a most substantial character,
the late owner having recently, altogether regardless of cost, greatly enlarged
and improved the entire establishment, making it as it now stands one of the
most complete English country residences. The whole of the Towers, North
Wing, Stabling, Coach-houses, Homestead and Outer Offices, are entirely
new."

These enlargements and improvements resulted in a big, rambling house,
vaguely classic in character, of which parts still survive, including the clock
tower, which is a notable landmark in the district. (See pages 32 and 33.)
It is now the Club House of the Huyton and Prescot Golf Club. In the catalogue
it is referred to as a "Noble Mansion, of imposing dimensions, approached
from the principal Lodge through a beautiful Serpentine Drive, standing in
the midst of a finely timbered picturesque Park, on a most commanding and
healthy elevation, giving most extensive views of the surrounding country."
At that date, the house stood in grounds that were about 100 acres in extent,

The clock tower, rising from
the inner court of Hurst House,
Huyton, Lancashire. *Drawn by
David Owen.*

with open country beyond the borders of the estate. From the various towers, the Mersey estuary could be seen, with the hills of Wirral and the Welsh mountains beyond, and fine views of Liverpool Bay, Knowsley and Croxteth Parks. A condensed description of the accommodation, without the laudatory adjectives, is as follows: On the ground floor a glass enclosed verandah, fitted with hot-water pipes, formed a sheltered walk and conservatory along the principal frontage. The main entrance on the West Front, approached through a vestibule or outer hall, 20 feet × 14 feet, led to the Grand Centre Hall, 21 feet × 17 feet 6 inches, from which two inner halls, each about 19 feet × 9 feet, and a glass roofed corridor, about 40 feet × 10 feet, were approached. These led to a suite of reception rooms, including a drawing-room, about 28 feet × 21 feet, and dining-room of similar dimensions. To the left of the main hall was the morning-room, 22 feet × 20 feet, with ante-room attached, and an oak sitting-room, 17 feet × 17 feet. From the corridor there was access to a second suite of apartments: a library, 29 feet × 20 feet, with a recess about 11 feet × 11 feet; billiard room, about 23 feet × 19 feet; magistrates' room, about 35 feet × 15 feet, with strong room adjoining, 15 feet × 11 feet, fitted with a Milner's door. There were also cloak-rooms, lavatories, and water closets.

On the same floor there were domestic offices, including the servants' hall, 29 feet × 15 feet; butler's pantry with strong plate safe; suites of kitchens, with vaulted roofs, fitted with dressers, cupboards, and open and closed cooking ranges; meat larders and pantries. Entered from the inner courtyard, detached from, but convenient to the other offices, were a large dairy and yard, kitchens, creamery, washing-room, fitted with coppers; ironing-room, with stove and two fitted drying-rooms attached.

On the upper floors, approached by a grand double staircase, from the main hall and secondary staircases there were ten principal bedrooms, mostly with a south and west aspect, with several dressing-rooms and ante-rooms. There was a "Noble Banqueting Hall," 55 feet × 22 feet, with a raised music plat-form, and lift communicating with kitchens; also an ante-room. In the main tower were several sitting and other rooms. Approached by independent stair-cases were the suites of servants' and housekeepers' rooms, night and day nurseries, baths, water-closets, dress and linen rooms, furnace and cistern rooms. The basement included three wine and two beer cellars, bottle, and four store cellars. "The Hot Water Heating Apparatus is on the best and most improved principle, and the Pipes are laid on for GAS throughout the new portion of the premises."

Such vast houses were lavishly furnished, luxurious and comfortable, and the standards set by their owners were copied, with diminished grandeur, by the middle classes in the suburbs. The small house in an undistinguished street would have a drawing-room and a dining-room on the ground floor, separated by folding doors, or perhaps a curtain or bamboo screen, each with its own fire-place, furnished for comfort and with an eye to what the owners considered to be fashionable taste. No matter to what grade of the middle class they belonged, they were usually without any standards that would enable them to appraise the aesthetic merit of their furniture, and were quite unaware of this deficiency. Charles L. Eastlake, in his *Hints on Household Taste*, said that: "The faculty of distinguishing good from bad design in the familiar objects of domestic life is a faculty which most educated people—and women especially —conceive they possess. How it has been acquired, few would be able to explain. The general impression seems to be that it is the peculiar inheritance of gentle blood, and independent of all training; that while a young lady is devoting at school, or under a governess, so many hours a day to music, so

many to languages, and so many to general science, she is all this time unconsciously forming that sense of the beautiful, which we call taste—that this
sense, once developed, will enable her, unassisted by special study or experience,
not only to appreciate the charms of nature in every aspect, but to form a
correct estimate of the merits of art-manufacture. That this impression has
gained ground so far as to amount to positive conviction, may be inferred
from the fact that there is no single point on which well-bred women are more
jealous of disparagement than on this. . . . It is, however, a lamentable fact
that this very quality is commonly deficient, not only among the generally
ignorant, but also among the most educated classes in this country."[6]

In 1833, John Claudius Loudon (1783–1843) had given a pre-view of
Victorian taste in his *Encyclopaedia of Cottage, Farm and Villa Architecture and
Furniture*, a huge compilation of over 1,150 pages, crowded with designs for
buildings of every description in every style, which became an indispensable
copy-book for speculative builders for over fifty years. The enervating effect
of the philosophy of comfort was disclosed by his illustrations, and the book
might well have been called *The Decline and Fall of Design*. In America, a few
years later, Andrew Jackson Downing (1815–52), whose training and career
resembled Loudon's, published two copy-books: *Cottage Residences* (1844), and
The Architecture of Country Houses (1850). Both men were landscape gardeners
and horticulturalists; both dabbled in architecture, writing and talking about
architectural styles with inexhaustible confidence, and they also designed a
few buildings. To Loudon belongs the credit of inventing the technique of
curvilinear glazing, which was used in the great conservatory at Chatsworth,
and ultimately for the Crystal Palace. Loudon and Downing specialised in
giving advice, and in their respective countries they exercised, through their
published works, an influence on taste that was far greater than their discrimination or abilities as designers. In dispensing advice they were not alone.

All classes were subjected to advice about the arrangement and furnishing
of their homes, in books, magazines and newspapers. One of the best-selling
works that had a far-reaching and detrimental effect upon popular taste was
The Young Ladies' Treasure Book, described in the sub-title as "A Complete
Cyclopaedia of Practical Instruction and Direction for all indoor and outdoor
occupations and amusements suitable to young ladies." In the Introduction
it was stated that "Those elegant Household Arts, for instance, by which a
home can be tastefully decorated, and made charming to the eye of taste, will
be here found elucidated; with plain practical instructions for all who wish
to cultivate their artistic tendencies for the embellishment of their homes, or
the gratification of their friends, or perhaps with the prudent design of turning
their skill to practical account in the future."[7] It was tacitly implied in such
works that the homes of their readers would be about the same size as Hurst
House, with a family income to match.

Whether a house was large or small, the size and treatment of windows

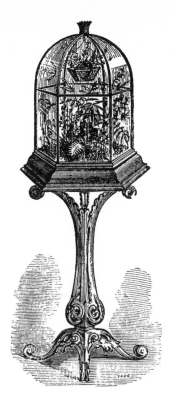

Leaves under glass, illustrated in *The Young Ladies'*
Treasure Book. The domed glass case, under which ferns
and other plants were grown indoors was used, as shown,
in conjunction with a small table supported by a pillar
resting on claws or a solid base, and was known as a
Wardian case. It was a popular item in Victorian
furnishing, introduced in the mid-nineteenth century,
and named after Nathaniel Bagshaw Ward (1791–1868),
who, in 1829, discovered accidentally the principle
which led to this method of growing and transporting
plants in glass cases.

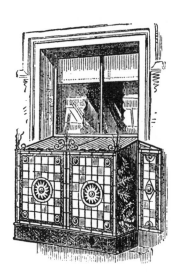

Right: A window arranged for flowers
or small plants. From *Sylvia's Home
Journal,* 1879.

affected the character of its rooms, and the Victorians liked big windows and
lots of them. After the abolition of the window tax in 1851, and as a result
of technical improvements in the manufacture of plate and sheet glass, large
uninterrupted expanses of glass were available. The double hung sash window,
as mentioned in the previous chapter, no longer consisted of twelve or more
separate panes, but of two large panes only. Bay windows were popular, and
their use increased the amount of daylight admitted to rooms, which would
have made interiors intolerably bright unless some method of diffusing daylight
had been adopted, so for this purpose, and to secure privacy, white lace curtains
were used. Every window was thus protected from prying eyes, and excessive
glare counteracted. Some windows were deliberately obscured with miniature
conservatories. (See above.) "Whenever it is possible, climbing plants should

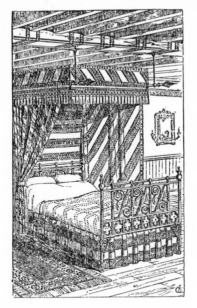

Iron bedstead with canopy, designed by Charles L. East-lake. "The design of metal bedsteads is generally very poor," he wrote, "especially where anything in the shape of decoration is introduced. For instance, it is usual to conceal the joint which occurs where the tie-rods intersect each other with a small boss. A circular rosette would be obviously the most appropriate feature to introduce at this joint, whether in wrought- or cast-metal. But, instead of this, the iron-bedstead maker (*elegantiae gratiâ*, as the gram-marians say) insists on inventing a little lumpy bit of ornament, which, possibly intended to represent a cluster of leaves, more closely resembles a friendly association of garden slugs, and this abomination is repeated not only a dozen times in one bedstead, but in some thousands of the same pattern." He recommended the suspension of the canopy from the ceiling, and shows this device in his design. From *Hints on Household Taste* (second edition, 1869), Chapter VIII, pages 187–88, and plate XXXII.

Below: A brass bedstead, with a canopy or half-tester, reproduced on a smaller scale from *Cassell's Household Guide*, Volume I, page 244 (1875).

be trained up the house and round the windows," said *The Young Ladies' Treasure Book*, adding that, "More than any invention of carving, friezes, stucco, paint, or other outward adorning, does nature's greenery decorate the house."[8] The same work also recommended a form of window decoration called "Vitremanie," which was applied to glass "to exclude unpleasing views seen through staircase or other windows." This could be prepared in the home, the designs drawn by any diligent young lady, and transferred to the glass surface by a fairly simple technical process.[9] Sets of window screens were often used, "of straw-colour and Bohemian-red glass, which cast a well-tempered and mellow shade throughout the room."[10]

The furnishing of the Victorian home was inclined to be haphazard; the chief unifying influence was the suite, but there were many supplementary articles, introduced as some new and novel contribution to comfort, or to satisfy a passing fashion. Increasing attention to comfort and cleanliness had a marked effect upon the standards of bedroom furnishing. In the early nineteenth century the warming pan had been used for airing sheets, but the stone hot-water bottle replaced it. Every bedroom had an ample wash-stand, with a marble top, splash-back and toilet set, basin, ewer, soap dish, tooth-

The suite was the unifying influence in furnishing: in the bedroom it included dressing table, wash-hand stand, wardrobe and chairs. The bed, a large, ornate affair in brass and iron, was often the disruptive element in the scheme. *Above* is a suite in black walnut and mahogany, made by Holland & Sons and illustrated on plate 19 of *Decoration and Furniture for Town Houses*, by Robert W. Edis (1881). *Left:* A brass bedstead, by Hoskins & Sewell, shown at the Furnishing Trades Exhibition, London, 1897. From plate 556, *Furniture and Decoration*, April, 1897.

brush stand, and chamber pots, highly decorated with floral and sometimes Oriental motifs. Bedroom equipment also included flat, shallow hip baths, usually painted and grained dark brown outside and cream inside, which were filled from large metal cans, either of polished brass or copper or painted and grained to match the baths. In the '50's and '60's bathrooms with taps for hot and cold water were rare. In *Mr. Sponge's Sporting Tour*, originally published in 1853, Surtees described a bedroom at Hanby House, furnished with "every imaginable luxury," including "hip-baths. and foot-baths, a shower-bath, and hot and cold baths adjoining, and mirrors innumerable. . . ."[11] John Leech frequently depicted the troubles of plumbing in the pages of *Punch*, and in one drawing showed an early oblong metal bath, enclosed in a wooden frame-work, with a gentleman pulling a bell cord amid clouds of steam and shouting: "Hollo! Here! Somebody! I've turned on the hot water, and I can't turn it off again!" A swell, with long, curling locks is advised by a close-cropped old gentleman to use a conical oil-skin cap when taking a shower bath: another gentleman, wearing such a cap, is interrupted in his shower by the maid knocking at the door and saying: "If you please, sir, here's the butcher, and missus says, what will you have for dinner today?" A schoolboy disgusts his sisters by announcing: "Do you know, all the pipes are froze, and we shan't be able to have any of that horrid washing these cold mornings! Ain't it prime!" Under the title of "A trifle the matter with the kitchen boiler," Leech shows a tragic breakdown of amenities, with a plumber and his mates taking out a kitchen range and piling bricks and rubble all over the floor, while the householder looks on in despair. But before the close of the century, bathrooms were common: every suburban "villa" had one, though respectable people doubted whether it was advisable to give the lower orders ideas above their station by permitting them to enjoy such conveniences.

Comfort in the bedroom was planned with minute attention to detail. A great though probably unrecognised increase in comfort and good health followed the replacement of the canopied four-post bed, with its tightly drawn curtains, by the bed with a half-canopy. Finally all traces of bed curtains disappeared. Although windows might be closed tightly against the night air, at least sleepers were not half-suffocated in a little tent of their own. The bed itself was cared for and kept in good condition, and the ritual of making it is described in the chapter on "Hints for Girl-Housekeepers," in *The Young Ladies' Treasure Book*, with some incidental reflections on the attitude of women to men in the home and on the ways of servants. "We spend at least a third of our time in bed," wrote the anonymous contributor, "and the care spent upon making them comfortable is far from being thrown away when it results in procuring an added measure of 'tired nature's sweet restorer, balmy sleep.' On rising, every girl should throw the bed-clothes over the foot of the bed, and open the bedroom window, if it has not been opened before, when she leaves the room, so as to allow of a current of air passing among them. In

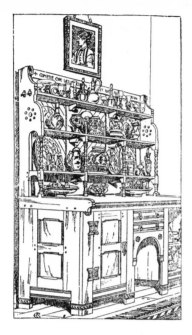

THE SO-CALLED "EASTLAKE" STYLE

Left: A dining-room sideboard. *Right:* A library bookcase. Charles L. Eastlake, who designed both examples, advocated the hand polishing of wood, and condemned French polishing, staining or varnishing. From *Hints on Household Taste* (second edition, 1869), plates XII and XXV.

The sturdy simplicity of Eastlake's designs was parodied in the 1890's, when the "Quaint" style became popular. The sideboard on the right is reproduced from *Furniture and Decoration*, March 15th, 1897, page 45, where the following remarks were made: "A few years ago such patterns as these would have been regarded as ridiculous, not to say cranky, had they emanated from the factory of a middle-class manufacturer, and in all probability they would have persistently remained in stock, whilst more ordinary and seemingly rational types

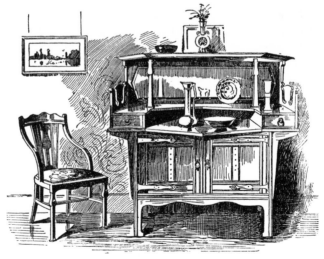

of small sideboards and chairs would have sold many times over. . . . The sideboard is original, if nought else be conceded in its favour, and it certainly bids fair to prove itself an inexpensive and somewhat effective production."

addition to this, it is advisable to toss back the feather bed, if one be used, or the mattress. This, however, is rarely done, even by women. As to men, it is of course absurd to expect anything of the kind from them. Their business at home is to make work for others, not to do it themselves. But, in cases of neglect of this good rule of shaking up the bed, the house-maid should go into every bed-room in the house while the family is at breakfast, open the windows, spread out the bed-clothes, and shake up the beds. This renders the mere making of the beds an easy matter. Many ladies make their own beds from

GLASS SHADES
For the Covering and Preservation of
Clocks, Statuettes, Wax Flowers, Alabaster, and other
Ornaments and Articles of Vertu.
CLAUDET AND HOUGHTON
having *considerably reduced their prices of Glass Shades*, they may be
appropriated advantageously not only as above, but also in
PROTECTING GOODS EXPOSED FOR SALE
from dust and the impurities of the atmosphere.
Wholesale & Retail Glass Shade Warehouse,
89 HIGH HOLBORN.

From the *Official Catalogue of the Great Exhibition*, Vol. I, page 65, advertisement section. (See plate 12.)

choice. Servants are not to be depended upon always even to give us the same number of blankets every night! They sometimes arbitrarily take one off the top of the bed and lay it beneath the under sheet. When asked to give a reason for such conduct, 'they can't think why they did it!' The person who has to sleep in it, very naturally makes no mistakes like these. With the help of the maid, she turns the mattress, or shakes the feather bed thoroughly, afterwards arranging it at the exact angle at which she likes it, lays on the under blanket smoothly and squarely, following suit with the under sheet, which is carefully tucked in. *Very* particular people turn the hem of the under sheet downwards, so that the right side of the hem comes uppermost, and take care to place the marked end of the sheet towards the top of the bed. The upper sheet is arranged with similar precision, with the right side of the hem uppermost instead of turned downwards, so that when the bed is occupied, the right side of all the hems is turned towards the person. 'I don't like the end of the sheet that is at my feet one night to be across my face the next,' say these good people. The bolster is then laid along the top of the bed between the sheets, the pillows upon it, then the upper sheet, the blankets placed with mathematical precision, and lastly, the quilt, which should be large enough to cover the pillows and then turn a little way, so that the fringe falls towards the centre of the bed.'[12]

Comfort was inseparable from tidiness. That account of bed-making, with its emphasis on *precision*, shows the importance housekeepers attached to every-thing being in its right place. Indeed, the interior of the Victorian home would have been hopelessly chaotic without a known and settled place for the innumerable objects that occupied every available space. Only men were expected to have untidy habits. There is a resigned note of protest in that sentence: "Their business at home is to make work for others, not to do it themselves." But men might well have complained that the home was always being disrupted by expensive novelties, that new fashions constantly intruded, and shelves and brackets and tables were cluttered up with knick-knacks, fancy goods and examples of "art-workmanship," sheltered by those glass domes, "for the covering and preservation of clocks, statuettes, wax flowers, alabaster, and other ornaments and articles of vertu," as set forth in the advertisement of Claudet and Houghton on the opposite page. Artificial flowers and leaves were not only modelled in wax, they were also cut from coloured cloth or made from knitting wool, stitched over wire frames. (See plate 12.) The pages of *The Young Ladies' Treasure Book* were thronged with ideas for increasing the ornamental contents of every room. In the chapter on "Taste and Care in the Household," it was stated that, "Girls who are clever with their fingers can do very much towards making the home beautiful, not only by needlework, painting, drawing, and the various kinds of fancywork, but by the practice of amateur upholstery, a pursuit which to some minds has a peculiar fascination. To these, little comes amiss. They make small decorative trifles out of the most homely materials. With a hammer, a box of nails and tin tacks, some yards of velveteen, cretonne, or serge, they will busy themselves to such purpose as would astonish their more helpless sisters."[13] Fretwork brackets and picture screens were produced by industrious girls who were "clever with their fingers," and all these additions to the furnishing of a house were accepted as evidence of good taste as well as diligence. America suffered from the same trouble: Downing gave many hints for transforming homely objects like barrels into dubious articles of furniture. (See pages 68 and 69.)

Furniture was usually made in the darkest woods available, in contrast with the taste of the early years of the century, when satinwood was in vogue and a light finish for mahogany was fashionable. Siddons in *The Cabinet-Maker's Guide*, a popular work for the use of those craftsmen, recommended a method for cleaning and finishing mahogany, and observed that it tended to darken the wood, and "according to the present fashion of furniture, that process which is most calculated to preserve the light appearance of the wood is preferred; but this is *taste*, and perhaps ere long it may be the fashion to admire dark in preference to light coloured wood. . . ."[14] That was published in 1830: the prediction came true within a few years, and dark mahogany with a reddish tinge (imparted by the use of brickdust), rosewood, black walnut, and bog oak were all used, while the growing taste for antique furniture, particularly old oak pieces, encouraged makers to stain and darken oak to simulate the rich, deep hue that age and generations of polishing gave to the surviving woodwork of the sixteenth and seventeenth centuries. Much of the furniture was monumental in effect, and copiously decorated with carving in high relief: flowers, fruit, animals, fabulous creatures and human figures, incongruously assembled, skilfully executed, and exhibiting a basic confusion of ornament with design. Although it was generally clumsy, ill-proportioned, and overpoweringly massive in character, the best of this furniture was as well made as the finest cabinet work of the Georgian period. Abundant skill was still available for making expensive furniture; cheaper variations of it were turned out in factories; but the solid, respectable furnishing of Mr. Bultitude's prosperous middle-class home in Westbourne Terrace, described in the opening chapter of F. Anstey's *Vice Versa*, was typical. The dining-room was long and lofty, "furnished in the stern uncompromising style of the Mahogany Age, now supplanted by the later fashions of decoration which, in their outset original and artistic, seem fairly on the way to become as meaningless and conventional. Here were no skilfully contrasted shades of grey or green, no dado, no distemper on the walls; the woodwork was grained and varnished after the manner of the Philistines, the walls papered a dark crimson, with heavy curtains of the same colour, and the sideboard, dinner-wagon, and row of stiff chairs were all carved in the same massive and expensive style of ugliness."(15) It accorded with the ideas expressed in one potent sentence in *The Young Ladies' Treasure Book:* "We enter the dining-room, and everything breathes of comfort and that repose which acts so beneficially upon the digestive organs when they are summoned into active service."(16)

By the 1880's, heavily carved, ponderous furniture was being replaced by lighter designs, often inlaid with marquetry. Rather flimsy bamboo furniture became fashionable, while Japanese screens and Oriental trifles, blue and white china, sunflowers and peacock feathers, joined the crowd of ornamental odds and ends. Meanwhile, the habit of collecting antique furniture had degenerated into a form of mania with many people, and was indirectly stimulated by the deliberate mediaevalism of the handicraft revival. The antiques that were "picked up" so avidly were occasionally spurious, and the dealer and the faker were very comfortable. Faking became a secret and most profitable industry. It developed some unexpected branches. For example, in the middle years of the century geologists and amateur archaeologists were provided with fossils and flint implements, counterfeited by a knowledgeable and subtle craftsman, popularly known as "Flint Jack," whose real name was Edward Simpson.(17) This was a highly specialised field for forgery, and not very rewarding, for "Flint Jack" remained poor all his life, becoming destitute, and ending his career in prison. The faking of furniture and interior woodwork was by far the most paying branch of the secret industry; detection was difficult, and the idea of prosecution distasteful to collectors who were proud of their acquisitions. The "expert" in old furniture did not as yet double the part of adviser and detective; he had hardly attained professional status, and was often almost as gullible as those who employed him. He would be able to spot the more obvious impostures, such as Eastlake described in his *Hints on Household Taste,*

The cover of *Punch*, designed by Richard Doyle, adopted in 1849, and used for over a century. It was a variation of a design by Doyle which was used between 1844 and 1849; there had been five earlier covers from the time the paper was first published on July 17th, 1841. (Reproduced by courtesy of *Punch*.) Of all the Victorian comic papers, *Punch* alone has survived, and it provides an authentic social and political history of the period, and, incidentally, an invaluable record of architectural and industrial design, changes in taste and fashion, and illustrates the consistent devotion of householders to "substantial comfort."

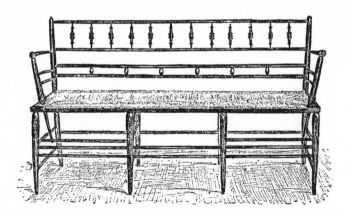

Examples of the work of Morris & Company. *Above:* A rush-seated settee, described as **a** "settle," and sold for £1 15s. *Below, left:* A rush-seated elbow chair of birch, stained black, and sold at 9s. 6d. The single chairs shown opposite in the *Punch* drawing are of the same design. *Below, right:* Bedroom chair with circular rush seat. From *The Decoration and Furniture of Town Houses*, by Robert W. Edis (1881), pages 28, 29 and 157.

REFINEMENTS OF MODERN SPEECH.

Scene—*A Drawing-room in "Passionate Brompton."*

Fair Æsthetic (suddenly, and in deepest tones, to Smith, who has just been introduced to take her in to Dinner). "ARE YOU INTENSE?"

"Art for Art's Sake" was already a tentative subject for daring and intense conversation. June 14th, 1879. (Reproduced by permission of *Punch.*) The single chairs shown above are of the same design as the elbow chair on the opposite page.

MRS. PONSONBY DE TOMKINS'S "DAY AT HOME."

Mrs. Ponsonby de Tomkins. "So good of you to take pity on us, Duchess! And you too, dear Lady Adeline! We were really feeling quite deserted, and——"

Footman. "Mrs. MacHallister!"

Mrs. MacAlister (an Aunt of Mrs. Ponsonby de Tomkins's—quite unexpected, and by no means a person of fashion). "Hech! ye didna think to set eyes on me the day, my Bonnie Bairnie! And hoo's a' wi' ye and the Guidman, Lassie?"

[*Sits down, and makes herself quite at home.*]

Stunned by the awful apparition, Mrs. Ponsonby de Tomkins mentally ejaculates, "Oh Heavens! what will the Duchess think?" *and loses all presence of mind.*

What the Duchess said to Lady Adeline, driving home:— "Nice Motherly Person that Mrs. MacAlister! She's the Wife of Lord Finsbury's Scotch Bailiff, it seems. I'd no idea Mrs. Tomkins had such Respectable Connections!"

Reproduced by permission of *Punch*, January 24th, 1880, page 30.

when he warned his readers "against the contemptible specimens of that would-be Gothic joinery which is manufactured in the back-shops of Soho. No doubt," he continued, "good examples of mediaeval furniture and cabinet work are occasionally to be met with in the curiosity shops of Wardour Street; but, as a rule, the 'Glastonbury' chairs and 'antique' bookcases which are sold in that venerable thoroughfare will prove on examination to be nothing but gross libels on the style of art which they are supposed to represent."[18] Eastlake was clearly unaware of the extreme rarity of any furniture earlier than the sixteenth century, and was ignorant of the fact that cabinet work,

NINCOMPOOPIANA.—THE MUTUAL ADMIRATION SOCIETY.

Our Gallant Colonel (who is not a Member thereof, to Mrs. Cimabue Brown, who is). "AND WHO'S THIS YOUNG HERO THEY'RE ALL SWARMING OVER NOW?"

Mrs. Cimabue Brown. "JELLABY POSTLETHWAITE, THE GREAT POET, YOU KNOW, WHO SAT FOR MAUDLE'S 'DEAD NARCISSUS'! HE HAS JUST DEDICATED HIS *LATTER-DAY SAPPHICS* TO ME. IS NOT HE *BEAUTIFUL!*"

Our Gallant Colonel. "WHY, WHAT'S THERE *BEAUTIFUL* ABOUT HIM?"

Mrs. Cimabue Brown. "OH, LOOK AT HIS GRAND HEAD AND POETIC FACE, WITH THOSE FLOWERLIKE EYES, AND THAT EXQUISITE SAD SMILE! LOOK AT HIS SLENDER WILLOWY FRAME, AS YIELDING AND FRAGILE AS A WOMAN'S! THAT'S YOUNG MAUDLE, STANDING JUST BEHIND HIM—THE GREAT PAINTER, YOU KNOW. HE HAS JUST PAINTED ME AS 'HÉLOÏSE,' AND MY HUSBAND AS 'ABÉLARD.' IS NOT HE *DIVINE!*"

N.B.—Postlethwaite and Maudle are quite unknown to fame.   [*The Colonel hooks it.*

Reproduced by permission of *Punch*, February 14th, 1880, page 66.

as such, was unknown before that time. But he knew the ways of the fakers. "A fragment of Jacobean wood-carving, or a single 'linen-fold' panel," he said, "is frequently considered a sufficient authority for the construction of a massive sideboard, which bears no more relation to the genuine work of the Middle Ages than the diaphanous paper of recent invention does to the stained-glass of our old cathedrals."[19] This diaphanous paper, introduced by a Frenchman named Vacquerel, was known as "Diaphanie," and its application to window glass was simpler than "Vitremanie," mentioned earlier: both were recommended in *The Young Ladies' Treasure Book.*

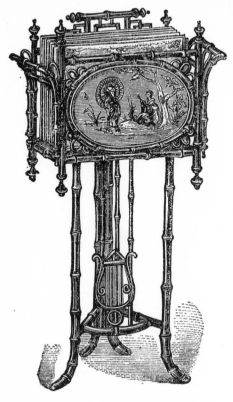

Left: A bamboo stand for newspapers, magazines or music. A variation of a Canterbury. (See page 82.) From *Sylvia's Home Journal,* 1879.

Below: A wicker revolving bookcase. From *Furniture and Decoration,* January, 1897, page 10.

The dark crimsons of fabrics and wallpaper, and the grained and varnished woodwork that pleased the eyes of Mr. Bultitude were succeeded by less soporific and more adventurous colour schemes. Velvet, serge or damask curtains trimmed with ball fringes and tassels, and heavy flock wallpapers in deep red, dark green or blue, covered with exaggerated damask patterns and almost hidden by large realistic paintings in wide gilded frames, were replaced by vivid colours, introduced with dazzling effect, for aniline dyes had been invented, which surpassed in harsh brilliancy the hues obtainable by vegetable dyes. These peacock greens and blues, magentas, violets and raw pinks were used with more enthusiasm than discrimination. Such strong colours were popular until the so-called "Aesthetic Movement" subdued everything, and olive greens and greys and dull blues were accepted as evidence of artistic rectitude. Some advanced people used white as a background, though this was rather daring. Such adventurers in decoration and furnishing were very different from respectable, comfortable, middle-class householders like Mr. Bultitude, or professional social climbers like Mrs. Ponsonby de Tomkins, depicted by that prince of Victorian de-bunkers, George du Maurier, in the pages of *Punch*. But even Mrs. Ponsonby de Tomkins allowed a slender, elegant tea table into her drawing-room, a forerunner of those light, slim associations of glass and metal and plastic that are called "contemporary" in the mid-twentieth century. (See page 46.) Hogarth and Rowlandson enlarged our knowledge of Georgian life and manners, but the accomplished black and white artists who contributed to the Victorian comic papers supplied a richer and more varied picture of life at many different levels, and from *Punch*, *Judy*, *Fun*, *Moonshine*, *Pick-me-up*, and, on a lower-class level, *Ally Sloper's Half-Holiday* and *Scraps*, we can learn more about the ideas and tastes, the prejudices and pleasures of Victorian life, than from any other source, particularly during the closing decades of the period. *Punch* alone has survived, and *Punch* is by far the most reliable record, for it abjured vulgarity and attracted artists of outstanding ability, Leech, Tenniel, Charles Keene, Linley Sambourne, George

A drawing-room cabinet sideboard, by Jackson & Graham, commended by Robert W. Edis in his *Decoration and Furniture of Town Houses* (1881), because it combined "general artistic merit of design with simplicity and practical common sense in form and arrangement. . . ." The cupboard fronts are decorated with paintings of Chinese subjects.

American "cottage furniture," *circa* 1850, made by Edward Hennessey, of Brattle Street, Boston, Mass., and illustrated by A. J. Downing in *The Architecture of Country Houses*, page 416. These sets were painted "drab, white, grey, a delicate lilac, or a fine blue—the surface polished and hard, like enamel." The set shown here sold for $37. It consists of: (1) A dressing bureau. (2) A small table. (3) A wash sink. (4) A French bedstead. (5) Four cottage chairs. (See opposite page.)

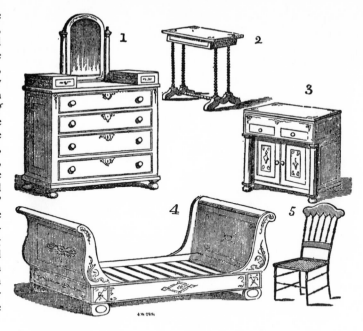

du Maurier, and, at the close of the age, Phil May. Of these, Leech and du Maurier were satirists of the stature of Hogarth, but without the savage anger of their eighteenth-century predecessor. Du Maurier's gentle contempt for middle-class follies, and his portrayal of types, from arrogant parvenues like Sir Georgius Midas to pitiful snobs like Todeson, uncover successive layers of social pretentiousness. He was far less impatient with honest Philistines than with the putative aesthetes, Maudle and Postlethwaite and their patrons, the Cimabue Browns, whose fatuous enthusiasms were presented under the label of "Nincompoopiana." As a contrast with such affectations, du Maurier occasionally introduced that stalwart symbol of common sense, a Colonel, who had strayed into an artistic gathering and couldn't understand what it was all about. (See page 47.) The Cimabue Browns had their own cherished standards of snobbery, their own ways of "keeping up with the Joneses," and an appetite for artistic novelty that would not be denied. In this they differed from Mr. and Mrs. Ponsonby de Tomkins, who were content to leave artistic innovations to their social betters, and to adopt new fashions only when they had been sanctified by at least one duchess. The Cimabue Browns might be "intense," and often remarkably silly and mistaken in their transient beliefs, but they were occasionally knowledgeable and well-informed about art, and intermittently sincere. The taste of such people had a marked effect upon the Victorian home in the '80's and '90's, and they were as eager to collect antiques, genuine or otherwise, as their solid and unimaginative contemporaries, though perhaps more discriminating in their choice of old furniture, but, like other collectors, impressed by the evidence of age rather than by excellence of design.

Other coteries, less aggressively conscious of their social leadership in matters

American "cottage furniture," *circa* 1850, by Edward Hennessey of Boston. This is in the same style as the set shown opposite, but is more complete and intended for a larger bedroom. It includes the following: (1) A commode or wash-stand. (2) A bureau dressing-table (this is not numbered, but is shown top right). (3) A zomno, or nightstand. (4) Bedstead. (5) Towel stand. Four cottage chairs go with the set, and a small table (bottom left). The price, without marble tops, was $68. With marble tops, $80. The wardrobe was extra, and cost $18. From *The Architecture of Country Houses*, by A. J. Downing, page 417. This furniture preserves traces of the classical tradition, and the bedsteads resemble the mahogany sleigh beds made by Duncan Phyfe in the 1830's.

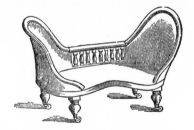

Two examples of so-called "cottage sofas," from *The Architecture of Country Houses*, by A. J. Downing, page 415.

of art, were frankly hedonistic. In that gruesome story, *The Diary of Mr. Poynter*, M. R. James mentions "one of those intelligent men with a pointed beard and a flannel shirt, of whom the last quarter of the nineteenth century was, it seems to me, very prolific."[20] That describes another type frequently lampooned in *Punch*, usually with disapproval or ridicule, though such people were often patrons or gifted amateurs of the arts and crafts. Happy intellectuals, inspired by William Morris, and fortified by a "hand-woven" outlook, they were blandly contemptuous of the good plain Philistines of the middle and upper classes, deploring their taste and laughing at their tidy, regulated lives. They were unconventional, inclined to socialism and statistics, not averse to comfort, though affecting to despise deeply-cushioned upholstery, far from austere in their private lives, and sometimes far from chaste. Their views and general approach to life differed from the intense "Art for Art's sake" aesthetes:

Furniture for a cottage dining-room, made by Edward Hennessey of Boston, Mass., and illustrated by A. J. Downing in *The Architecture of Country Houses*, page 419. The set consisted of "an extension-top dining-table, which, when closed, measures 4 feet, and when extended . . . measures 12 feet and will seat 12 persons; a side table, 3 feet long and 2 feet 4 inches wide, with drawers; and 8 arm-chairs with cane seats. The whole is furnished at $50, made of oak, maple, or birch as may be preferred. This set is in a mixed style—rather Flemish or Elizabethan than Grecian, but will not be out of keeping with a cottage or a plain country house. The chairs are strongly braced, and not so slender as they appear in the engraving." Those chairs are attenuated versions of the smoker's bow type, illustrated in the centre of page 54, one of the many nineteenth-century variations of the Windsor chair.

they were devoted to country life, not the established hunting, fishing and
shooting life of the county families and their parvenu imitators, but the simple
life, idealised by the pastoral poets. Many of them, like Morris himself, spent
much of their time in the country, where they acquired old houses and adapted
cottages, and partly furnished them with their own works. This generated a
new version of the "cottage" style in furniture, for the magic word "cottage"
had bewitched furniture makers long before the handicraft revival.

In the title of his *Encyclopaedia of Cottage, Farm, and Villa Architecture and
Furniture*, Loudon gave significant precedence to the word cottage, allotting

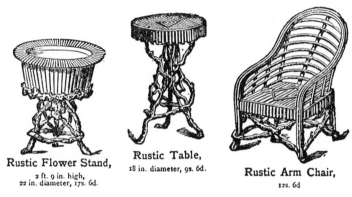

Rustic Flower Stand,
2 ft. 9 in. high,
22 in. diameter, 17s. 6d.

Rustic Table,
18 in. diameter, 9s. 6d.

Rustic Arm Chair,
12s. 6d

From an advertisement by Oetzmann & Co., Hampstead Road, London, in *The Graphic*,
August 25th, 1883, page 194.

345 pages to the subject, of which just over 54 had illustrations and descriptions
of furniture. Many of the designs he suggested were, in 1833, far beyond the
means or ambitions of cottagers, but Loudon explained that the term included
"not only labourers, mechanics, and country tradesmen, but small farmers
and cultivators of their own land; and the gardeners, bailiffs, land stewards,
and other upper servants, on gentlemen's estates."[21] He anticipated "a new
era" for the British cottager or workman, "and a condition very different
from that in which he now is, at no great distance of time. All the evils which
have for so long afflicted him have arisen from his own moral and political
ignorance, and from his consequent incapacity for self-government, either
individually or collectively; and they will be dispelled by the education of
the rising generation, and the new order of things which will thenceforth be
established. The working classes will then be able to take care of themselves;
and never, till this shall be the case, will they obtain those comforts and enjoyments which ought to be in the possession of the industrious labourer, as well
as of the wealthy capitalist."[22]

The middle class, which possessed such comforts and enjoyments, was
attracted by the word cottage; and had been supplied by the furniture trade,

Left: Double bow back, with pierced baluster splat, cabriole legs in front, and a spur stretcher. *Centre:* Comb back type. Both examples are mid-eighteenth century. *Right:* Mendlesham or Dan Day chair: late eighteenth- and early nineteenth-century type, an obvious ancestor of the Victorian kitchen chair.

THE CHAIRS WITH SHAPED WOODEN SEATS AND TURNED SPINDLES, KNOWN AS WINDSOR CHAIRS, REPRESENTED AN AUTHENTIC "COTTAGE" STYLE.

Left: Plain double bow back type. *Right:* Smoker's bow.

643

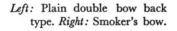

644

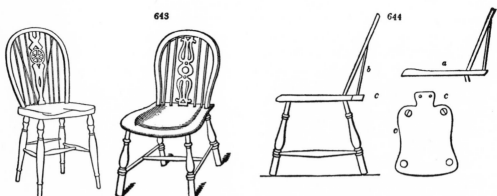

Left: Wheel back type, with V-shaped brace. *Centre and right:* Windsor chair with constructional details, from Loudon's *Encyclopaedia* (1833), page 319.

Left and centre: Baluster-and-spindle and plain spindle types of mid-nineteenth-century chair, variations of the basic Windsor model. *Right:* Decorative spindle-back chair, of the 1860's, illustrated by Eastlake in *Hints on Household Taste*, page 54. (Second edition, 1869.)

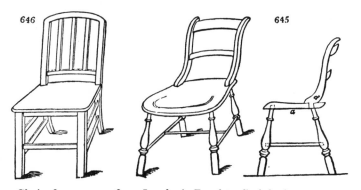

Chairs for cottages, from Loudon's *Encyclopaedia* (1833), page 319.

both in Britain and America, with inexpensive designs sold under that label; and the simpler furniture in the new suburban homes of that increasingly prosperous class was often based on the prototypes Loudon had illustrated. There was nothing particularly rural about the "sideboards, dumb waiters, bookcases, book-shelves, wardrobes, chests of drawers, chairs, stools, benches, sofas, beds, cribs," and so forth, which, Loudon said, "pretend to nothing more than what could be invented by any joiner who could read and draw, and derive ideas from books."[23] The so-called "cottage" furniture which Downing illustrated in *The Architecture of Country Houses* in 1850 was no more rustic than Loudon's examples, and preserved some traces of the classical tradition, associated with the American interpretation of the French Empire style. There was a family resemblance between some of the dining-room furniture shown by Loudon and Downing, and the chairs surrounding the dining table, made by Edward Hennessey of Boston, reproduced on page 52, are slender variations of the "smoker's bow" type of Windsor chair, which

"In the hall or entrance passage of small houses the folly of overcrowding is very prevalent. A hall which is 6 feet wide is capable of some artistic treatment, and it would be well if this width (which is little enough) could be generally recognised as the minimum of respectability in suburban villas as is the presence of a bathroom." This view was expressed in an article on "An Arch Fitment for a 6 feet Hall," published in *Furniture and Decoration*, June, 1897. An "artistic hall screen" was described and illustrated. The screen spanned the hall "with narrow pieces on either side. The archway should be draped at the back of either wing, there would be an angle wardrobe enclosed by a curtain for coats, umbrellas, etc.; whilst to the front a small shaped shelf and a plate rail above might be arranged and worked into the general scheme of decoration." Vol. XXXIV, page 107.

was popular in England as an arm-chair in cottages, inns, institutions and offices. Hennessey's version had a cane seat, decorative cresting on the top rail of the back, straight turned front legs, slightly curved back legs, and seven stretchers bracing the legs instead of three as in the "smoker's bow." Loudon did not include this type in his *Encyclopaedia*, though he showed a single Windsor chair with a pierced back splat, describing it as "one of the best kitchen chairs in general use in the midland counties of England."[24]

Windsor has become the generic name for chairs and seats with turned spindles socketed into solid wooden seats to form the legs and backs. The name has been traced back to 1728, when a Windsor chair was included in a sale catalogue.[25] In England and America the two main types, the hoop back and the comb back, were developed during the eighteenth and early nineteenth centuries with many regional variations of the basic form, and the Windsor chair survived the transition from production by hand to mechanical production without injury to the character of its design. High Wycombe in Buckinghamshire was the chief centre of manufacture, and the term "White Wycombe" was used as a description of a Wycombe turned or Windsor chair, "in the white," that is unstained and unpolished. These "White Wycombes" were stacked on farm wagons, and hawked through the Midlands, sales being made for a few shillings a chair from door to door in villages and the new suburbs of old towns. Such chairs represented an authentic "cottage" style, and their merits were not recognised until late in the Victorian period, when new versions of that style followed the handicraft revival. (See pages 54 and 55.) Apart from his passing reference to their use as kitchen chairs, Loudon ignored them, though he illustrated many examples of Gothic chairs for the furnishing of cottages, some of which Downing reproduced in *The Architecture of Country Houses*.[26]

The furniture in pleasure cottages differed little from that considered suitable for villas, and the *cottage ornée*, with its contrived rusticity, differed only in external character from the villa, for in size and plan they were often identical. Downing said that a country house "should always be furnished with more chasteness and simplicity than a town house; because, it is in the country, if anywhere, that we should find essential ease and convenience always preferred to that love of effect and desire to dazzle, which is begotten, for the most part, by rivalry of mere wealth in town life." He believed that furniture for such a house "should be essentially *country-like*—which, we think, is attained only when it unites taste, comfort and durability in the greatest degree."[27] In the '60's a demand existed for plain, undecorated furniture. Eastlake recorded that "a well-known firm in Tottenham Court Road has for some years past been

Bamboo furniture was fashionable throughout the last quarter of the nineteenth century, and by the late '90's it had become so attenuated that its initial attempt to suggest Oriental elegance was defeated by flimsiness. From *Furniture and Decoration*. May, 1897, page 92.

selling bed-room wardrobes, toilette-tables, &c., which (I suppose, from their extreme plainness of construction) are called *mediaeval*. They are executed in oak and stained deal, and are certainly a great improvement on the old designs in mahogany." Such articles were "actually dearer than their more ornate and pretentious predecessors. The taste no doubt, requires to be popularised to render it profitable to trade; but whether it will ever become popular while people can buy more showy articles at a less price, may be questioned."[28] The firm Morris founded in 1861 was able to produce some simple furniture that was reasonable in price. Edis describes and illustrates other examples of the firm's work in *The Decoration and Furniture of Town Houses*, such as "an excellent arm-chair in stained wood, comfortable, and artistic, although perhaps some-

The cosy interior, with a large and flourishing aspidistra supported by a rustic pot stand. The legend that each leaf of the aspidistra represented a hundred pounds of the family's annual income is probably apocryphal. Reproduced from *Judy*, September 2nd, 1885. The caption runs as follows:

NOT SUCH A BAD NOTION EITHER

Young Married Man.—Upon my word, my dear, *I* can't think where we ought to go to. But we really ought to make up our minds. Everybody's out of Town.
Wifey-pifey.—Suppose *we* stop in Town then, dear, and go the rounds of all the Music Halls, and have little suppers at the restaurants. As everyone else is gone, no one can see us, you know; so it's a good chance.

what rough in make, for 9s. 9d.," and " a plain rush-bottomed settle . . . 4 feet 6 inches long, which is quite good enough for any ordinary hall, and costs only 35s. complete."[29] Such furniture appealed alike to the supporters of the Arts and Crafts movement and the "intense" aesthetes; the rush-seated single chairs in the drawing reproduced from *Punch* on page 45 are of the same design as the elbow chair and settee on page 44, which Edis used as examples of the work of Morris and Company; but only a few discriminating people were prepared to accept something countrified in appearance and "somewhat rough in make," so the cottage style stimulated by the handicraft revival attained only a limited popularity towards the end of the century. The individual work of the artist-craftsmen whom Morris had inspired was superbly made and fabulously expensive. They produced "collector's pieces" for a small number of wealthy patrons, and their work had no effect on the furnishing of the Victorian home, where comfort and elegance contended for the mastery, until elegance became identified with flimsiness, and comfort solidified.

CHAPTER III

COMFORT AND ELEGANCE

IN nearly every type of home, furniture was unmistakably masculine or feminine: the dining-room and smoking-room were emphatically male, the drawing-room and the bedroom female. Comfort before elegance was a manly requirement, and although ladies preferred elegance, they did not reject comfort in furnishing, though they certainly did in costume. Their practical regard for comfort in the bedroom has been mentioned in the previous chapter; and their desire for some equivalent to the easy-chairs in which their menfolk lounged was met by such acceptable compromises as the lady's easy-chair—almost, but not quite a full-blown easy-chair—with buttoned uphol-stery, low arms, circular seat, and padded shell back, a type sometimes called "The Prince of Wales," though why it is difficult to say. An advertisement for this model is reproduced on page 63, where, in contrast with its modest com-fort, the "Wolsey," displays voluptuous curves. (See also page 75 and plate 9.) The American and English lounging chairs shown on the upper part of the opposite page, hardly encouraged such abandoned relaxation as the "Wolsey," though the adoption of inelegant attitudes did not depend wholly on soft, deeply cushioned upholstery. The angle of the back and the shape of the seat of any chair, could tempt an indolent or tired man to put comfort before elegance, like the languid gentleman in the drawing from *Fun* on page 62. He is sprawling in a folding, six-legged steamer chair, a type introduced late in the 1850's, which remained popular for over half a century. Such chairs often had a detachable leg-rest, so they could be used as a form of day bed. Two varieties are shown on the lower part of page 62, one appearing as an illustration in an article on furniture in *Cassell's Household Guide*, which included some advice about easy-chairs. "There is more care required in the selection of these necessary articles than in almost any other," said the anonymous contributor. "Some appear as if they were arranged rather for penitential chairs than anything else. The back aches, or the neck becomes stiff, when sitting in them, although perhaps they look truly comfortable till they are tried. The cane-seated arm-chairs are useful and inexpensive, but are a nuisance if they creak. The very best of them may be had for 17s. 6d.; also one of the same kind termed the Derby chair, which is with-out arms, and if not cane-seated to match the arm-chair, is made of laths,

COMFORT BEFORE ELEGANCE:
EASY-CHAIRS DESIGNED FOR
LOUNGING

Left: The American easy-chair of 1850, described by Andrew Jackson Downing as a "lounge, better adapted for siesta, than to promote the grace or dignity of the figure." *The Architecture of Country Houses*, New York, 1850, pages 452–53. *Right:* An English lounging chair, illustrated in *The Adventures of Mr. Verdant Green*, by Edward Bradley (who used the pen name of Cuthbert Bede), published, 1853–56, page 152.

In 1833 Loudon illustrated and described "easy reclining chairs for a library, parlour, or other sitting-room." They were "covered with morocco leather, with button tufts," and were "very easy to sit upon." *Encyclopaedia*, Chapter VI, page 1057.

COOL, VERY!

Young Lady :—"WHAT IS LAZY LAWRENCE READING? ARCTIC EXPLORATIONS! NOT MUCH IN YOUR LINE, SURE-LY!"

L. L. :—"OH, ISN'T IT? WHAT CAN BE PLEASANTER IN THIS WEATHER THAN TO LIE OUT HERE WITH A CIGAR AND A 'COBBLER,' AND FANCY YOURSELF ONE OF AN ICEBOUND AND DEVOTED BAND!"

Reproduced from *Fun*, June 12th, 1875, page 244. The folding "steamer" chairs shown below encouraged inelegant attitudes and deplorable manners.

Left: These cane-seated folding chairs were described, in *Cassell's Household Guide*, as "useful and inexpensive, but are a nuisance if they creak. The very best of them may be had for 17s. 6d. . . . ." Volume I, page 126 (1875). *Right:* Steamer chair in mahogany with slatted back. (Formerly in the author's possession.)

the cost being about 4s. 6d. This can be padded, cushioned, and covered in chintz or worsted rep, and thus it makes a most comfortable easy-chair for a lady, in which she can work or read; quite as pleasant to sit in as many of the more expensive."[30] A lath or slatted back steamer chair in mahogany with a cane seat is also shown on the opposite page. With or without arms, such chairs were described as early as 1858 as Derby folding chairs.[31]

Chairs and seats are more revealing than any other articles about the postures and manners encouraged by the philosophy of comfort. Arm-chairs and

COMFORT FOR
LADIES

The Prince of Wales'
Lady's Easy Chair,
Very comfortable . . . . 32s.
Superior ditto, all hair, 36s.

The "Wolsey" Easy Chair.
Spring Seat, very soft and comfortable, £3 3s.
Extra size ditto, £3 17s. 6d.

Left: The Lady's easy-chair, with the upright shell back and the buttoned upholstery did not permit lounging, though its comfort was undeniable. It was a type known as "The Prince of Wales'" easy-chair. (From an advertisement by Oetzmann & Co., Hampstead Road, London, in *The Graphic*, August 25th, 1883, page 194.)

Right: The circular seated arm-chair was designed purely for comfort: deeply sprung, with buttoned upholstery, and with arms and back inclined to promote relaxation and after-dinner sleep. (From Oetzmann's advertisement in *The Graphic*, March 31st, 1883, page 331.)

easy-chairs were not always clumsy and corpulent. Tenniel's drawing on page 65, shows Alice curled up in a robust arm-chair that is by no means ill-proportioned; and old Redburn, chatting with the Colonel in the illustration from "The Missing Rubies" on page 67, sits back in a heavier, leather-covered type with open arms, that obviously belongs to the dining-room or the breakfast-room. He is pleasantly relaxed, but is not lounging. The room in which these characters appear is probably furnished with a mixture of comfortable articles. The oak seventeenth-century press cupboard in the background has the same reassuring air of comfort as the arm-chair; and its appearance in an illustration to a serial story published in 1887 indicates the

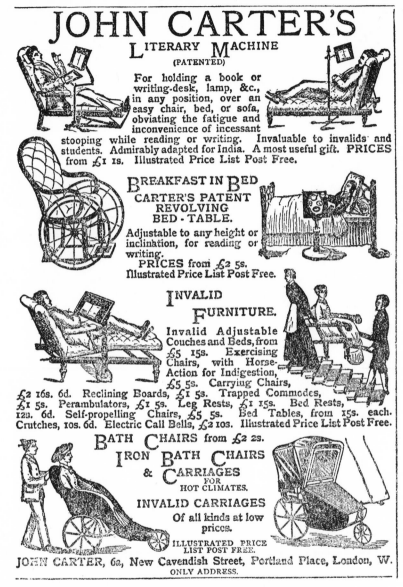

JOHN CARTER'S

LITERARY MACHINE
(PATENTED)

For holding a book or writing-desk, lamp, &c., in any position, over an easy chair, bed, or sofa, obviating the fatigue and inconvenience of incessant stooping while reading or writing. Invaluable to invalids and students. Admirably adapted for India. A most useful gift. PRICES from £1 1s. Illustrated Price List Post Free.

BREAKFAST IN BED

CARTER'S PATENT REVOLVING BED - TABLE.

Adjustable to any height or inclination, for reading or writing.
PRICES from £2 5s.
Illustrated Price List Post Free.

INVALID FURNITURE.

Invalid Adjustable Couches and Beds, from £5 15s. Exercising Chairs, with Horse-Action for Indigestion, £5 5s. Carrying Chairs, £2 16s. 6d. Reclining Boards, £1 5s. Trapped Commodes, £1 5s. Perambulators, £1 5s. Leg Rests, £1 15s. Bed Rests, 12s. 6d. Self-propelling Chairs, £5 5s. Bed Tables, from 15s. each. Crutches, 10s. 6d. Electric Call Bells, £2 10s. Illustrated Price List Post Free.

BATH CHAIRS from £2 2s.
IRON BATH CHAIRS & CARRIAGES FOR HOT CLIMATES.

INVALID CARRIAGES
Of all kinds at low prices.

ILLUSTRATED PRICE LIST POST FREE.

JOHN CARTER, 6a, New Cavendish Street, Portland Place, London, W.
ONLY ADDRESS.

COMFORT BEFORE ELEGANCE

Men could lounge and loll: invalids were made as comfortable as wheels and cushions and adjustable seats and tables could make them, and the bath chair, a wheeled descendant of the Sedan chair, could be drawn by a pony or pushed or pulled by a chairman. Bath chairs for hire were a feature of many seaside resorts. From an advertisement in *The Graphic*, November 17th, 1883, page 503.

The philosophy of comfort is perfectly expressed by the lines of this chair: it could support equally well a lounger or the conscious dignity of those who sat bolt upright. When Tenniel drew Alice curled up in it, the date was 1870, and by that time easy-chairs had lost some of their clumsy corpulence. While comfort has been attained, an understanding of good proportions has been recovered. The form is robust, the scroll supports of the elbows are related to the curves of the back, and carved ornament has been used discreetly. Buttoned upholstery is indicated on the back and seat; and the exposed frame and legs would almost certainly have been of rich red polished mahogany. (Reproduced from *Through the Looking Glass*, by permission of Macmillan & Company Ltd.)

growing interest in antiques. The dining-table would probably be of heavy mahogany, the chairs, leather-seated and buttoned, would resemble those on page 66, from a trade catalogue of the 1840's. There might even be a semi-circular social or "sociable" table, that agreeable survival from the Georgian period, which Loudon illustrated and described. (See page 68.) It was, he said, "chiefly used by gentlemen after the ladies have retired to the drawing-room," and was then "placed in front of the fire, with its convex side outwards, and the guests sit round that side with their feet to the fire."(32)

During the last quarter of the nineteenth century, the high-backed winged easy-chair was reintroduced. Such chairs came into use originally during the latter part of the seventeenth century, and were perfected in the Georgian period. No Victorian variations of the underframing or the convolutions of the arms and sides could detract from the basic excellence of the ancestral design, though upholsterers did their best to mask it with trimmings and repellent

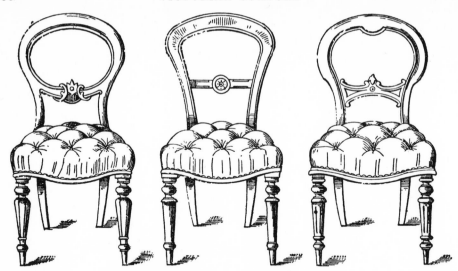

Three balloon-back dining-room chairs in mahogany with buttoned leather seats. From a trade catalogue, of the 1840's. Uncompromisingly masculine in character, like the leather arm-chair on the opposite page, which is occupied by old Redburn, such types would also appear in the study and the smoking room.

covering materials. At some time in the '80's the sentimental name of "grand-father" became popular for winged easy-chairs, shortly after "grandfather" was adopted as a term for long-case clocks. That term may be dated, for in 1878 Henry C. Work's song, "My Grandfather's Clock," was published and became a great favourite in the drawing-room. The opening lines of the first verse ran thus:

> "My grandfather's clock was too large for the shelf,
>   So it stood ninety years on the floor;
>   It was taller by half than the old man himself
>   Though it weighed not a pennyweight more."

The association of the term with the song is explicitly recorded by a trade magazine, *Furniture and Decoration and the Furniture Gazette*, in an article on "Grandfather" Clocks, published in May, 1897, in these words: "It is a worthy tribute to the workmanship of our predecessors that so many of these 'Grand-father' clocks have even exceeded 'ninety years without slumbering' and are still hale and fit to do reliable work. . . ."[33] The term was still new enough to appear in quotation marks. A few months later the same magazine said: "The most fashionable type of easy-chair at the present time is that known as the 'Fireside' or 'Grandfather.' The elegance and comfort of this kind of seat warrant the expectation that it will enjoy lasting favour, and it is therefore

FRANK DADD.   R. TAYLOR.

"BY GEORGE, LINDRICK," OLD REDBURN HAD SAID TO THE COLONEL,
"IT SEEMS THAT YOU MISLED ME ABOUT YOUNG EARLE."

An illustration from "The Missing Rubies," by Sarah Doudney, which appeared in *The Argosy*, November, 1887. The press cupboard in the background suggests the growing interest in antique furniture, particularly when it came from such a romantic period as the seventeenth century: it had the same, reassuring air of comfort and solidity as a well-upholstered leather-covered arm-chair, like the one old Redburn is using, or the mahogany dining-room chairs on the opposite page.

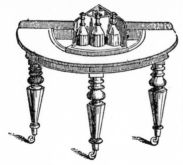

A survival from the Georgian Age, exclusively masculine in character, and known as a social table. From Loudon's *Encyclopaedia* (1833), Fig. 1888, page 1049. (See page 65.) Jawleyford, in *Mr. Sponge's Sporting Tour*, "rang the bell, and desired Spigot to set in the horse-shoe table. . . ." (Chapter XXI.) The book was published in 1853.

highly probable that easy-chairs with high backs and side shoulders will long continue to be regarded as standard patterns among fashionable upholstery."(34) Certainly the comfort of a high padded back to a seat appealed to everybody, and in 1850 Downing had illustrated and described a home-made high-backed barrel-chair, one of "the cheapest and simplest seats for a cottage," ingeniously constructed from a barrel, with "the seat and back . . . stuffed with any cheap material, covered with strong coarse canvas, and covered with chintz."(35) That early example of "do-it-yourself" furniture did not escape crudity: it owed too much to its humble origin, and the high back, severely vertical, was unrestful. (See opposite page.) American chairs tended to have a certain severity of line; even the lounging chair shown on page 61 lacks the gentle rake of the back which makes its English counterpart so much more comfortable. Both date from the 1850's, the decade when the so-called "French style" was popular in America, which reproduced in black walnut and rosewood, a heavy parody of rococo. The rococo revival began in the 1840's, and the best examples of it came from the New York workshop of John H. Belter, a cabinet maker and chair maker whose workmanship was superb, but whose addiction to an excessive use of ornament blunted the sinuous lines of his furniture. Earlier, in the 1830's, an easy-chair with a continuous back and seat of buttoned fabric or leather, was admirably designed for lounging or dozing. The inclined support for the back and the hollow seat were pre-eminently restful; the scrolled arms were open and not upholstered; and the frame, supported by two arched members, looked, from the side view, like a mediaeval X-framed seat. An example, reproduced from Loudon's *Encyclopaedia* (1833), is shown on page 61, bottom left. Sometimes wrongly called a "Sleepy Hollow" chair, which is an American term for a small, tub-backed arm-chair

1897

A leg-rest, called "an ease and comfort," used by old gentlemen after the ladies had left the dining-room. It was shaped and stuffed to fit the calves of the legs. From Loudon's *Encyclopaedia* (1833), Fig. 1897.

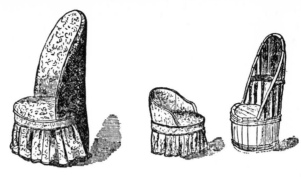

The *barrel-chair*, described by Downing as "the cheapest and simplest" seat for a cottage. From *The Architecture of Country Houses* (New York, 1850), Section XII, page 414.

with buttoned upholstery, which invited "the listless repose" associated with the "sequestered glen" described in Washington Irving's "Legend of Sleepy Hollow".

Easy-chairs and settees began to put on weight after the coiled spring had been patented in 1828 by Samuel Pratt, a maker of camp equipment, of New Bond Street, London. The device was applied at first to mattresses, but by the early 1830's Birmingham factories were making thousands of single and double cone spiral springs for use in upholstered furniture. Corpulence had come to stay, though nobody recognised this bloated aspect of "substantial comfort" until late in the '90's.

Seats that accommodated two or three people had an amplitude of form that often excluded all pretensions to elegance, whether they appeared in the drawing-room or the smoking-room. That decorative method of attaching the covering material to the backs and seats of chairs and sofas, known as buttoning, gave an air of slightly explosive plumpness to upholstered furniture, like the

Almost a "Grandfather," but wingless. This design "suggests an effort to combine the formal character of the Empire style with the comfort of the modern dining-room easy-chair. This combination could not be entirely effected by a change of outline or proportion merely. It would be needful to requisition the aid of colour to complete its appearance. In this particular instance we would suggest that the chair be covered with a dull maroon cloth or ruby velvet, and that a broad braid of dull red and gold silk be fixed all round the front edges. . . ." From "A Chapter on Easy Chairs," *Furniture and Decoration and the Furniture Gazette*, October 15th, 1897, page 201.

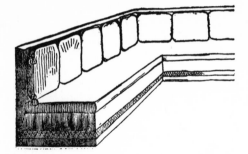

An ottoman, in the form of a continuous seat, extending round the wall. This type may have originally suggested the idea of the "cosy corner." From Downing's *The Architecture of Country Houses* (New York, 1850). Section XII, page 428.

paunch of a stout man protesting against the restraint of a waistcoat; indeed, the seats of the chairs on page 66 and the circular ottoman on page 75 have an almost indecent resemblance to bulging flesh too tightly clad. Sofas and settees, which derived their basic shape from the settle, were introduced in the latter part of the seventeenth century, and by the end of the nineteenth had disappeared under layers of fat, yielding upholstery, culminating in the Chesterfield, which was described by Rosamund Mariott Watson, in *The Art of the House*, as "an indirect descendant of the Empire sofa, with the comfort kept, but all the grace left out," that "obese, kindly-natured couch . . . about as comely as a gigantic pin-cushion, and as little convenient in a room of moderate dimensions as an elephant; plethoric and protuberant with springs and stuffings . . . at best a tiresome piece of goods, decoratively worse than worthless, and not so very easeful after all."[36] That was published in 1897, and in the same year the August issue of *Furniture and Decoration and the Furniture Gazette* included

an article welcoming the introduction of thin stuffing in upholstery, which, said the writer, "has not only created a novelty and helped to reduce the price of manufacture, but it has also an aesthetic value in that it compels the upholsterer for the first time in recent years to observe that golden rule of industrial art, viz., that we should ornament construction, and not construct ornament. It is necessary now that the system of thin stuffing has become prevalent to pay more careful attention to the frames of our couches than was commonly done a few years ago. The frames of some of the old-fashioned thickly-stuffed Chesterfield sofas bore little or no relation to the finished piece of upholstery. The lines of the wood formed merely a skeleton which

THE "CAVENDISH" DOUBLE SETTEE.
In Walnut, Dark Mahogany, or Ebonized. Best make and finish. Stuffed all hair, and covered with Gobelin Cretonne in contrasting colours. Price 6 Gns. In Rich Tapestry, Plain Silk, Plush, and Fringe, price 9½ Guineas.
Coloured sketches and patterns of covering materials sent for selection. For Easy and Occasional Chairs to match, see our Furniture Catalogue, page 30, sent free on application.
DEBENHAM and HEWETT,
FURNITURE MANUFACTURERS,
CAVENDISH HOUSE, CHELTENHAM.

From *The Graphic*, June 16th, 1883, page 616.

THE ROCOCO REVIVAL IN AMERICA

This revival began in the 1840's, and the best examples of the style came from the New York workshop of John H. Belter: his work was imitated, not always successfully. The illustrations on this page are reproduced from Downing's *The Architecture of Country Houses* (New York, 1850). *Above, left:* "A sofa which unites graceful form and good ornamentation, with luxurious ease in the seat." From Roux's in New York. *Above, right:* This couch was described as "awkward and destitute of grace," and Downing refrained from naming its maker. *Below:* This group is by Platt, of 60, Broadway, New York. "It consists of a chair, fire-screen and ottoman, in the Louis XIV style. The ottoman is remarkable for its elegance and an expressive dignity arising from its large size and good proportions. It is octagonal in shape, and in the centre of a large, square, octagonal or circular saloon, would have a fine effect. There are, of course, several pillows, though only two are shown in the engraving." Figs. 240, 241 and 242, pages 433–35.

was padded out and completely extinguished in an envelope of horsehair, flock, alva, shavings, or even cheaper and nastier fillings according to the wishes of the customer and the honesty of the manufacturer. The construction of the article was completely hidden from the lay eye, and one of the primal laws of industrial art was outraged."[37] The best elements in the teaching of Ruskin and Morris were obviously having a delayed-action effect on the furniture trade, and the anonymous writer of the article just quoted was also reflecting, perhaps unconsciously, the belief that structure should be acknowledged, not concealed, which was then being expressed by such pioneers of the modern movement in architecture and industrial design as van de Velde in Belgium, Louis H. Sullivan and Frank Lloyd Wright in America, and C. F. A. Voysey in England.[38]

During the '90's, fitted furniture increased in popularity and convenience: incorporated in a scheme of interior decoration it could provide such comfortable treatments for flanking a fire-place as the library fitment on page 74. Such designs resumed an ancient structural partnership between furniture and walls, which had been dissolved in the early part of the sixteenth century when free-standing furniture came into fashion. This resumption of dependence on the wall encouraged the use of long, high-backed seats, and at last comfort was married to seclusion in the cosy corner, which was developed either concurrently with or shortly after the reintroduction of the winged easy-chair. It was really a luxurious form of upholstered high-backed settle, designed to accommodate two or more people, with shelves or miniature cabinets for ornaments above, forming a decorative feature in the corner of a drawing-room. Essentially a seat to be shared, its inviting shape and rather remote position implied a delicate intimacy that no sofa, settee, or divan could suggest. Three lines from a popular song about it, indicate that it could also encourage rather bold conduct:

> "My heart's in a whirl,
> As I kiss each curl
> Of my cosy corner girl."

A chair that combined comfort with occasional elegance of design and formed a new social habit, both soothing and decorous, was the rocker. The earliest type was an ordinary ladder-back or spindle-back chair, with the front and back feet connected by two curved members, called bends, which allowed the chair to be rocked. Introduced in England and the American Colonies at some time between 1760 and 1770, this invention of an entirely new additional function for a seat has been attributed to Benjamin Franklin, though a Lancashire origin has also been suggested. Rockers had been used on cradles throughout the Middle Ages, and even earlier, but the principle was not applied to chairs until this comparatively recent date, possibly because chairs had hitherto been regarded as static and almost ceremonial articles, associated with dignified attitudes and important occasions if they had arms, and still closely related to stools if they were single or side chairs, the term "back stool" being used for the latter by Ince and Mayhew as late as 1762.[39] Compared with Georgian England, manners were certainly more free and easy in the thirteen American Colonies which became the United States, and the rocking chair was correspondingly popular. During the nineteenth century it became an American domestic institution; rockers were in nearly every home, in the parlour and on the back porch. Several regional variations of form were

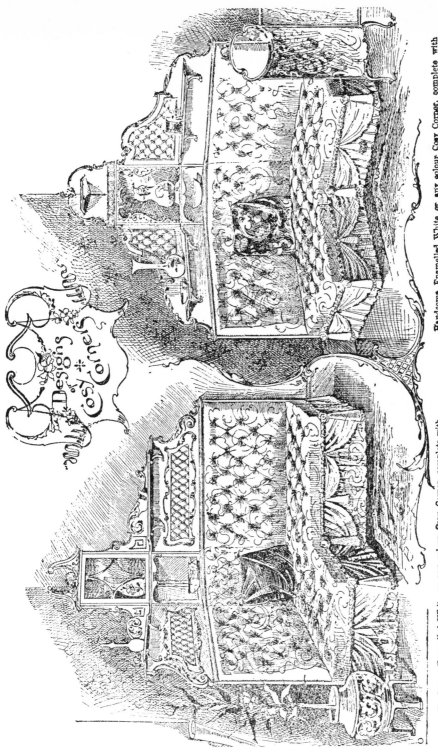

"Designs in Cosy Corners"

Handsome Enamelled White or any colour Cosy Corner, complete with drapery of cretonne ... ... £9 9s.

Handsome Enamelled White or any colour Cosy Corner, complete with drapery of cretonne ... ... £8 3s.

The Cosy Corner, which was sometimes called a Turkish Corner, was a typical expression of the Victorian love both of comfort and ornament. These two examples are from an advertisement published during the 1890's by Oetzmann & Company, Hampstead Road, London.

A fitment for a recess in a library, with accommodation for books, stationery and writing materials, and a low-seated settee. In combining such various functions, this design anticipates some characteristics of the unit furniture that became popular fifty years later. Reproduced on a reduced scale from *Furniture and Decoration*, September, 1897, page 175. This was almost a cosy corner, but predominantly functional. (See page 73.)

developed, notably the Salem and Boston rockers which evolved from the Windsor chair, with high comb backs, curved seats, dipped from back to front, and an ornamental panel on the comb-shaped top rail, decorated with paintings or stencils of fruit and flowers, in the manner of Hitchcock chairs, which were named after their maker, Lambert Hitchcock, who first produced them at Hitchcocksville, Connecticut during the 1820's. The Boston rocker became and has remained the standard American type, and a variation of it appears in Caldecott's sketch of Washington politicians made in 1886 and reproduced on page 76.

Early in the Victorian period, two new forms of rocking chair were introduced, which became popular both in Britain and the United States, though they did not supplant the basic American Boston type. These new types gave structural expression to the function of the rocker; they were not, as all earlier designs had been, ordinary upright chairs fitted with rockers; they represented a complete break with the original form and traditional materials, for they were made either of curved metal strips or of bentwood. As early as 1831 a patent was taken out in America for an improved rocking chair, with wagon springs inserted between the rockers and the seat to increase the resiliency,[40] and during the 1840's some English manufacturers attempted to make rocking chairs with cast-iron frames, but the material was too brittle and unyielding to resist the constant strain on the bends, so brass or steel strips were used. A brass rocking or lounging chair, with morocco furniture, was shown at the Great Exhibition of 1851, by R. W. Winfield & Company of Birmingham,[41] also an "improved iron rocking chair for the drawing-room, in gold, and

Left: A low chair, with a continuous seat and back: a type that came into fashion in the Regency period, and remained popular for over half a century. This example is from a trade catalogue of the 1840's. *Right:* A so-called "Spanish" chair, which obviously owes something to the Regency design, but has exchanged grace for corpulence. From *Practical Upholstery*, by "A Working Upholsterer." (London: Wyman & Sons, second edition, 1883), Chapter IV, page 24. These low, armless chairs were, like "The Prince of Wales" model on page 63, sometimes called ladies' easy-chairs.

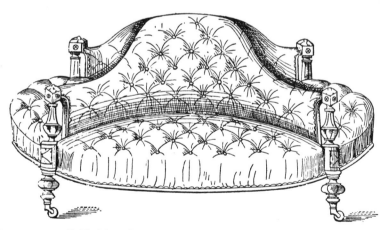

A circular ottoman, divided into four seats, with buttoned upholstery. From a trade catalogue of the 1840's.

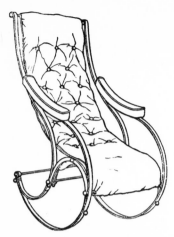

Ebonized Rocking Chair,
Stuffed all hair, 42s.
Ebonized and gold ditto, in velvet or satin, any colour, 72s. 6d.

Rocking chair made from bent steel strips. Chairs of this type, made of brass, were shown at the Great Exhibition of 1851. They were sometimes called "Digestive chairs."

Bentwood rocking chair, reproduced from an advertisement by Oetzmann & Co., London, in *The Graphic*, March 31st, 1883, page 331.

"TAKE IT EASY." Specially adapted for rest and comfort. Recommended by scores of gentlemen. The ladies are enthusiastic about them. Graceful, Easy, Fashionable, and Inexpensive. Visitors to the U.S. will recall the luxury of these chairs, which are to be found in every American home, and no family can keep house without them. They are made in variety of styles, so that any one's taste can be suited. Try a "Common Sense" easy chair, and you will have solid comfort. Price of Rockers, from 25s. to 35s. Price of Arm Chairs, from 25s. to 30s. Lists free. London Agents, RICHARDS, TERRY, and CO., 46, Holborn Viaduct, E.C.

A BRACE OF WASHINGTON POLITICIANS

The American type of rocker was popular in England, and was quite different in design from the bentwood types which had originated in Europe. From an advertisement in *The Graphic*, May 17th, 1884, page 487.

This was one of the last sketches made by Randolph Caldecott, who died during a tour in the United States, early in 1886. Two items essential to American comfort are shown: a cuspidor and a rocker. From *The Graphic*, February 27th, 1886, page 229.

covered with French brocatel" by William Cunning of Edinburgh.[42] The makers claimed that the latter was "a useful invention for invalids and others." This type, with a curved, continuous back and seat in buttoned upholstery is shown opposite, and it is identical with a chair of bent steel strips, produced under the direction of a certain Doctor Calvert, who called it a "Digestive" chair. Bentwood rocking chairs with canework or upholstered seats and backs were made in large quantities during and after the 1860's by Michael Thonet (1796–1871), a gifted Austrian designer, who had exhibited bentwood furniture in London in 1851. The length of the seat, the rake of the back, and the

Left: Bentwood rocking chair with canework in seat and back. *Centre:* An American "Rocker," of the late '90's, designed by Clarence R. Hills of Grand Rapids, which owes some of its character to the Windsor prototype. From *Furniture and Decoration*, February, 1897, page 31. *Right:* A rocking chair with a fixed base, known as a "swing" rocking chair. It was introduced to the furniture trade by the firm of H. & A. G. Alexander & Co. Ltd., of Eastfield, Rutherglen, near Glasgow. From *Furniture and Decoration*, April, 1897, page 72.

convoluted underframing gave far more comfort and stability to the chair than the Boston rocker ever attained; but although this design popularised rocking chairs in England, so that by the 1880's they were an accepted item in the furnishing of any well-equipped home, America remained faithful to the original models or adaptations of them. Late in the '90's a swing rocking chair was introduced by the furniture trade. A descriptive paragraph in *Furniture and Decoration and the Furniture Gazette* claimed that "the action is different to that of any other chair in the market, and it is possible to sit in the chair and be gently rocked to and fro without shifting its position."[43] This swing type depended on a heavy underframing, for the chair rocked on a fixed base which remained stationary, and not on bends resting on the floor. Compared with the Boston or bentwood types it was a complex contrivance.

Footstool,

In Walnut, Mahogany, Oak, or
Ebonized, 9s. 6d.
Ebonized and gilt ditto, 12s. 6d.
Post Free, 6d. extra.

Two items from an advertisement by
Oetzmann, in *The Graphic*, August
25th, 1883, page 194. The footstool,
left, is for the drawing-room: the
salivarium, *right*, for the smoking-
room. It is a genteel spittoon or cuspidor, with a hinged lid covering the
porcelain or metal container.

Inlaid Walnut Salivarium,
6s. 9d.

A variety of patterns in stock in
Walnut, Oak, or Mahogany, 4s. 11d.,
5s. 9d., 6s. 9d., 9s. 9d., 12s. 6d., 18s. 9d.
Post free, 1s. extra.

The rocking chair was not identified with either sex: it was equally acceptable in the drawing-room, the boudoir, the study, or the smoking-room.
Comparatively few articles could be shared so satisfactorily by men and
women; and about some articles used by and expressly designed for men,
there was a coarse exclusiveness which made delicately-bred women shudder.
Of these, the spittoon was accepted reluctantly as a necessity in England, but
in America it was regarded as an essential item in the home, and generally
called a cuspidor, a term derived from the Portuguese *cuspidore*, which presumably came from the Latin *conspuere*, to spit upon. Mark Twain, describing a
sumptuously furnished pilot house on a Mississippi steamboat, mentions
"bright, fanciful, 'cuspadores' instead of a broad wooden box filled with
sawdust" . . .[44] A brass or pewter cuspidor, shaped like a miniature vase,
appears in Caldecott's drawing on page 76. Gentlemen who smoked were
expected to use a spittoon: the lower orders dispensed with such refinements.

Smoker's chairs with a drawer below the seat, containing a spittoon. These chairs were
introduced late in the '90's, and the spittoon which had been out of favour for some years
was restored to smoking-rooms and dining-rooms. These examples were made by Tarn &
Company, and illustrated in *Furniture and Decoration*, February, 1897, pages 26–27.

Comfort in the study. An enclosed wash-hand stand, "commonly placed in a library closet, or in a gentleman's study or business room. There is a slip of wood on the under side of the top, which drops down in front, and completes the panel; thus shutting the whole up close. A glass is fixed on the under side of the cover, which rises with a rack and horse. There are two doors below, in the inside of which are shelves, and a space for keeping the ewer with the water, or it may be fitted up with any appropriate convenience that may be desired." Loudon's *Encyclopaedia* (1833), page 1057, Fig. 1910.

1910

A reading chair, "of a simple and good form, a very useful piece of furniture, having a desk for a book on one arm, and a stand for a candle on the other—both being movable—and easily lifted out and put away, when not in use." *The Architecture of Country Houses*, by A. J. Downing (New York, 1850), page 426, Fig. 218.

In a short story that appeared in an annual called *The What-Not; or Ladies' Handy-Book*, for 1861, there was a description of a ship's cook, known as ship's cooks generally were, as the "Doctor." He was entertained on Christmas Day at the home of his former captain, and was unused to polite society. "One thing annoyed him considerably, and that was a spittoon. The 'Doctor' was in the habit of expectorating while smoking, and Mrs. Goodall had placed a spittoon by his side. Now this said spittoon was a modern one, recently purchased at the neighbouring market town, and was resplendent with paint and gold. The 'Doctor' who had never seen such an elaborate affair, did not use it, but kept every now and then expectorating into the fire. Mrs. Goodall, who thought he did not see it, and yet not wishing to make him uneasy by calling attention to this lapse in his manners, removed it from one side to the other in the hope of his using it. On two or three occasions he had been on the point of so doing; but at last he said, 'I beg yer pardon, mum, but if you don't take that thing away I shall spit into it;' and he was quite taken aback when she replied, 'That's just what I want you to do, Doctor, if you will.' "(45)

In England the spittoon was usually a circular pan of metal or porcelain, either open or enclosed in a wooden case with a hinged lid, which was covered with leather or some patterned material, so it could masquerade as a footstool. The genteel name of *salivarium* was invented, and thus disguised the appliance could and did appear in the dining-room and the study. (An inlaid walnut salivarium advertised by Oetzmann in 1883 is shown on page 78.) By the '90's the spittoon was on the way out; either because it was condemned as an unhygienic nuisance, or because more men were smoking cigarettes and spat less than cigar and pipe smokers; but it was reintroduced surreptitiously. Its resurrection was thus described in *Furniture and Decoration and the Furniture Gazette*: "Under the seat of an ordinary standard chair, a club divan, or an upright arm-chair, is placed a drawer. This drawer is kept normally closed by means of spiral springs, and is brought forward by means of a cord, terminating in a small button. A pan (which for cleaning purposes is made removable) is contained within the drawer. Thus, when required, the spittoon may be drawn forward, and then released, when it returns to its place automatically."[46] Two examples of such smoker's chairs are reproduced on page 78.

THE DESK OF THE AGE

THE WOOTON CABINET.

Comfort and Tidiness. From *The Graphic*, May 17th, 1884, page 487.

Low, curved armless chairs, of which some types were known as "Spanish," were recommended as particularly suitable for ladies, whose vast framed and inflated skirts could overflow on either side. Feminine taste was supposed to favour slender if not positively flimsy furniture; but this was a late development. In the '30's and '40's drawing-room chairs still retained a Georgian stability, and a few traces of the classic tradition remained in their lines and ornament; but after the '50's they became gross. Even Eastlake, who thought he was regenerating design, produced a drawing-room chair of loutish proportions, which, he asserted, would "at least, be in better taste than the elaborate deformities" produced by the furniture trade.[47] It was made of oak, "covered with velvet, and trimmed with silk fringe." Buttoning was used on the seat and back, and although in general design it was simpler than comparable trade productions, Eastlake in common with furniture manufacturers, identified comfort with solidity. It is shown with a typical trade model on page 91.

Towards the end of the century, the restless anarchy of the fashion known

Above: Two varieties of the pre-Victorian type of small writing desk, called a davenport. From Loudon's *Encyclopaedia* (1833), where the name is spelt devenport. Later and more elaborate examples are shown on plates 14 and 15.

Right: Writing desk with slender twisted under-frame. From *The What-Not; or Ladies' Handy-Book* (1861).

Below: The comfort of the davenport type of desk was obvious. From *The Young Ladies' Treasure Book.*

Right: An ornate, late Victorian development of the davenport. From an advertisement by Oetzmann & Co., in *The Graphic*, March 31st, 1883, page 331.

Ebonized and Gilt Early English Davenport.

With Morocco Top, any colour, 5 Guineas
A variety of Davenports in stock from £3 10s. to £11 14s.

A canterbury in papier-mâché, by Jennens & Bettridge. From *The Crystal Palace and its Contents*, 1851, page 212. The canterbury had at least two quite separate functions. Sheraton in *The Cabinet Dictionary* (1803) described and illustrated two forms, one a small music stand, the other a supper tray, really the forerunner of the trolley table. At some time in the Victorian period the term was also used to describe a music stool with a hinged seat and a box below for music.

as "New Art" reached England, where for a few years in valiant defiance of tradition and the philosophy of comfort, it imposed the most disturbing ideas on furniture and interior decoration. In 1897 "van de Velde was startling Europe with his celebrated *art-noveau* Rest-Room at the Dresden Art Exhibition,"[48] and the transplanted forms of *art-noveau* startled staid Victorian England far more than any European country. Master designers like Charles Annesley Voysey (1857–1941) and Charles Rennie Mackintosh (1868–1928) could control such exotic, naturalistic forms, and use them with discretion; and in America, before he repudiated all forms of ornament, Louis H. Sullivan employed them to embellish some of his buildings. But those florid, wriggling plants and exuberant blossoms and arabesques, the heart-shaped apertures,

Waste paper basket of brown lacquered osier work, lined with red velvet cloth. Outside the basket are crossway bands, embroidered, and lines of balls of olive green Oriental wool and old gold silk. From *Sylvia's Home Journal*, 1881.

An ottoman with a lid, covered with decorative fabric, and trimmed with braid, fringes and tassels. From *Sylvia's Home Journal*, 1879.

The natural beauty of polished wood was often deliberately hidden by cloths and covers. This table is covered with "nut-brown Java canvas, embroidered in cross-stitch with pale brown and maize filoselle." From *Sylvia's Home Journal*, 1879, pages 339 and 352.

the inlays of enamel, mother-of-pearl and burnished copper, the carved scrolls and loops and painted and stained patterns degenerated into what the furniture trade called the "Quaint" style, which encouraged many people who lacked both imagination and taste to make incompetent contributions to the universal confusion. Architects, who were also great teachers, like William Richard Lethaby, rejected this strenuous fashion, realising that its superficial

Left: An *étagère*, "of French design, suitable for the drawing-room of a villa." The large, semi-circular headed mirror is flanked by shelves, intended "for articles of *virtu*—bouquets of flowers, scientific curiosities, or whatever else of this kind the owner may indulge his taste in." *The Architecture of Country Houses*, by A. J. Downing (New York, 1850), Fig. 300, page 456. *Below:* A carved *étagère* and a lady's escritoire, from Roux's, in New York. From the same work, Figs. 248 and 249, page 436.

Centre table, described by A. J. Downing as "the emblem of the family circle," which "draws all talkers to a single focus." From *The Architecture of Country Houses* (New York, 1850), Fig. 223, pages 428–29.

An *étagère* sideboard and a dining-room chair, both exhibiting Gothic features. They were made in oak, by Roux's in New York. From Downing's *The Architecture of Country Houses* (New York, 1850), Figs. 282 and 283, page 448.

cleverness which seduced so many students and young designers was not based on the good workmanship which could inspire rational design. In 1898, when Edward Johnston, who revived the art of calligraphy in England, asked Lethaby, the principal of the newly-formed Central School of Arts and Crafts in Upper Regent Street, if he could become a student, he was warned: "If you draw a straight line with a heart at the top and a bunch of worms at the bottom and call it a tree, I've done with you!"[49]

The "Quaint" style had a debilitating effect on the comfort and shape of chairs and seats; and although the fashion appealed to a few advanced artistic intellectuals, its feverish extravagance repelled most people. Not many householders desired to live in surroundings that suggested a stylised mangrove swamp; and such rootless modernity led to a reaction in favour of period furnishing; instead of picking up oddments of antique furniture and bits of old panelling and carved chimney-pieces and admiring them as isolated "finds," people who could afford it commissioned careful reproductions of seventeenth- and eighteenth-century interiors, so that large town or country houses might have a Jacobean dining-room, a Queen Anne boudoir, an Adam drawing-room, and late Stuart, William and Mary, and early Georgian bedrooms. As usual, on a cheaper and flimsier scale, the suburban homes attempted to follow this fashion for period styles, and although comfort was preserved all vitality was drained from design, while elegance was incidental and generally accidental. *Art-noveau*, although it was

1898

A candlestick stand used on dining tables to raise the candlesticks, "in order, by elevating the light, to throw it better over the dishes." Loudon's *Encyclopaedia* (1833), Fig. 1898, page 1050.

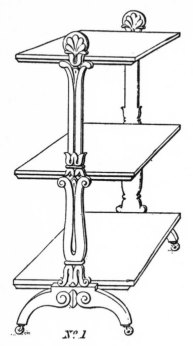
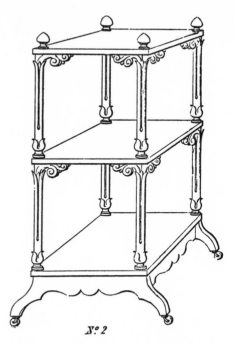

Two types of whatnot. The design on the left could also be used as a running sideboard or dinner wagon. From *Designs of Furniture*, an undated trade catalogue issued by William Smee & Sons at some time between 1830 and 1840. This firm of cabinet makers and upholsterers were established at The Pavement, Moorfields, London, from 1817 to 1851, and later became Smee & Cobay, moving to Wardour Street. (*The London Furniture Makers*, by Sir Ambrose Heal, page 170.)

Two moving sideboards from Downing's *The Architecture of Country Houses* (New York, 1850), Section XII, page 420. These light articles were mounted on castors and could easily be wheeled about the dining-room.

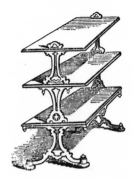

Left: A pedestal sideboard, with an open wine cooler below. The carved decoration at the back is becoming a little coarse, like that above the cornice of the bookcase on plate 13. *Right:* A chiffonier pier table which could also be used as "a sort of morning sideboard for containing any light species of refreshment." It lacks the good proportions of the small sideboard shown on plate 15, with its restrained ornament. From Loudon's *Encyclopaedia* (1833), Fig. 1871, page 1044, and Fig. 1942, page 1066.

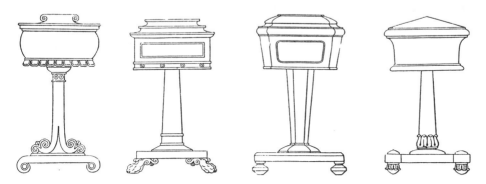

Four designs for teapoys, from plate 3 of *The Modern Style of Cabinet Work* (London: T. King, 1832, Second edition). These small pillar tables, with three or four feet, supported a tea chest or tea caddy, and were probably introduced in the late eighteenth century: two designs for them, with tray tops, are shown in George Smith's *Household Furniture* (1808), and they were usually included in the furnishing of Victorian drawing-rooms. They were made of various woods, mahogany, rosewood, black walnut, and occasionally of papier-mâché.

DRAWING-ROOM AND DINING-ROOM CHAIRS

Right: The classical tradition still persists in the ornament used on these chairs, and the sabre leg (which, after 1815, was sometimes called a Waterloo leg) is used on both examples, though unhappily associated with ill-proportioned, turned and fluted legs in the first. From *The Modern Style of Cabinet Work*, Second edition, 1832, plate 34.

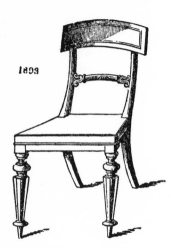

Left: Only rudimentary traces of the classic tradition have survived in these chairs, and the use of ill-proportioned front legs, totally unrelated to the back legs, has been carried a stage further. From Loudon's *Encyclopaedia* (1833), Figs. 1893, 1894, page 1050.

Right: A dining-room chair, with a stuffed back and tufted seat, covered with morocco. Loudon's *Encyclopaedia*, Fig. 1895, page 1050.

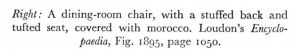

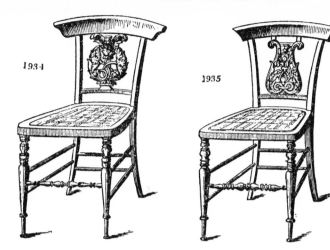

DRAWING-ROOM CHAIRS

These rather fragile designs, with the legs braced by stretchers, are in maple or satinwood, with matted seats. The back splats are carved with a complicated mixture of the rose, thistle and shamrock. From Loudon's *Encyclopaedia*, Figs. 1934, 1935.

Right: Chairs to be executed in rosewood or mahogany. Of all the examples shown on this page, Loudon said: "Not one of these chairs can have been designed by an architect, or other artist; they are much more like the efforts of a mechanic in search of novelty." *Encyclopaedia*, Figs, 1936, 1937, page 1063.

a genuine attempt to create a non-historical style, became an ephemeral fashion, not because of its complete independence of tradition, but because it was wholly ornamental in character, and was not attuned to the real revolution in architectural and industrial design which was then beginning to trouble the minds and quicken the thoughts of a number of gifted young men in Europe and America.

Other reasons, less recondite, caused the failure of this experiment in England. It was incompatible with the canons of "substantial comfort," it collided with the brusqueness of masculine taste, and when it was commercially interpreted as the "Quaint" style, the end was near. It became just one more symptom of

D*

Mahogany drawing-room chairs, upholstered in leather. From a trade catalogue of the 1840's. Other examples from this catalogue are on pages 66 and 75.

the general degradation of design, and was occasionally recognised as such by the more outspoken contributors to *Furniture and Decoration and the Furniture Gazette* which, for a trade magazine, was in advance of its time and followed an intricate editorial policy of compromise, illustrating, describing and praising the productions of manufacturers, irrespective of their merit, but also publishing articles that were waspishly frank about the general condition of taste. Critical comments by anonymous writers were interspersed with puffs for the wares of various makers, news about new companies and issues, legal cases, fires, bankruptcies, applications for patents, obituary notices, and toothsome scraps of flattery about leading figures in the trade, often accompanied by rather painful portraits. The year 1897 was particularly rich in revelations about the paucity of inventive powers in the trade. Censorious articles were copiously illustrated, frequently by designs that obviously contradicted everything their writers were trying to say. As the readers were largely manufacturers and retailers whose outlook was unaffectedly commercial, it was strong stuff for them to digest, especially when they were told about "the general degradation art has suffered through commercialism. . . . " In the course of a general accusation about lack of originality in design, one writer asserted that, "We do not seem to have a staple force to build up a consistent style or form a rational basis for the expression of our national character. We are will-o'-the-wisp in our fancies for the most part, and crazy in our hobbies. This being so we must go on supplying goods according to demand, and so long as Louis Quinze, Chippendale, Sheraton, Adams, or that new style called 'Quaint', which seems to be the carcase without the spirit of the new style promulgated by the Arts and

Crafts and other Societies, are popular we shall continue to harp upon all of them."

Exactly what the "Quaint" style did to chairs and seats is shown on page 92. No wonder such objects were rejected by men, and found no place in the study or the smoking-room.

Apart from chairs and seats, many articles enhanced the feminine elegance of the drawing-room. Among them were screens and stands and occasional tables of papier-mâché; the whatnot, often known by its French name, *étagère*, or, more pretentiously, an omnium, which originated in the 1790's[50] but only came into its own in the early Victorian period; the teapoy, another Georgian inheritance; and that small, compact writing desk called a davenport, named after a Captain Davenport for whom the prototype was made by the firm of Gillow in the late eighteenth century.[51] The davenport took up very little room and was designed to encourage tidiness, for it had several drawers and ample space below the sloping desk. (See page 81 and plates 14 and 15.) In the United States the term was also used to describe an upholstered sofa; a davenport bed was a couch which could be transformed into a bed; and a long, narrow table standing in the centre of a room behind a sofa was called a davenport table. There were innumerable varieties of writing desks, and many of them attained a spurious elegance by the sacrifice of

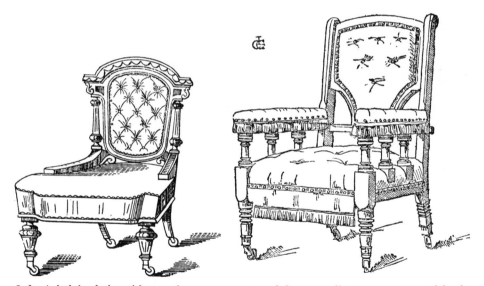

Left: A lady's chair, with a mahogany or rosewood frame, rudimentary arms, and leather upholstery. Like the other chair on this page, it lacks the feminine character appropriate for drawing-rooms. From a trade catalogue of the 1840's. *Right:* A drawing-room chair designed by Charles L. Eastlake, and illustrated on page 157 of *Hints on Household Taste* (second edition, 1869). The frame was oak: seat, back and arms were covered with velvet, trimmed with silk fringe. (See page 80.)

elementary comfort. "The aesthetic advantages of modern writing tables have, in many instances, been obtained at the expense of convenience," said *Furniture and Decoration*. "In other words, the present day escritoires, although admittedly more interesting in appearance, are as a rule less useful in service. The prevailing taste for 'Quaint' furniture is, in no small measure, responsible for this. The advent of eccentricity among our household goods has banished from our midst such commodious contrivances as the old-fashioned cylinder fall and capacious pedestal writing table. Happily American desks cannot as yet be regarded as sufficiently beautiful to ornament the private study or the homely dining-room how ever much their indisputable merits may fit them for commercial offices. Hence it behoves us to see that in increasing the prettiness of our writing tables, we do not allow our new productions to deteriorate in point of usefulness."[52]

When elegance was identified with attenuated versions of French and Georgian period furniture, and desks and occasional tables, china and curio cabinets exhibited an exiguous complexity of form, the confusion of elegance with eccentricity inevitably followed. In an article on new designs for cabinets and vitrines, *Furniture and Decoration* said: "Perhaps one reason why the middle-class 'Louis' cabinets that are now being so plentifully made in this country do not please the fancy as well as they might, is that they are invariably designed on what may be called Old English lines."[53]

One of the English manifestations of *Art-nouveau* was the "Quaint" style in furniture, which haunted the '90's. The work of master designers like Voysey and Mackintosh was imitated by the furniture trade. Here are some examples of designs by Sidney Robinson, which are reproduced on a reduced scale from plate 564 of *Furniture and Decoration and the Furniture Gazette*, May 15th, 1897.

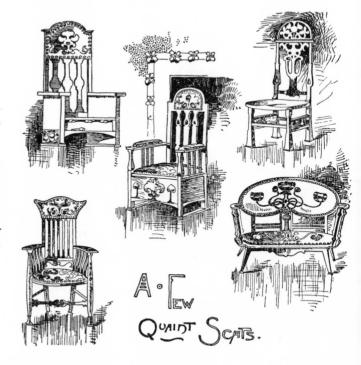

The premises of Spiers & Son at the corner of Oriel and High Streets, Oxford. (See page 101.) From *The Adventures of Mr. Verdant Green.*

These hybrid inhabitants of the drawing-room were devoid of character, and were often badly made. But they satisfied feminine taste, and Victorian women pursued elegance, or what they thought was elegance, with fervid enthusiasm. In addition to the rich and heady mixtures of styles the retail furnishing houses could supply, there were other shops to tempt them, "crowded with a costly and glittering profusion of *papier mâché* articles, statuettes, bronzes, glass, and every kind of 'fancy goods' that could be classed as 'art-workmanship.' "(54) That is a description of the shop of Spiers & Son, at the corner of Oriel Street, Oxford, written in the 1850's. (See above and page 101.) Every city of any size had such shops, Bath, Bristol, Cheltenham, and the fashionable seaside resorts, while in London there were hundreds of them. The female appetite for fascinating inutilities never flagged, and after the Great Exhibition it was fed for fifty years on a meretricious diet that atrophied the critical faculties.

In their clothes women renounced comfort, and whether they were hampering their freedom of movement in crinolines, or imitating the steatopygous Hottentot with bustles, they subjected their bodies to the rigid confinement of tightly-laced corsets. Doctors protested, but no doctor or health specialist could hope to deflect the course of fashion. Victorian women wore far more clothes than their grandchildren and great-grandchildren, but they did achieve elegance, as the ballroom scene, reproduced on plate 9, testifies. Part of the price they paid for that achievement is shown on the next five pages.

ELEGANCE BEFORE COMFORT. I.

THE WAIST.—BELTS.—SASHES.

A BOOK on dress would be incomplete without some allusion to the unfortunate habit of tight-lacing, which is only too prevalent in Great Britain. So much has already been written and said upon this subject, that we do not intend to enter very fully into detail as regards the consequences of pinching in the waist by means of corsets. A study of the accompanying little illustrations will give a clear idea as to the natural position of the internal organs and the manner in which they are displaced by the continuous practice of tight-lacing.

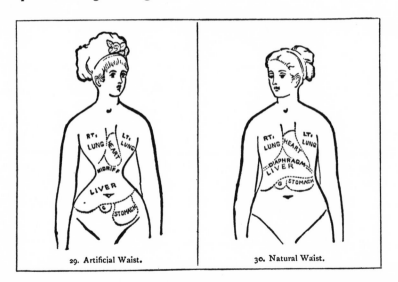

29. Artificial Waist.   30. Natural Waist.

It is small wonder that fashionable women, and working girls who are foolish enough to follow their bad example in this respect, feel languid, oppressed, and causelessly low-spirited. Even in cases where serious illness has not supervened, the languor and depression resulting from tight-lacing in time induce a feeling of hypochondria which in its turn leads to confirmed illness.

In Chapter LXX of *The Young Ladies' Treasure Book*, various articles of dress were discussed with commendable frankness and sense. The case against tight-lacing was forcibly made, and the opening of it with the warning diagrams, reproduced above from page 718, was reinforced by the views of Sir Erasmus Wilson. He admitted his inability to compete with fashion.

ELEGANCE BEFORE COMFORT. II.

THE Y AND N PATENT
DIAGONAL SEAM CORSET.

NEWEST INVENTION. EXQUISITE MODEL. UNIQUE DESIGN.
**Perfect Comfort. Guaranteed Wear. Universal
Adaptability. Free from complication.**
ADVANTAGES OVER ANY OTHER MAKE OF CORSETS.
THIS CORSET HAS BEEN INVENTED to supply what was really
wanted—viz., a Corset warranted not to split in the seams, at the same time
combining every excellence required in a lady's Corset. All the parts are
arranged diagonally instead of the ordinary upright pieces, the seams being
thus relieved of a great portion of the strain. The material is also cut on the
bias, and yields to the figure without splitting. The bones are arranged to
give support to the figure where required (avoiding undue pressure), and by
crossing the diagonal seams prevent the utmost strain in wear tearing the
fabric. The *specialité* of construction gives the freest adaptability to the
figure, making it unrivalled in its graceful proportions, and meeting the
requirements of the latest fashions without any complication of belts, straps,
&c. To prevent imitations every Corset is stamped. *To be had of all high-
class Drapers and Ladies' Outfitters; through the Principal Wholesale Houses.*

**This Corset has gained the Gold Medal at the
New Zealand Exhibition.**

From *The Graphic*, January 5th, 1884, page 23.

BROWN'S PATENT
"DERMATHISTIC" CORSET

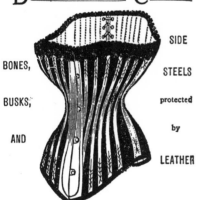

SIDE

BONES,

STEELS

BUSKS,

protected

by

AND

LEATHER

The mechanics of elegance were studied by
specialists who advertised in a way that must
have saddened authorities like Sir Erasmus
Wilson, who admitted that when he asked
ladies what was the *use* of stays was met by the
reply that they gave "a *roundness of waist* which
we could not otherwise obtain." (*The Young
Ladies' Treasure Book*, Chapter LXX, note on
page 719.)

The *Queen*, November 17, says:—
"There is nothing like leather, and the novel idea of
covering with kid those parts which wear out first
seems a most practical idea. The DERMATHISTICS
are shapely, neatly sewn, and the leather adds but
little to their weight."
Myra, December 1, says:—
"An ingenious method for ensuring durability. The
leather adds in no way to the bulk, while it gives a
decided added support to the figure, besides preventing
wear. They are very comfortable."
BLACK, and all Colours, 5s. 11d. to 15s. 6d. Satins, 8s. 6d.
to 21s. SOLD EVERYWHERE. AVOID WORTHLESS IMITA-
TIONS.

Above: From *The Graphic*, Summer Number,
1884, page 17. *Right:* From *The Graphic*,
May 17th, 1884, page 487.

ROSENTHAL'S SANITAIRE
CORSET.

This CORSET is constructed to
obviate the debilitating effects of
ordinary Corsets by relieving the
delicate and vital organs of the female
structure by preventing the damag-
ing mechanical pressure, while still
affording a healthy and comfortable
support to the wearer. By its use
the following results of great importance are attained. The support to
the figure is properly distributed,
and the distressing effects of Tight
Lacing neutralised; and in all other
respects it is one of the most perfect
and useful Corsets ever offered to the
REGISTERED public.
D. ROSENTHAL and CO., 5, Cripplegate Buildings,
London, E.C.

ELEGANCE BEFORE COMFORT. III.

The slender line of the post-crinoline and pre-bustle period. A half-mourning dress from *Sylvia's Home Journal*, 1879. The figure, the hair-style, the metal pot stand, and the aspidistra exhibit elongated curves.

ELEGANCE BEFORE COMFORT. IV.

Above: From *The Graphic*, January 30th, 1886, page 123. *Right:* From *The Graphic*, April 11th, 1885, page 363.

The above made to measure for the same price For Patterns of Material and form of self-measurement apply to

W. P. STOCKBRIDGE, MANTLES, COSTUMES, AND FANCY DRAPERY, 204, 206, and 262, OXFORD STREET, W.

"Too small a waist is as great a fault in proportion as one that is too large," said *The Young Ladies' Treasure Book*, "and it should be looked on with greater disfavour than the latter, as indicating either something wrong with the internal organs or the practice of violent measures to reduce the natural size." (Chapter LXX, page 719.) But if you wanted to look as modish as the figure on the right, you had to take the "violent measures" depicted on the left, and put yourself into an unbreakable metal frame. (See pages 94 and 95.)

ELEGANCE BEFORE COMFORT. V.

WORTH ET CIE.,
"ARTISTES EN CORSETS."

WORTH et CIE
have added a separate
DEPARTMENT for GEN-
TLEMEN, and every class of
Corset, riding, surgical, spinal,
for corpulency, made to measure.
The LADIES' DEPART-
MENT is still carried on as
before, and special attention is
given to the Dressmaking
Department.
CORSETS (Patented) made
for all figures, also for embon-
point, deformities, curvature,
and spinal complaints. Orders
from abroad receive every attention. Instructions for country
orders and self-measurement on
application to

WORTH et CIE.,
4, Hanover Street, Regent Street, W.,
BRANCHES: 15, SLOANE ST., LONDON;
74, KINGS ROAD, BRIGHTON.

Above: From *The Graphic*, August 18th, 1883,
page 179.
Left: Men also kept their waistlines under
control. Though tailors were skilled in the art
of disguising or modifying corpulency, it was
sometimes necessary to resort to corsets. From
The Graphic, August 11th, 1883, page 147.
(Continued on pages 167 and 168.)

CHAPTER IV

THE COSY HEARTH

SINCE the thirteenth century the private chambers of English houses have had wall fire-places with flues; only the great halls had open hearths near the centre of the floor, with louvres in the roof through which the smoke ultimately found an exit; and a six-hundred-year-old tradition of comfort has been associated with the sight of a fire, which, as Sir Henry Wotton said, added to a room "a kind of *Reputation*."(55) From the reign of Henry VIII to the end of the Georgian period, the chimney-piece attained an ornate magnificence; it was often the principal feature of a room, and was always a focal point, though by the 1830's it had lost its decorative dominance. "The chimney-piece of the present day has been reduced in height to allow the introduction of the chimney-glass," said the Editor of *Domestic Life in England*, writing in 1835, "the jambs are no longer enriched with sculptural embellishments, but exhibit plainness and severity of style, especially when we recollect the exuberant fancies of our forefathers in this branch of internal decoration."(56) But it remained the focal point of comfort, and in a sitting-room was always generous in size, though not perhaps as spacious as the one that warmed the best sitting-room at Manor Farm, which Dickens described as "a good, long, dark-panelled room with a high chimney-piece, and a capacious chimney, up which you could have driven one of the new patent cabs, wheels and all."(57) Robert Kerr, in *The Gentleman's House*, published in 1864, said, "for a Sitting-room, keeping in view the English climate and habits, a fireside is of all considerations practically the most important. No such apartment can pass muster with domestic critics unless there be convenient space for a wide circle of persons round the fire, embracing indeed in some degree the table; and this without inconvenience or disturbance being created at any point by the passing out and in and to and fro of all parties. It is the placing of the fire-place with relation to the door or doors, windows, sideboard, closets (if any), and furniture generally which constitutes the problem."(58) In the dining-room the problem was different, for there, said Kerr, "the only purpose of the fire is to warm the room throughout, and if possible equably, without purposely constituting what is invaluable in a Sitting-room, a comfortable fireside; so that, but for our pardonable prejudices in favour of the open grate, the best mode of heating for the special

" A ROLAND."

[*Officer of Volunteers having requested the Serving Man to put a Screen on his Chair.*
Wife of Regular. SORRY TO SEE THAT VOLUNTEERS CAN'T STAND FIRE.
O. of V. OH, YES, THEY CAN; BUT NOT AT THEIR BACKS.

Detachable screens of woven canework could be fixed to chair backs, like the example
illustrated above. From *Judy*, March 25th, 1868, page 282.

purpose would be by hot-water apparatus or the like. Consequently, the
fire-place has simply to be placed where it shall best warm the room and
least scorch the company. To place it in a recess sometimes helps the matter;
to bring it forward with a chimney-breast does the reverse. In any room over
30 feet in length two fire-places are generally provided. Both ought to be on
the same wall, opposite the windows, unless there be special circumstances to
prevent it."[59] Robert W. Edis, at the beginning of the 1880's after observing
that the mantelpiece "should be an important feature in any room," described
the most suitable treatment for the dining-room mantelpiece and overmantel.
It could be, he said, "of unpolished wainscot, mahogany, American walnut,
or painted deal, with a lining of black or golden Sienna marble; the lower
panels may be filled in with good painted subject tiles, or delicate carving of
fruit or flowers, the main shelf sufficiently broad to take, if necessary, the

various ornaments, useful or otherwise, which are wanted, with perhaps a centre panel for a good portrait or subject picture, enframed in boldly carved moulding; round it, on either side, might be plain panelling, carried up to the ceiling line, with recesses for sculpture or bronzes, or tiers of shelves for those whose tastes lie in china or other *bric-à-brac*, the top perhaps finished with a bold curved cove, filled in with stamped leather or decorative enrichment."[60]

Whether there was one fire-place, or two as Kerr specified for a large room, the heat was nearly always unevenly distributed. Some guests were almost roasted, others half-frozen. At the dinner in Hanby House, given by that "am*aaz*in instance of a pop'lar man," Mr. Puffington, to celebrate the splendid run with his hounds, described by Sponge and Jack Spraggon and

printed with so many errors by the *Swillingford Patriot*, "after the usual backing and retiring of mock modesty, Mr. Puffington said he would 'show them the way,' when there was as great a rush to get in, to avoid the bugbear of sitting with their backs to the fire, as there had been apparent disposition not to go at all."[61]

Protection from the heat of the fire was provided by screens: detachable, like the example on the opposite page, fixed or adjustable. The latter gave the ladies of a household opportunities for exercising their artistic talents. Many traditional forms were used. For example, the sliding pole or banner screen

An ornamental fire screen of papier-mâchè, framing a view of the Martyrs' Memorial at Oxford. This was shown at the Great Exhibition by the Oxford firm of Spiers & Son, whose premises on the corner of Oriel and High Streets are shown on page 93. Reproduced from *The Official Catalogue*, Volume II, page 734.

had survived from the eighteenth century, and variations of those illustrated
in Chippendale's *Director* were made, for that copy-book was used by Victorian
cabinet makers and upholsterers, as well as a best-selling forgery, published
by John Weale, who passed off Thomas Johnson's designs as Chippendale's
work.[62] Weale issued the first book of alleged Chippendale designs in eleven
plates, sold for seven shillings, without any letterpress or title page or publisher's imprint. This appeared at some time prior to 1834, at which date
Weale published another and larger forgery. By some means he had acquired
the old plates engraved for Johnson's book of designs, and these he rearranged,

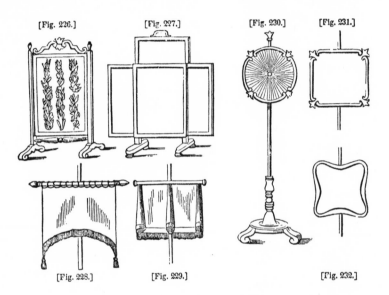

[Fig. 226.]   [Fig. 227.]   [Fig. 230.]   [Fig. 231.]

[Fig. 228.]   [Fig. 229.]   [Fig. 232.]

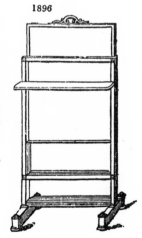

1896

Above: Fire screens from Downing's *The Architecture of Country
Houses* (New York, 1850), described as follows: Fig. 226. A cheval
screen for the parlour, with a mahogany frame. (Downing in
error mixed up the descriptions of Figs. 226 and 227: they have
been corrected here.) Fig. 227. An extension fire screen, the sides
and top drawing out when required: used chiefly in dining-rooms.
Figs. 228 and 229. Drawing-room fire screens, of the banner type.
Fig. 230 shows the complete banner screen. Figs. 231 and 232 are
formed "by a single piece of plate-glass." (Section XII, pages
429–31.) For an "American Rococo" example, see page 71.

Right: A sliding fire screen from Loudon's *Encyclopaedia* (1833),
page 1050.

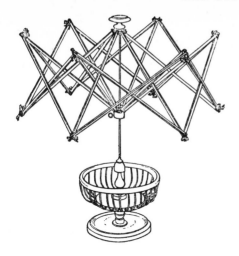

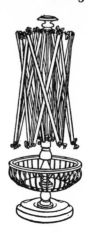

Somebody was always knitting by the fireside, but an obliging man was not always present when wool had to be wound. This wool-winder, shown open and closed, was a slender and elegant design. *Circa* 1840. *Drawn by Marcelle Barton.*

removing the signature "T. Johnson" on each plate, and engraving "T. Chippendale" in its place. He took the title page of Johnson's book, retained the ornate, rococo design, and substituted Chippendale's name for Johnson's and his own in place of the original publisher, Robert Sayer. In 1858–59 he published another edition, with additional plates, entitled *Old English and French Ornament*.[63]

There were other copy-books, with plates directly or indirectly based on Georgian designs, which were interpreted with ornamental additions by the furniture trade on both sides of the Atlantic. Loudon included sliding fire-screens and a design with two swinging leaves in his *Encyclopaedia* (1833), and Downing illustrated seven forms in *The Architecture of Country Houses* (see opposite page). The type Downing described as a "cheval screen" is almost identical with Loudon's design with the swinging leaves. *The Young Ladies' Treasure Book* was prolific in suggestions for home-made fire screens. "A pretty little banner-screen is made by cutting cretan embroidery into strips, and inserting between them strips of black velvet embroidered in filoselle. A sapphire-blue velvet border will serve as a frame, and combed crewels in tufts will furnish it with a fringe at the bottom." Another recommendation was "a fire-screen of nasturtiums embroidered in silks upon slate-grey Pongee silk, framed in cherry-wood. . . . The colours may be orange, yellow, scarlet or 'maroon.' "[64]

Those capacious fire-places, heaped up with coal, gave out scorching heat. Fresh air, in the form of whistling draughts, came into the room from the sash windows and from beneath the doors, and cooled the backs of those seated round the fire. But such uncomfortable ventilation was often modified by the use of long, sausage-shaped draught-excluders, of fabric—generally red in colour—filled with sawdust, which were placed along the joint between the upper and lower window sashes and on the floor in front of doors. Ventilation

was then provided by a cast-iron box, with an iron-valve that was opened by
the pressure of impure air in the room, and closed automatically to check the
emission of smoke from the chimney. This valve was usually inserted at the
side of the chimney-breast near the ceiling, the front flush with the wall, and
painted or white-washed the same colour.

With the reduction in height and importance of the chimney-piece, the
mantelpiece acquired a new decorative significance. "In a well-lighted apartment, with light furniture, white marble is decidedly preferable," said
Richardson, in *The Englishman's House*. In rooms moderately lighted, "serpentine, black, or coloured marbles, grey and even red granite, may all
agree. . . ."[65] Those sepulchral white marble mantelpieces were partly
concealed by valances, like the one in Tenniel's drawing of Alice beginning
her adventure *Through the Looking Glass*, reproduced opposite. "Mantel
hangings, or valances, have now become an accepted portion of household
decoration, wherever the mantel remains, instead of the new style mantel-
shelf or the 'gallery' chimney-place, with its 'wall-laid' historical or religious
painting above the hearth," said the writer on "Taste and Care in the House-

Gentlemen stood gracefully in front of the fire, resting an arm on the mantel-shelf, comfortably warm and strategically placed for addressing a "captive" audience, for no member
of the audience wished to move too far away from the fire. From *The Adventures of Mr. Verdant
Green*, by Edward Bradley (published 1853–56), pages 133 and 164.

The arched fire-place, with its grey, black, or white marble surround, the draped mantel-shelf with a tall, arched looking-glass above in a carved and gilded frame, the French clock of gilded metal, protected in a glass case, the ornaments, also protected by glass, are typical of the sedate comfort of the fireside in the 1870's, when Alice began her adventure through the looking-glass. The mantel-shelf was not over-crowded, though it is possible that Tenniel omitted the usual array of ornaments in this example, to allow Alice to climb up. (Reproduced from *Through the Looking Glass*, by permission of Macmillan & Company Ltd.)

hold," in *The Young Ladies' Treasure Book*. "Nothing is considered too costly a material upon which to paint or embroider a mantel-valance, no pains ill-bestowed that serve to beautify these hangings, which are considered to constitute an elegant and highly acceptable bridal, Christmas, or birth-day gift. White velvet, for example, decorated with a wreath of orange blossoms and leaves in oils, intermingled with fronds of that most exquisite of ferns, the 'maiden-hair,' is a late bridal gift. It is heavily edged with white and green silk fringe, below which falls a row of balls of white carved wood fastened to the fringe, and which serves to keep the valance in place. For mantel-decoration above this superb hanging are two vases, four feet high, of 'irridescent amber' glass-ware, over the rainbow-like surface of which trail smilax and white honeysuckle, imitated from the 'Assyrian' pattern. The central ornament is peculiarly beautiful, being a large and unusually perfect conch shell, with a lining of pure colour, in which reclines the figure of a nymph, sleeping. Above her is a cupid, who has climbed to the top of the shell and gazes at the sleeper. The mantel-valance, the vases, the nymph and

Left: Design for mantelpiece shelves, by Charles L. Eastlake, intended for use in a library. "Few men care for a mirror in such a room," said the designer; "but if it is indispensable to the mantelpiece, let it be a long low strip of glass, stretching across the width of the chimney-breast, about eighteen inches in height, and divided into panels. Over this may be raised a capital set of narrow shelves—say six inches wide and twelve inches apart—for specimens of old china, &c. The plates should be placed upright on their edges, and may easily be prevented from slipping off by a shallow groove sunk in the thickness of each shelf. A little museum may thus be formed, and remain a source of lasting pleasure to its possessors, seeing that 'a thing of beauty is a joy for ever.' " From *Hints on Household Taste* (second edition, 1869), Chapter V, page 122, plate XXVI. *Right:* Some thirty years later, complicated mixtures of this kind were being produced by the furniture manufacturing trade. This mantel and overmantel, a single fitting, shown at the Furnishing Trades Exhibition, April, 1897, was made by C. F. Finch & Co., of Bethnal Green Road. From *Furniture and Decoration*, Volume XXXIV, April, 1897.

A mantel-valance, from *Sylvia's Home Journal*, 1881. The design of the mantelpiece was often completely concealed by decorative fabrics.

Eastlake's idea of "a little museum" above the mantel-shelf certainly appealed to Robert W. Edis, who published this illustration of his own dining-room mantelpiece on plate 11 of *Decoration and Furniture of Town Houses*. He had "a cluster of shelves specially made to take blue and white china" with the shelves "moulded on the edge and made narrower as they rise in height, and the whole cluster . . . fastened to the wall with strong wrought-iron brackets. . . ." (See page 106.)

This dining-room, designed by Robert W. Edis, was described by him "as an example of simple treatment for wall decoration and furniture." It is reproduced from plate 16 of *Decoration and Furniture of Town Houses*, and the description continues as follows: "In this room the mantelpiece, with the *étagère* over, is made to form an important feature of the general design; the wall space is divided by a high dado or picture rail slightly moulded with ½ inch gas piping under, as a picture rod. The frieze is painted in plain vellum tone of colour, and decorated with stencil pattern enrichment. The woodwork generally is of deal varnished, the panels of the doors and shutters filled in with stencil decoration in a light shade of brown under the varnish. The general wall surface is hung with an all-over pattern paper of good warm golden brown tone of colour, admirably adapted for pictures. The furniture throughout is executed in Spanish mahogany, and designed to harmonise with the general character of the decoration." (Lecture IV, pages 171–72.) Such a restless conflict of form and colour and pattern could hardly provide the sort of dining-room specified in *The Young Ladies' Treasure Book*, where "everything breathes of comfort and that repose which acts so beneficially upon the digestive organs when they are summoned into active service." Old Redburn, in the interior on page 67, enjoyed far more comfort in his severely masculine dining-room, which was free from what Edis called "high art-decoration."

A mantelpiece, designed by Robert W. Edis and illustrated on plate 10 of *Decoration and Furniture of Town Houses*. The arrangement of cupboards and shelves "for guns, fishing-rods, swords and china, cigars, tobacco, and pipes" was for his own library. "This work was done in deal, painted, at a moderate cost, the tiles and figure plaques after Teniers, being from an old German stove, and utterly unseen until placed as I have shown." (Page 126.)

shell, all harmonise with each other most perfectly."(66) A mantel-valance which completely conceals the mantelpiece is shown on page 107.

Clocks of a monumental kind in black or white marble occupied the centre of the mantel-shelf, and with vases and other ornaments were reflected by the tall chimney-glass. Such glasses generally had an arched head and an enriched, moulded and gilded frame. Tenniel shows Alice climbing through just such a glass, having carefully threaded her way between the ornament and the clock under their transparent domes. (See page 105.) More elaborate chimney-glasses were flanked by sets of shelves, rather like slender versions of the *étagère* Downing recommended for the drawing-room of a villa, illustrated in the previous chapter on page 84. Eastlake preferred shelves, and for masculine rooms like a library, suggested an arrangement for the display of old china and other ornaments, which

Stove by Robertson, Carr & Co., of Sheffield, shown at the Great Exhibition, 1851. The upper part is of cast-iron, the grate of polished steel. (From *An Illustrated Cyclopaedia of the Great Exhibition*, pages 326 and 329.) A fading loyalty to classical architecture and ornament has influenced the proportions and decoration, but has not allowed the designer to overcome his dread of blank space.

The Alhambra stove, manufactured by Stuart & Smith of Sheffield, and shown at the Great Exhibition of 1851. It was purchased by Queen Victoria. "The pattern is arabesque of the richest description, in ormolu and bright steel." (From *An Illustrated Cyclopaedia of the Great Exhibition*, pages 323 and 328.)

would allow "a little museum" to appear above the mantelpiece. (How Eastlake's prototype ultimately affected the ideas of the furniture trade is illustrated on page 106.) Over a decade later, Robert Edis elaborated the idea of "a little museum" (page 108), but for his own library or study he devised a manly arrangement of glass-fronted cupboards to contain guns, fishing-rods and swords, shelves for china, and little cabinets for tobacco and cigars (page 110).

For small bedrooms or dressing-rooms where space was restricted, Edis suggested that there was no reason "why the mantelpiece should not, to a

IMPROVEMENTS IN THE OPEN FIRE-PLACE

An improved form of fire-grate, an early example of convection heating, described and illustrated in a paper read by Mr. John Taylor, Junior, M.A., F.S.A., at the Ordinary General Meeting of the Royal Institute of British Architects, January 12th, 1863. "An Englishman's love for his fire-place," he said, "is so deeply rooted, that, even supposing it could be shewn that a close stove possessed greater advantages, I am sure he would most reluctantly relinquish all the comfortable associations with which it is connected, although he is accustomed to turn his back upon it (one of the Peculiar privileges of our sex)."

Above: Diagram showing the action of the grate. (See page 115.) *Right:* The front of the grate, surrounded with small radiating china tiles with serrated edges, "which, being brought together, form ornamental perforations through which the warm air enters the room. . . ." From *Papers read at the R.I.B.A., session 1862–63, pages 90–93.*

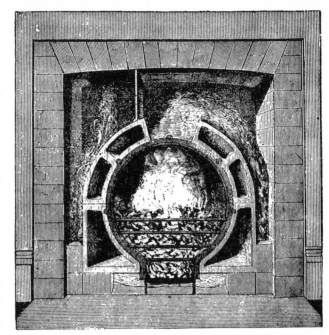

certain extent, be formed into a sort of dressing-table. Above the shelf, which adapts itself easily for all dressing paraphernalia, on either side, might be formed small cupboards, useful for many purposes, the centre space between being filled up by a sufficiently large looking-glass, flanked with light movable brackets for gas or candles, the whole made of deal stained and polished, or painted and varnished, or of some other inexpensive wood." He added that such an arrangement would be unsuitable "for the more important work of a lady's toilet; but in small bachelor or dressing-rooms, it would, I venture to think, be found sufficient for all purposes, and infinitely better than the movable table. . . ."[67]

The fire-place opening was generally arched, either rounded or slightly pointed, of cast-iron or polished steel with applied ormolu mouldings; the grate was blackleaded, or kept bright with Brunswick black; the surround and the hearth were often tiled. The hob grate survived, and was very popular in bachelors' apartments, and the basket grate, standing independently on the back hearth, was used in large fire-places; and for those types the opening was usually rectangular. A prodigious amount of coal was consumed, for it was cheap, abundant, and of excellent quality; but after several years of experiment, slow-combustion grates were introduced and became popular during the '70's. "The fire-place suits our climate," said Richardson; "it is cheerful and attractive, but it gives its heat only by radiation."[68] He believed that "the common fire-place has held its own, and will continue to hold its own, against the best-contrived stove that can be introduced in lieu of it. But it still remains to find such a construction as will remedy its serious defects. These are chiefly such as pertain to the flue; it is not to the stove that these belong, for that, thanks to our excellent makers, is quite perfect."[69] He

Dining-room fender, designed by Arthur William Blomfield (see page 115), and illustrated in *Hints on Household Taste* (second edition, 1869), Chapter V, page 127. Eastlake commended the extreme simplicity of construction, contrasting this design with those produced by manufacturers who persisted "in decorating them with a species of cast-iron ornament, which looks like a bad imitation of rococo carved work."

enumerated the defects of flues, and the effect of the remedies on the skyline of towns. "In our sluggish winter atmosphere," he said, "the smoke leaves the open flue with tolerable certainty unless the flue is foul with soot; but when high winds prevail and the atmosphere is anything but sluggish, it teaches us the faults of the open flue, and volumes of smoke descend into our apartments. There are few occurrances in domestic life more vexatious and annoying than this; the numerous unsightly appendages in the form of cowls, turncaps, and windguards which appear alike on our houses, churches, and palaces, whilst they exhibit the ingenuity of our builders and workmen in remedying the trouble of smoky chimneys, demonstrate also the frequency of the misfortune."[70]

Although Richardson was such a forthright champion of the fire-place, he illustrated and described a stove for the entrance hall of a Baronial Mansion, externally a romantic evasion of function, calculated to surprise and perhaps injure anybody who took it for a suit of armour and touched it, especially as it was intended to appear in a group "of ancient armour, pikes and helmets, and the other warlike implements of ancient times. . . ."[71] A side view and a section through this stove are given on page 117.

The improvement of flues and fire-places received constant attention from architects, builders, manufacturers, and a host of inventors; but very few improvements were adopted. The smoky chimney and the wasteful fire remained with householders, although the consumption of coal was reduced by the introduction of fire-clay linings to grates, and the use of fire-clay balls. In 1863 a form of convection heating was described at a meeting of the Royal Institute of British Architects,[72] and illustrations of the device are reproduced on page 113.

Poking the fire was a national pastime, and when fire-irons—shovel, poker, tongs and long-handled brush—were made of polished steel or brass and elaborately decorated, a spare poker was often kept for use, the one belonging to the set being merely for show. Curbs of marble or metal, cast-iron, brass or polished steel, moulded and ornamented, bordered the hearth; but low, shaped or pierced fenders were also used, like those shown on pages 61, 104 and 106. Eastlake complained of the way manufacturers decorated fenders "with a species of cast-iron ornament, which looks like a bad imitation of rococo carved work."[73] He illustrated two designs, by Arthur William Blomfield, an architect who built several churches, was knighted in 1889 and awarded the R.I.B.A. gold medal in 1891. One of these designs is reproduced on the opposite page: it is high, simply constructed, and, as Eastlake observed, fully answers "the purpose for which (as its very name signifies) a *fender* is intended, namely, to protect dresses, &c. from the chance of becoming ignited by close contact with the fire—an accident, unfortunately, of too frequent occurrence while the dangerous and ungraceful crinoline was in fashion."[74]

High fenders fitted with leather seats were introduced during the latter part of the century. There were two principal types, the seat curb, and the club fender, and both were incorporated with the metal structure of the fender. The seat curb consisted of padded box seats at each end of the fender, which provided two receptacles, one for coal and the other for slippers. The club fender was a continuous seat, supported by vertical metal bars rising from the front and sides of the curb. A small supply of fuel was kept in a coal vase or box, with a detachable metal lining and a metal slot or socket at the back to take a small shovel with a wooden handle. Made in mahogany, walnut or oak, and sometimes of metal, japanned black and decorated with painted flowers and leaves or gold arabesques, these boxes were sometimes described as a purdonian or purdonium, fancy names that appear in trade catalogues during the second half of the century. (See below.) Brass, copper and iron scuttles and cauldrons had been used during the Georgian and early Victorian periods, but they had no permanent place by the fireside, as it was then customary for servants to carry coal into a room in some such receptacle, make up the fire, and take it down to the cellar again. As domestic labour was less plentiful and far more expensive after the 1850's, a scuttle or coal box always stood at one side or other of the fire-place.

The fireside might be cosy, but it was not always well-lit, for the little hot jets of flame that sprouted from gas burners on wall brackets and on the form of chandelier that was known as a gaselier (sometimes spelt gasalier or gasolier) lacked the mellow softness of wax candles and lamps, and until the power and purity of gas lighting was improved by the incandescent mantel, it was decidedly inferior to the paraffin oil lamp. The incandescent mantel and the atmospheric burner, introduced at the close of the century, gave six times the amount of light of the jet burners without increasing the consumption of gas. Owing to some ill-considered legislation, the development of electric lighting by private enterprise was discouraged until the Electric Lighting Act of 1888 was passed, and thereafter the development of this new form of

A coal vase or box, japanned black, made by Orme, Evans & Company of Wolverhampton, and illustrated in *Furniture and Decoration*, October, 1897, page 212. These boxes, made of metal or wood with a detachable metal lining, were sometimes called a purdonian or purdonium, a name introduced at some time during the second half of the nineteenth century.

A stove for an entrance hall. It was "intended to fill a recess in the hall of a Baronial Mansion, placed on a marble pavement with groups of ancient armour, pikes and helmets, and the other warlike implements of ancient times, surrounding it." This shows the side view and a section through the stove. "A movable box is placed within the pedestal to receive the ashes; the smoke flue leaves at the back; the helmet opens to receive a cup of water. . . ." From *The Englishman's House from a Cottage to a Mansion*, by C. J. Richardson (1870), Design No. 12. pages 120–23.

THE FIRE-PLACE IN SUMMER

Artificial flowers or aprons of folded paper usually filled the empty fire-place. A long article in *Cassell's Household Guide* described a variety of alternative methods, of which two, shown to the left and opposite, are described in detail below and on pages 119 and 120.

artificial light went ahead, though other countries, notably the United States, had enjoyed the brightness of it in their homes for a long time.

All the year round the fire-place was the principal feature of a room, but during the summer it was not allowed to keep open a black, gaping mouth; nor was it enough to hide that sooty yawn with a fire screen; the whole fireside scene had to be transformed. *Punch* frivolously suggested that discarded crinolines should mask the empty grate,(75) but writers on interior decoration took the matter very seriously and poured out ideas for disguising and adorning the grate and hearth. Many were included in a long article on "Household Decorative Art," published in *Cassell's Household Guide*, and the writer had something to say about the summer-time defects of Victorian flues. "Some sitting-rooms during the summer emit so much draught, damp, earthy smell, and falls of soot into a room, as to render curtaining the grate a very useful process; as much air as is desired can be admitted by the windows or doors."(76) Aprons of folded paper and artificial flowers were popular, but as the writer of the article observed: "For handsome steel grates fire papers are not generally used." For the filling of the grate shown above, the following directions were given: "Purchase a yard and a half of tarlatan, and pull it entirely to

THE FIRE-PLACE IN SUMMER

Here a framed looking-glass conceals the fire-place opening and reflects the plants and blossoms that occupy the hearth. From *Cassell's Household Guide*, Volume II, pages 168–69 (1875). Flowers in the grate are also shown in the illustration from *Sylvia's Home Journal* on page 107.

pieces, thread by thread. [Tarlatan was a fine, open transparent muslin of coarse texture, used for dresses.] Fill the grate and fender entirely, as full and lightly as possible. The fire-irons are removed, greased with mutton fat, rolled in paper, and put away in a dry closet for the season. Arrange a slight wreath of myrtle on top of the shavings, or carelessly throw a few well-made muslin roses about the tarlatan in the manner shown. . . . It is very tasteful to use pale-coloured tarlatan, the shade of the furniture, for this purpose, but the tint should be extremely light. A little gold, sold for the purpose, looks well on the coloured cloud thus arranged in the stove. Nothing can be prettier than the palest shade of pink tarlatan, unravelled, in the grate, with a few moss roses carelessly arranged about it, and the lace window curtains lined with pink tarlatan throughout, a couple of shades deeper in tone."[77]

For the fire-place above a "piece of looking-glass in a plain gilt frame" was fitted as a chimney board, reflecting an array of blooming plants that stood in a gilt rustic fender, "with a green tin inside." Instead of the mantel-shelf valance of fringe, "point lace in deep vandykes mounted on silk" was

recommended, "edged with a narrow silk fringe, the colour of the furniture."
On each side "curtains of fine lace, lined with coloured tarlatan or thin silk"
were to be hung and looped back.[78] The sort of fringed mantel-shelf valance
referred to appears in Tenniel's drawing on page 105. Another summer treatment for the fire-place, published in *Sylvia's Home Journal*, is given on page 107.
The dining-room fire-place, on page 108, designed by Robert W. Edis, had
a light rod under the lower shelf from which depended "russet-brown Utrech
velvet curtains to hide the modern mantelpiece, and to shut in the whole
space when a fire is not required."[79] They were a sombre substitute for the
cheerful fire, and had no decorative pretensions: but then Edis had the male
approach to the problem: his solution, like most of the designs he produced
and found good, was uncompromisingly masculine. But except for exclusively
male rooms, the cosy fireside was a family affair: it was the epitome of
Victorian comfort.

CHAPTER V

COMFORT IN TRAVEL: THE ROAD

NOBODY pretended that coach travel was comfortable; exhilarating and romantic, perhaps, but even those emotions emerged retrospectively, when travellers in the railway age looked back regretfully at their youthful stoicism. Sir George Gilbert Scott, in the early stages of his career as an architect, was constantly on the road with his partner Moffatt. He described those strenuous days when he wrote his autobiography some forty years later. "I lived, like Moffatt, in a constant turmoil," he said, "though less so than he. The way in which we used to rush to the Post Office, or to the Angel at Islington, at the last moment, to send off designs and working drawings, or to set out for our nocturnal journeys, was most exciting, and one wonders, in these self-indulgent days, how we could stand the travelling all night outside coaches in the depth of winter, and in all weathers."[80] The comparison with latter-day comforts was inevitable; everybody who related their own experiences of coach travel did so in a way faintly detrimental to their own time, though Scott was not so blatantly hearty as Thomas Hughes, the author of *Tom Brown's Schooldays*. Hughes appeared to revel in tribulation; but then he was an early Victorian, a pupil of Dr. Thomas Arnold, and uncorrupted by the philosophy of comfort. "I sometimes think that you boys of this generation are a deal tenderer fellows than we used to be," he wrote. "At any rate you're much more comfortable travellers, for I see every one of you with his rug or plaid, and other dodges for preserving the caloric, and most of you going in those fuzzy, dusty, padded first-class carriages. It was another affair altogether, a dark ride on the top of the Tally-ho, I can tell you, in a tight Petersham coat, and your feet dangling six inches from the floor. Then you knew what cold was, and what it was to be without legs, for not a bit of feeling had you in them after the first half hour. But it had its pleasures, the old dark ride. First there was the consciousness of silent endurance, so dear to every Englishman—of standing out against something, and not giving in. Then there was the music of the rattling harness, and the ring of the horses' feet on the hard road, and the glare of the two bright lamps through the steaming hoar frost, over the leaders' ears, into the darkness; and the cheery toot of the guard's horn, to warn some drowsy pikeman or the hostler at the next change; and the looking forward to daylight; and last,

The Birmingham and Oxford coach, which made its final journey in the last week of August, 1852, after the opening of the Birmingham and Oxford Railway. It was a great favourite with undergraduates returning to Oxford, and the coachman often gave up his seat and the reins to a sporting box-passenger. From *The Adventures of Mr. Verdant Green* (published 1853–56), page 19.

but not least, the delight of returning sensation in your toes. Then the break of dawn and the sunrise, where can they be ever seen in perfection but from a coach roof?"[81]

That description has often been quoted, but Sir George Gilbert Scott said very much the same thing in fewer words and without any moralising. "These were the last days of the integrity of the old coaching system," he wrote, "and splendid was its dying perfection! It was a merry thing to leave the Post Office yard on the box-seat of a mail, and drive out amidst the mob of porters, passengers, and gazers. As far as Barnet on the north road seven mails ran together with their choicest trotting teams passing and repassing one another, the horns blowing merrily, every one in a good humour, and proud of what they were doing. Then the hasty cup of coffee at midnight, and the hurried breakfast had joys about them which I seem even now to feel again. One coach I travelled by—'the Manchester Telegraph'—cleared eleven miles an hour all the way down, stoppings included. It was a splendid perfection of machinery, but its fate was sealed, the great lines of railway being in rapid progress. Our shorter journeyings we did by gig and on horseback, though they often extended through the length and breadth of a county.''[82]

The Manchester *Telegraph* was the first coach to be fitted with springs, and thereafter they were known as Telegraph springs. Those crack coaches had exciting names: the York *Highflyer*, the Shrewsbury *Wonder*, the Devonport *Quicksilver*, the Birmingham *Tantivy*; but those names were not confined to individual vehicles, they were common to the whole fleet of coaches on a route.[83] Mail coaches were introduced by the Postmaster General in 1784,

The mails were given to the railways in 1841, and by the following year most of the stage coaches had stopped running. The highways were deserted, and coaches were driven only by gentlemen for recreation. One of the last regular coaches to survive until the 1850's was the Oxford and Birmingham. (See opposite page.) Reproduced by permission of *Punch* from the issue of May 15th, 1858, page 193.

TOUCHING.

Groom (to Old Coachman). "WHY, GUV'NR, WHAT HEVER 'S THE MATTER?"
Old Coachman (sobbing). "AH, WILLIAM! MOST AFFECTIN' SIGHT!. I'VE JUST SEEN THE FOUR-IN-HAND CLUB GOING DOWN TO GREENWICH! TEN ON 'EM! BEAUTIFUL TEAMS! AND DRIVEN BY REG'LAR TIP-TOP SWELLS! IT 'S BIN A'MOST TOO MUCH FOR ME!"   [*Is relieved by tears.*

and from these the fast stage coach developed during the first three decades of the nineteenth century. By 1825 coaches had attained a functional perfection of design, and established remarkable standards of speed, timing and comfort, compared with the earlier types they displaced. Their liveries were gay and varied, as the colour prints of the 1820's and '30's testify; they delighted the eye by the grace of form that fitness confers, which was shared by nearly everything made by skilled craftsmen, working with traditional, pre-industrial techniques, from all types of passenger vehicles to the unmatched beauty of the tea clippers and the frigates of the Royal Navy.

High speeds for coaches became possible when the gradients and surfaces of roads had been improved, "every effort being made, by straightening and shortening the roads, cutting down hills, and carrying embankments across valleys and viaducts over rivers, to render travelling by the main routes as easy and expeditious as possible."[84] The work of two gifted Scotsmen changed the character of the highways: Thomas Telford (1757–1834), a civil engineer, and a great builder of bridges and canals, and John Loudon McAdam (1756–1836), who invented the system of road making that was afterwards known as "macadamizing." Their roads had hard surfaces, without ruts, and with a crown, following Telford's specification for a metal bed "to be formed in two layers, rising about four inches towards the centre—the bottom course being of stones (whinstone, limestone, or hard freestone), seven inches in depth."[85] McAdam's method for surfacing was to have stones broken "into angular fragments, so that a bed several inches in depth should be formed," using for this purpose "fragments of granite, greenstone, or basalt," and watching the repairs carefully "during the process of consolidation, filling up the inequalities caused by the traffic passing over it, until a hard and level surface had been obtained, when the road would last for years without further attention."[86] The roads that were completed did last for many years, but the advent of the railways interrupted all the schemes that were in hand for road improvements throughout the country, and when, in 1841, the Post Office gave the contract for carrying mails to the railways, the golden age of the stage coach ended, and the highways and their famous inns declined. The inns never recovered, and the grass on the deserted highways was kept under only by local traffic, for such artificial revivals of coaching as the Four-in-hand Club, started in 1856, and the Coaching Club founded later in 1870, catered only for a form of sport beloved by members of the wealthy classes. (In America, the New York Coaching Club was established in 1875.) So the great age of coach travel lasted little more than fifteen years, but the memory of it left a permanent mark on the national imagination, becoming identified with "the good old times." It was idealised by Washington Irving in *The Sketch Book*, five years before it really began, and by Dickens in *The Pickwick Papers*, five years before it ended. "A Stage Coach . . . carries animation always with it, and puts the world in motion as it rolls along," Irving wrote

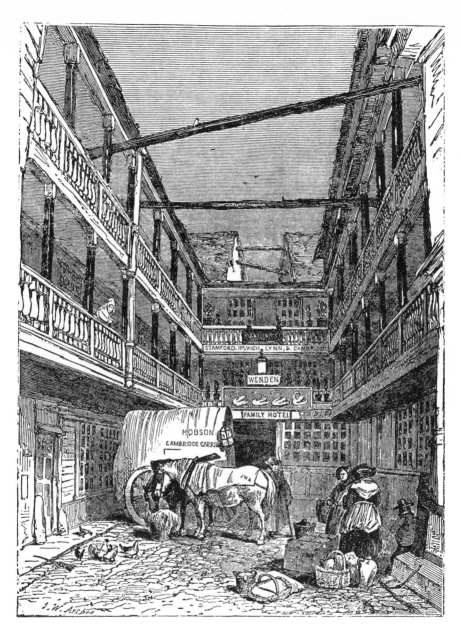

The Four Swans Inn yard, Bishopsgate Street Within, London, in the mid-nineteenth century.
A double row of galleries, giving access to the bedrooms, overlooks the yard; and the form
of the building dates from the sixteenth century. "There are in London several old inns,"
Dickens wrote in *The Pickwick Papers*, "once the headquarters of celebrated coaches in the
days when coaches performed their journeys in a graver and more solemn manner than they
do in these times; but which have now degenerated into little more than the abiding and
booking places of country wagons." (Chapter X.)

The London streets were bright with omnibuses, painted in various colours. The gay character of Georgian coaches and private vehicles was inherited by the democratic 'bus, and the comments of drivers and the patter of conductors reminded passengers at all times that the 'bus was a jovially democratic institution. From *Judy*, May 22nd, 1867, page 39.

Conductor. Go a-head, Bill, our dinner's ready, and we've only a Monster left.

in 1820.[87] Even then coach travel had its compensations, for the manners of coachmen and guards were improving; they no longer looked down on outside passengers as people of no account because they paid less than the "insides," and the passenger on the box seat might have the luck to sit next to a Tony Weller, though even when he had paid for that privilege he didn't always enjoy it, as David Copperfield discovered after he had booked his place from Canterbury to London, and had taken the trouble to have " 'Box Seat' written against the entry, and had given the book-keeper half-a-crown."[88] Passengers could smoke, an indulgence forbidden by the railway companies for many years. The "insides" were tolerably warm, the seats were well upholstered, the windows adjustable. The Telegraph springs and the new road surfaces minimised jolting and swaying, and some outside passengers were able to sleep soundly. Scott said that his partner Moffatt snored so loudly "on the box of the mail" that he kept "the inside passengers awake."[89]

Some experiments were made with steam-driven coaches, or land-carriages as they were called, and although they were mechanically successful, popular prejudice stopped their development. Despite this, several steam-traction companies were formed in the 1830's, and for a few years steam-carriages ran in London. They were a gift to caricaturists, and were consistently lampooned, and their dangers exaggerated. Horse-drawn traffic remained on the streets, and was, if anything, denser than in the Georgian age. Public transport enterprises began to cater for people who could not afford to hire a private

The first passenger tramcars in Europe were introduced by George Francis Train, an enterprising American, who found encouragement for his ideas at one place only, namely Birkenhead, where the first street railway, as it was called, was opened on August 30th, 1860. A year later trams were introduced in London, and for the next twenty years they were considered aggressively modern compared with the horse-drawn 'bus. They were certainly more commodious and ran very smoothly. From *Fun*, July 25th, 1874, page 35. Typical examples of horse-drawn trams are shown in John O'Connor's painting on plate 1.

CONVERSATIONS OF THE ROAD.

Tram Conductor (to 'Bus ditto) :—" GO ON, TAKE IT AWAY; TAKE IT DOWN TO THE SEASIDE AND MAKE A BATHING-MACHINE OF IT."

[*The answer was lost in the distance.*

vehicle or keep a carriage; and in July, 1829, Shillibeer introduced the omnibus from Paris, where it had appeared a year earlier, and was known as *voiture omnibus*. Drawn by three horses abreast, it had inside accommodation for twenty-two passengers. Those early omnibuses were quick and comfortable, although they looked clumsy, but they took up too much room on the streets, and were replaced by smaller types carrying twelve passengers inside. The knife-board seat running lengthways along the roof was added in 1849, and after the London General Omnibus Company was formed in 1856 'buses increased in numbers, and other companies were started. The humour of the old stage coachmen and guards was revived by the drivers and conductors of the 'buses, and, on the evidence of *Punch* and other comic papers, it was brisk cockney humour, lively and cheerful. The driver's conversation could be enjoyed only by the outside passenger on the box-seat of the 'bus; but when the knife-board seat was abolished early in the 1880's, the passenger's seat by the driver went too, and garden seats, each accommodating two people, were placed transversely on the top, with a central passage, and a curved staircase at the rear rising from the conductor's platform. This was the final type of the horse 'bus, which carried twenty-six passengers, twelve inside and fourteen on top, and the garden seats with the long, protecting boards each side of the upper deck, allowed ladies to enjoy the pleasure of riding on top, as their feet and ankles were decently hidden.

Trams came to London in the '60's, after they had been tried out experimentally at Birkenhead. They were introduced by an enterprising and irrepressible American named George Francis Train, whose excessive powers of showmanship and persuasion had failed to impress any town or city in Europe with the advantages of "The People's Carriage," as he called the tram, until he came to England, and found in Birkenhead, the prosperous opposite number of Liverpool, receptive and far-sighted municipal authorities. That critical mid-Victorian writer of guide books, Samuel Sidney, described Birkenhead as "a great town which has risen as rapidly as an American city, and with the same fits and starts."[90] Perhaps that was why Train was allowed to lay down the first tramway in Europe, from the Park, which Paxton had planned for the town in 1843, to Woodside Ferry. It was opened on August 30th, 1860. The following year London followed the lead of Birkenhead, and a line for horse-drawn tramcars was laid along the Bayswater Road, from the Marble Arch to Notting Hill Gate, followed by a second running from Westminster Abbey to Victoria Station, along Victoria Street. Both were Train's enterprises, and he celebrated the opening of each with lavish hospitality, issuing invitations to a great many important and prominent people: some of them were accepted. The wording of those invitations was unusual, and the one he sent out for "An American Breakfast" to be held at 10 a.m. on April 15th, 1861, to inaugurate the Victoria Street Tramway, began as follows:

The manners of 'bus conductors were variable: their powers of comment and repartee were considerable, but were nicely adjusted to suit the characters and deflate the pretensions of their passengers. Reproduced from *Moonshine*, January 3rd, 1885, page 11.

A FACT.

'Bus Conductor (to stout old lady, who has just handed him a sixpence).
"AND WHERE HAD WE THE PLEASURE TO PICK YOU UP, MA'AM?"

"I arrived in England in October, 1859. I opened the Birkenhead street railway (with a Banquet) in August, 1860; the Marble Arch street railway (with a Turtle Lunch) in March, 1861; and to-day I inaugurate the third street railway this side the New World with a Yankee breakfast.

"I cannot better shew my appreciation for the great kindness I have received in this Country, than by calling my friends about me whenever occasion offers. Several kind friends (I wish I had more enemies and fewer friends) say that I am running the thing into the ground,—that they talk about it in the Clubs,—and so forth; such nonsense is unworthy of intelligent minds. I intend to give Dinners, Lunches, Suppers, Breakfasts, just when I please, and if those I invite object, they of course will not honor me with their distinguished company. I maintain that a man has a perfect right to spend his own money, in his own way, providing he breaks no law, and laws are not yet made for Street Railways."[91]

Unfortunately they soon were. Tramcars were certainly more commodious and smooth-running than 'buses. Train's cars in Birkenhead had a knife-board seat on the upper deck, and in London the outside passengers were protected by a canopy. The cars seated twenty people inside, with room for twelve standing; looped leather straps hanging at intervals from the roof helped standing passengers to remain upright, so the straphanger began his century of suffering. Train had ended the invitation just quoted by saying: "I cannot think that any one would wish to throw any impediment in the way of introducing so great a luxury as THE PEOPLE'S CARRIAGE." But after Train's initial successes the development of tramways by private enterprise was consistently hindered. The cost of laying the track demanded a large capital outlay, which municipal authorities were reluctant to invest, but although

WINDOW STUDIES
June. The Festive Hour, 7.45 p.m., Piccadilly

Reproduced on a slightly reduced scale from *Punch*, June 5th, 1886, page 270. (By permission of *Punch*.) Chesterton once described the hansom cab as "a piece of English architecture; a thing produced by the peculiar poetry of our cities, a symbol of a certain reckless comfort which is really English. . . ." *Charles Dickens*, by G. K. Chesterton. (London: Methuen & Co., 1906.) Chapter VII, page 157. The hansom was designed by an architect who worked in the classic idiom. (See pages 20, 21, 162, 210, plate 1 and opposite.)

A CAB WITH A VIEW

This is what passengers saw from the comfortable little cabin of the Hansom cab, which could be closed or open as desired. Reproduced by permission of *Punch*, from the issue of August 18th, 1863, page 157. (See opposite page.)

Our friend Browne, the fashionable Portrait Painter, occupies this Hansom, going to dine in Carlton Gardens, April 7th—it was annoying under these circumstances, to meet Stodge, who was taking his Pictures to the Academy on the top of a Bus, and to be violently recognised by that low Bohemian all the way down Piccadilly.

they recognised the comfort and convenience of trams they put every obstacle in the way of private companies who wanted to construct lines through the areas they administered. An Act of 1870 gave local authorities extensive rights to place unjust and indeed intolerable burdens on tramway companies that sought permission to use their streets.(92) Concessions, if granted, were valid for twenty-one years only; after that the local authority was entitled "to buy the entire plant and all the stock at the appraised value, regardless of the revenues of the company at the time."[93] Despite the fact that trams were considered almost aggressively modern compared with 'buses, their comfort was made available to the ever-increasing travelling public so slowly that England, which had encouraged the pioneer of tramways, soon lagged far behind the cities of the Continent.

Private carriages were still as elegant as they had been in the Georgian period, and until the last quarter of the nineteenth century they were decorated with chaste colours: for example, a family landau shown by Silk & Sons of Long Acre at the International Exhibition of 1862 had a body of "a dark transparent green" with the under carriage and wheels "of a rich crimson

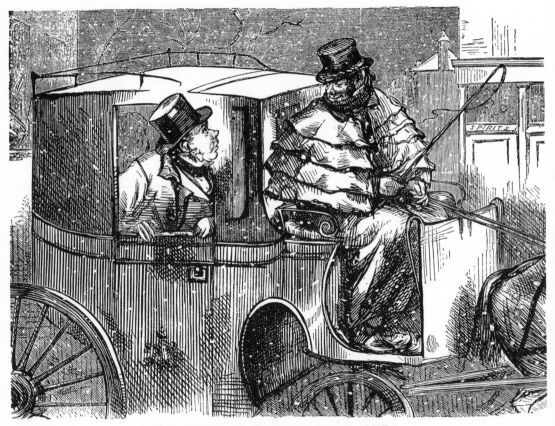

PREVENTION IS BETTER THAN CURE.

Nervous Party. IT SEEMS TO BE VERY SLIPPERY, CABBY.
Cabby. AH! IT'S ALL THAT, SIR; AND IF I DON'T 'AVE A HOPPERTUNITY O' DRINKING SOMEBODY'S 'EALT AFORE LONG, I SHOULDN'T BE SURPRISED IF VE 'AD A HACCIDENT.

Reproduced on a slightly reduced scale from *Judy*, December 30th, 1868, page 108.

A sociable, with interchangeable heads, allowing the vehicle to be converted "as pleasure or convenience requires, either into a coach, a landau, or a barouche." Shown by Rock & Son, of Hastings, at the International Exhibition of 1862. See examples on page 137. (From *The Art Journal*, illustrated international catalogue, 1862, page 94.)

colour." The barouche illustrated at the top of page 135, shown by Corben & Sons of Great Queen Street, at the same Exhibition, was painted "ultramarine blue, relieved with fine lines of vermilion . . . ." Coachmen and footmen wore gorgeous liveries, but by the close of the period they had been exchanged for sober fawns and browns and dark grey; and carriages like the brougham, victoria and landau were painted a uniformly respectable black, with some thin lines of colour, crimson or dark green or blue on the door panels and wheels.

Those light private vehicles were well sprung, far superior in comfort to the carriages of the Georgian age; and their makers, who achieved on a smaller scale the same functional perfection of design as the stage coach, exhibited a sensitive regard for good proportions. The brougham was a closed carriage with two or four wheels, introduced in 1838, and named after the First Baron Brougham and Vaux (1778–1868), Lord Chancellor of England, who was reputed to have been largely responsible for the design. He certainly placed the original order for such a vehicle with Hoopers, the coach-builders. The victoria, a graceful open carriage without doors, was so called because it was used by the Princess Victoria before she came to the throne. It had four wheels and was drawn by a pair of horses. Late in the '90's, the electrically-propelled brougham and victoria came into use. They had none of the explosive, uncertain adventurousness of the early motor cars, but were smooth-running, silent and odourless, though limited in range. They survived in Edwardian times until the motor car replaced them.

Hackney coaches, drawn by two horses, had been on the road since the early days of the nineteenth century, but in London their numbers were legally restricted. In 1831 such restrictions, which had also applied to cabs, were removed, and as a result many more light, one-horse cabs came into service. Their drivers had a reputation for recklessness and pugnacity. When Sam Weller brought Mr. Pickwick's luggage to the yard of the Bull Inn at Whitechapel, ready for the Ipswich coach, Tony Weller said: "He's cabbin' it, I suppose?" And Sam replied: "Yes, he's a havin' two mile o' danger at eight-pence."(94)

The four-wheeled cabs lost their reputation for speed, and became known by such unflattering names as *crawlers*, because of their slow pace, or *growlers*, because of the surly arrogance of their drivers. They were pervaded by a damp, musty, leathery smell. The upholstery was adequate, but usually rather grubby; the side windows were ill-fitting, with the adjusting straps often missing or damaged, so that one or both windows had to be wide open or tightly shut; the bare boards on the floor were sometimes covered with straw, which was not changed until it was matted with mud and filth. To communicate with the driver the passenger had to lean out of one of the windows and shout until he attracted his attention, at the risk of crushing or losing his top hat. The old gentleman shown on page 132 has successfully emerged; getting back was the trouble. The driver cultivated a mordant turn of humour, quite unlike the light-hearted banter of the 'bus crews. There was often an implied threat in his remarks; he was convinced that the customer was always wrong; and, if he dared, he browbeat his passengers into paying more than his legal due. He was never satisfied with the fare tendered; and was a brutal specialist in bullying women, particularly when they had children with them. " 'Ere, wot's this?" was the opening gambit of his complaint about the fare. If the passenger asked "How much is it?" there was usually one of two answers: the naming of an amount far above the legal fare, or, if the hirer was an obvious "soft touch," the smiling suggestion, "I leave it to you, sir." Blarney as often as not was used instead of bullying. In *Punch's Almanack* for 1860 there is a cartoon by John Leech entitled "Irresistible," showing an elderly lady disputing the amount a cabman has named. "What! Two shillings! and eighteenpence for waiting three-quarters of an hour? Nonsense, man! It was only ten minutes by my watch!" The cabman replies (insinuatingly): "Wasn't it, Miss? Well, then, I s'pose it was a missin' o' your pretty face as made it *seem* three kervarters of an hour!" (Fare pays, and thinks the cabman an extremely nice person.)

The cabman's habits and savagery were consistently castigated by *Punch*, whose pages showed up these blackguards year after year: they never improved.

In 1834 a new type of "Safety" cab with a single pair of large wheels was

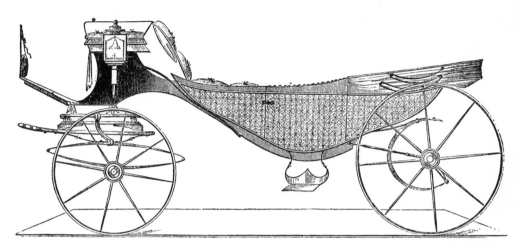

The elegance of the Georgian period was preserved and amplified in the design of private and public vehicles, and was transmitted after the Victorian age to the motor car; and here the lightness and grace of the private carriage is illustrated. *Above* is a design shown by Corben & Sons, of London, at the International Exhibition of 1862, and described as "a luxurious, sociable Barouche" painted "ultramarine blue, relieved with fine lines of vermilion, and glazed with carmine; the lining is of rich drab silk and satin, the lace white silk, with blue figures, elaborately plated lamps and door-handles. . . ." *Below* is an "improved light 'Craven' barouche" exhibited on the same occasion by Hooper & Company, of London. (From *The Art Journal*, illustrated international catalogue, 1862, pages 94 and 96.)

patented by Joseph Aloysius Hansom (1803–82), an architect who, in partnership with Edward Welch, had built churches in Liverpool and Hull, and designed the Town Hall at Birmingham, but had become involved in bankruptcy over its building. His original design for the Safety cab established the subsequent character of these vehicles, though the raised back seat for the driver was a later addition, and there were several other details and fittings which did not appear on the earliest model. Light, fast and comfortable, the hansom cab had a dashing, stylish air; it was also a cab with a view; the passenger could see where he was going, and by closing the half-doors and lowering the glass, could protect himself completely from the weather; also he could give directions to the driver through a little trap door in the roof. (See pages 20, 21, 130, 131 and 162.) Everybody used hansoms, even ladies a few years after crinolines went out, and their mobility and independence increased. The drivers had far better manners than the barbarians who drove the growlers; their clothes were smarter, and they wore well-cut overcoats instead of the heavy coat with many capes which the older drivers had inherited from the stage coachmen. Nearly all cab drivers wore top hats, but the hansom cabbies often preferred the more sporting bowler, and in summer affected light clothes, with a check pattern. Their cabs, as smart as their clothes, were always well-kept, with brightly polished brasswork; their

Left, above: Patent Park Phaeton, by Cook, Rowley & Co., of King Street, Regent Street. The body is attached to the car by plated snake hoops. *Left, below:* Pony carriage, by William Henry Mason, Kingsland Road. (See pages 133, 135 and opposite.)

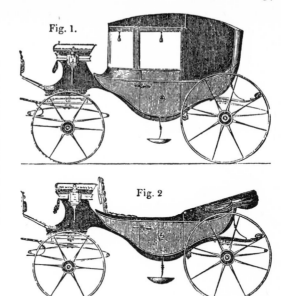

Fig. 1.

Fig. 2

When there was no imagined obligation to disguise an article, the Victorian designers proved their competence, and exhibited a sensitive regard for good proportions and functional excellence. The examples on this page and opposite were shown at the Great Exhibition and illustrated in *The Official Catalogue. Right:* The "Amempton" carriage, by Kesterton of Long Acre, which could be converted "into a light, open, step-piece barouche, adapted for summer or winter."

humour was akin to that of the 'bus drivers and conductors, and they were helpful to their passengers, especially when they were drunk, as gentlemen often were in the evening.

The hansom, most famous of all Victorian vehicles, was also the most comfortable. It outlasted its period, lingering on in London until the 1914–18 War, but, as the stage coach was killed by the railways, the hansom, in common with nearly all other forms of horse-drawn vehicle, succumbed to the internal combustion engine, and London and every city in the world began a new phase of traffic congestion.

"LUSITANIA"

"MEXICAN"

"ARIZONA"

Steam was not wholly accepted or relied upon by ocean-going passenger liners, even as late as 1885. In design they were still in the hybrid stage: their form was dictated by the needs of the sailing vessel. Only small craft, like ferry boats or the river steamers on the great waterways of the United States were expressly designed for steam power. (See pages 141 and 142.) The ships shown above were among the vessels taken over by the British Government when war with Russia was threatened. From *The Graphic*, May 16th, 1885, page 500.

CHAPTER VI

COMFORT IN TRAVEL: THE RAILWAY

SUCCESSFUL experiments in steam navigation had been made in the United States thirty-five years before the Stockton and Darlington Railway started to run a daily passenger-carrying coach on October 10th, 1825. At Philadelphia in May, 1790, an English sea captain named Samuel Kelly noted in his journal that he had seen a steamboat, "stemming the tide at the rate of about four miles an hour."[95] In 1798 Robert R. Livingston, the American statesman, had been granted the exclusive right to navigate the waters of New York State with steamboats, and when he was appointed United States Minister to France in 1801, he met his compatriot Robert Fulton (1765–1815), a gifted inventor and engineer who was then living in Paris. Fulton had succeeded in running a paddle-wheel steamboat on the Seine, and in 1803, when Livingston's monopoly of steam navigation in New York was renewed, he held it jointly with Fulton, who returned to America and shortly afterwards built a steamboat with engines made by Boulton & Watt of Birmingham. This was named the *Clermont*, after Livingston's home, and in 1807 she began to run between New York and Albany on the Hudson. Within a few years large, fast and luxurious paddle-wheel steamboats were carrying freight and passengers on the inland waterways of the United States. On great rivers like the Mississippi they raced each other, always trying to make new records, and covering immense distances. For example, in 1815, the *Enterprise* completed the 1,440-mile run from New Orleans to Louisville in twenty-five days, two hours and forty minutes; by 1819 the *Paragon* had cut the time to eighteen days and ten hours; in 1837 the *Sultana* reduced it to six days and ten hours; and the *Eclipse* brought it down to four days, nine hours and thirty minutes in 1853.[96]

The design of these river steamers had a permanent effect on American standards of comfort in travel. Describing the interior of a big New Orleans boat in *Life on the Mississippi*, Mark Twain said: "She was as clean and as dainty as a drawing-room; when I looked down her long, gilded saloon, it was like gazing through a splendid tunnel. . . ."[97] Alexander Mackay, in his account of travels in the United States during 1846–47, gave a detailed description of the first-class steamboat that carried him from New Orleans to St. Louis. "One might reason himself into the belief that she had a hull," he wrote, "knowing how necessary such things are to steamboats; but, viewing her from an ordinary position, the eye could detect none; all that was visible for her to rest upon being her paddle-wheels, which were very large. She was of immense width, the enormous protrusion of her lower deck on either side being the cause of the invisibility of her hull. This was so constructed as to accommodate in front the greatest possible quantity of cotton and other merchandise which she could carry without sinking her; whilst above it, resting on very slender pillars, rose the promenade decks, covered abaft the engine with an awning. She was named the 'Niobe,' and was like Niobe, all *tiers*. The saloon, which was between decks, occupied nearly the latter half of the vessel, the state rooms lining it, being entered both from within, and by means of a door, with which each was provided, entering from the walk between decks, which completely surrounded the saloon, the latter part of which was divided off into a cabin for the ladies. She carried a prodigious quantity of white and black paint upon her; had two enormous funnels, as most American boats have; and consumed a tremendous supply of wood, shooting up flame at night, and leaving a double train of brilliant sparks behind her. . . ."[98]

The spaciousness and luxury of the American river steamboats were not to be found in the coastal steamships that began to ply between British ports after 1815. For over three-quarters of a century both coastal and deep water steamships remained in a hybrid stage of development, their external form dictated by the needs of the sailing ship, their funnels dwarfed by tall masts with yards and rigging, so that sails could supplement the engines or supplant them in case of a breakdown. Only small craft, like the ferry boats on the Mersey and other rivers, and tugs, were designed solely for steam power. Britain had no waterways comparable with the Ohio, Mississippi or Missouri, so that nothing on the scale of the American steamboats could have developed to supply a prototype, or to suggest a basic form, for the new type of vehicles needed for railways. That daily passenger coach on the Stockton and Darlington Railway was named the *Experiment*: it carried six passengers inside and fifteen to twenty on the roof, but it was a solitary vehicle; only when the Liverpool and Manchester Railway was opened in 1830 were trains of coaches made up to cater for passenger traffic. With the opening of that line, the Railway Age really began: the public recognised it as a portent: even the Duke of Wellington, who abhorred change, condescended to preside at the opening ceremony, and although the Right Hon. William Huskisson, one of the Members for Liverpool, was run over by the *Rocket* and died the same night, that in its way was a portent too, for the old superstition about ships requiring a blood sacrifice during their building or launching seemed now to have a new application.

The Woodside Ferry Boat, 1886

Small craft, such as ferry boats and tugs, were designed for steam without any provision for auxiliary power. *Above:* A Mersey ferry boat in service during the 1880's. Reproduced from *The Graphic*, January 30th, 1886, page 121. *Left:* The trim type of vessel that succeeded the twin-funnelled paddle boats. *Drawn by David Owen.*

The *Rocket*, designed by George and Robert Stephenson, had become famous as a locomotive when it won the £500 prize, offered by the directors of the Liverpool and Manchester Railway for the best engine, and showed its superiority at the trials held at Rainhill in October, 1829. On that occasion it was driven by Edward Entwistle, a lad of under fifteen, who worked in the engineering shop where many parts of the *Rocket* had been made, and was recommended to George Stephenson by the shop foreman. Nobody then knew what special qualities an engine-driver should have: obviously he should be familiar with machinery, but driving experience had to be acquired: there were no guiding precedents, for the character and performance of the steam locomotives in service on slow freight-hauling jobs—like *Puffing Billy*, built in 1813 by William Hedley—were as different from those of the *Rocket* as a cart-horse from a crack coach team. This new type of skilled mechanic was destined to inspire generations of schoolboys with romantic ambitions and to assume responsibilities that would have shaken the nerves of the most

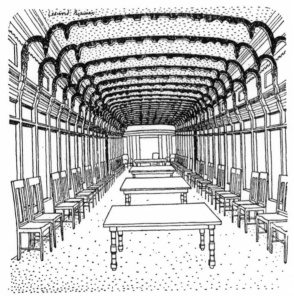

The inland waterways of the United States were developed by steam power over twenty years before the first American railroads. The river steamboat had its own characteristic form; was expressly designed for the new kind of power, and never passed through a hybrid stage like coastal and ocean-going craft. (See page 138.) The long spacious saloons may well have been the prototypes for the American railroad cars. Drawn by Leonard Rosoman and reproduced from *Industrial Art Explained* (1946 edition), by courtesy of George Allen & Unwin Ltd.

experienced stage coachman. The young Lancashire boy, who was born at Tilsey's Bank during March, 1815, was the first of the passenger-train engine-drivers; and after two and a half years on the Liverpool and Manchester line, making from two to four daily trips, his nerve broke under the strain, and he exchanged the job for the relatively tranquil life of an engineer on a coasting steamer. In 1837 he emigrated to the United States, and spent the rest of his

The American railroad cars had open platforms at each end, and a saloon with a central aisle, a form probably suggested by the river steamboat. (See opposite page.) The type shown here could be transformed into a sleeping car by night with two tiers of berths, the upper tier pulled down from the roof, the lower formed from the seats. This type of car was perfected by George Mortimer Pullman. (See pages 150, 151 and 155.) Drawn by Leonard Rosoman and reproduced from *Industrial Art Explained* (1946 edition), by courtesy of George Allen & Unwin Ltd.

life there, ultimately buying a small farm and settling down at Des Moines, Iowa. When he was eighty-seven an interview with him was published in *The Strand Magazine*, entitled, "The Man who Drove the 'Rocket.' "(99)

The safety of the passengers was in the hands of the engine-driver, though after signalling systems were introduced that responsibility was qualified, but not seriously diminished. Men of this new class had to be tough, and little was done by their employers to ease the strain of driving day and night in all

A train of first- and third-class coaches on the Liverpool and Manchester line, hauled by a famous early locomotive, the "Lion." This basic form of railway coach with separate compartments was used throughout the Victorian period, even when the length of the coach was increased by mounting it on flexible, four-wheeled bogies. Drawn from materials supplied by the former London, Midland and Scottish Railway, and reproduced from *Industrial Art Explained* (1946 edition), by courtesy of George Allen & Unwin Ltd.

weathers. No vestige of protection for the driver appeared on the *Rocket*, which was admittedly a pioneer design, nor on its successors on the Liverpool and Manchester line, like the famous *Lion*, or any of the early Great Western and London and North Western engines. Their designers may have thought that because coachmen had never been protected from wind and rain that engine-drivers could resist such exposure; but their working conditions were in no way comparable. Coachmen did not drive along the roads at speeds of half a mile a minute or more, subjected to constant alternations in temperature, like the driver and fireman on the footplate who endured heat from the proximity of the boiler and furnace, and rain, icy wind, sleet and snow in winter, converging on that cramped space between the back of the boiler and the tender. The *Rocket* and the *Lion* are illustrated opposite and above; and two of the engines shown at the Great Exhibition on page 146. The absence of protection may have arisen from the streak of puritanism that chilled the characters of the leaders and engineers of the Industrial Revolution: the lower orders were inured to hardship: any idea of pampering them would have seemed like impiety, and, worse still, unpractical impiety, to dedicated men like the Stephensons, father and son, and the stern, upright members of the new rich class who financed railways and conducted industrial enterprises. The slightest indulgence might have tempted the new types of mechanic to have ideas above their station, and to become less tractable than farm labourers and other comparatively docile workers. No workman, however novel and untried his occupation, should be allowed to forget or ignore the injunctions in the Catechism, "to order myself lowly and reverently to all my betters" and "to learn and labour truly to get mine own living, and to do my duty in that state of life, unto which it shall please God to call me."

Even when wind screens were at last introduced to shield drivers, they were of meagre dimensions, giving frontal protection only, and pierced by two circular glazed apertures, which gave a view ahead along the top of the boiler. Such shields were used during the 1840's on some of the engines running on the London and Southampton line, which became the London and South Western Railway; but several years passed before side extensions were added, and the cab with the half-roof only became general in the 1860's. A large and comfortable cab for driver and fireman was a feature of American loco-motives when they were designed and built by their own engineers. (Many of the early models on American railroads had been ordered from England, notably the Stourbridge *Lion*, which completed its first run in America on August 9th, 1829.) The commodious cab, the big smoke stack tapering down-wards to the boiler, and the cow-catcher projecting like the ram of a battleship in front of the swivelling bogie-truck with its four wheels, were characteristics of design that, however varied the accessories and livery, became identified with locomotives on every road in the United States. Two of those accessories never varied: the bell mounted on the boiler abaft the smoke stack, tolling mournfully throughout the whole journey, and the whistle that emitted a penetrating wail when approaching grade crossings or depôts. (This latter sound still haunts all American railroads, preserved by the sirens used on contemporary Diesel locomotives.) The provision of good shelter for the engineer and fireman by the early use of the cab, demonstrated in terms of design a proper and progressive evaluation of human needs; but apart from

The "Rocket," which won the £500 prize offered by the directors of the Liverpool and Manchester Railway in 1829 for the best engine. From *The Life of George Stephenson and of his son Robert Stephenson*, by Samuel Smiles. (London: John Murray, 1868 edition, page 324.)

F

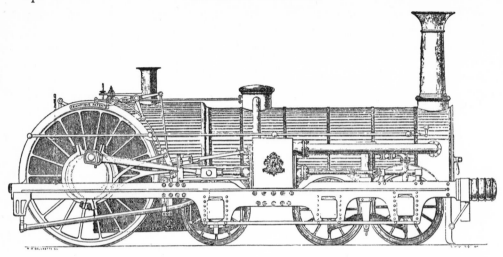

The design of the classic locomotives of the late Victorian period was forshadowed in the early '50's. *Above:* The express locomotive, "Liverpool," patented by Thomas Russell Crampton who designed it for the London and North Western Railway Company. *Below:* Tank engine, constructed to run light express trains, by Kitson, Thompson & Hewitson, Leeds. Both examples shown at the Great Exhibition and illustrated in *The Official Catalogue*, on plate 50, and page 240, Volume I. Although locomotive design had improved, no protection in the form of a wind screen or cab was provided for the driver and fireman: they worked in the open, as they did on the "Lion" and the "Rocket." (See pages 144 and 145.)

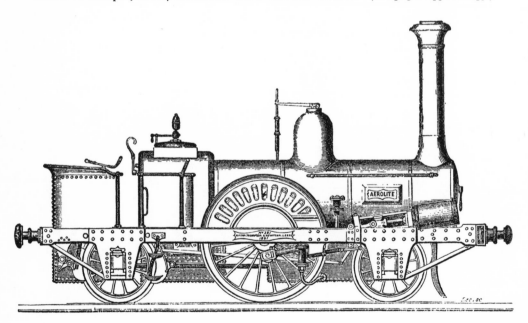

all humane considerations the severity of American winters demanded such protection on long runs.

The comfort of the passengers was attended to by the directors and managers of the various British railway companies: the former, presumably, settling the policy, and the latter carrying it out. The results exhibited a class-consciousness that astonished American railroad chiefs whose democratic approach to the problem was based on the belief that spaciousness and relative comfort should be available for everybody, as opposed to the British idea of exclusive comfort for first-class travellers, partial shelter for second class, and cattle-truck standards for third. This variance of outlook profoundly influenced the design of railway coaches in Britain and railroad cars in the United States: the difference in those terms, *coaches* and *cars*, signified an irreconcilable divergence of view about the character of such vehicles, despite their common function. In both countries the stage-coach was used as a prototype, and American builders had at first mounted stagecoach bodies on trucks, developing from this crude beginning a vehicle with three compartments with a seat on the roof for the conductor;[100] but the compartment system was soon abandoned and forgotten in the United States. In Britain the long-lasting loyalty of designers to the stage coach prototype set definite limits to the comfort of passengers. First-class carriages were merely three conjoined stage coaches, and the memory of the coach was also preserved by the persistence of old coaching terms: in Britain trains had *guards* and *drivers*; in America, *conductors* and *engineers*.

Externally the carriages were as bright and gay as stage coaches. The arrival of Mr. Jorrocks and his family at Datton Railway Station, gave Surtees an opportunity for describing a train with the same devotion to detail that he lavished on men's clothes. "Precisely at three-quarters of a minute before three, a wild shrill whistle, that seemed to issue from the bowels of the earth and to run right up into mid-air, was heard at the back of Shavington Hill, and, in an instant, the engine and long train rounded the base, the engine smoking and snorting like an exasperated crocodile. Nearer and nearer it comes, with a thundering sort of hum that sounds throughout the country. . . . The guard's red coat on the engine is visible . . . next his gold hat-band appears . . . now we read Hercules on the engine, and anon it pulls up with a whiff, a puff, and a whistle, under the slate-covered shed, to give Hercules his water, and set down and take up passengers and goods. Seven first-class passenger carriages follow the engine, all smart, clean, and yellow, with appropriate names on each door panel—The Prince Albert, Queen Victoria, and The Prince of Wales, The Venus, The Mercury, The Comet, and The Star; next come ten second-class ones, green, with covered tops, and half-covered sides, but in neither set is there anything at all like the Jorrocks' party. Cattle-pens follow, holding sheep, swine, donkeys, and poultry; then came an open platform with a broken britzka, followed by a curious-looking nondescript one-horse vehicle, containing a fat man in a low-crowned hat, and a versatio or reversible coat, with the preferable side outwards. Along with him were two ladies muffled up in cloaks, and at the back was a good-looking servant-maid."[101]

Private carriages were often taken on a rail journey, mounted and tied down on flat trucks, with their owners riding inside, enjoying a far smoother run than they could possibly have in a horse-drawn vehicle, even on the improved roads of Telford and McAdam. But apart from a guarantee of absolute privacy, and the convenience of having their own carriage immediately available when the railway journey was over, with their own horses which had travelled by the same train in a horse-box, this practice had few advantages in terms of comfort that a first-class compartment could not provide. Harriet Beecher Stowe, writing in 1853, made some instructive comparisons between the comfort of English and American trains. She liked the "snug compartment of the railroad car," and had either forgotten or was unaware that the compartment system had been tried and discarded in her own country twenty years earlier. "The English cars are models of comfort and good keeping," she wrote. "There are six seats in a compartment, luxuriously cushioned and nicely carpeted, and six was exactly the number of our party. Nevertheless, so obstinate is custom that we averred at first that we preferred our American cars, deficient as they are in many points of neatness and luxury, because they are so much more social."

The American saloon cars were certainly more spacious, and although American railroads used the English narrow gauge of 4 feet 8½ inches, their loading gauge for rolling stock was broader and higher. Both countries had experimented with broader gauges: the Erie railroad had a 6-foot gauge, but nothing approached the magnificent scale of Brunel's 7-foot gauge on the Great Western, which was not finally abandoned until 1892. Like the saloons of the river steamboats, those long American railroad cars with open platforms at each end were sociable places. (See pages 142, 143 and 149.) Mrs. Stowe observed that in England "every arrangement in travelling is designed to maintain that privacy and reserve which is the dearest and most sacred part of an Englishman's nature. Things are so arranged here that, if a man pleases, he can travel all through England with his family, and keep the circle an unbroken unit, having just as little communication with anything outside of it as in his own house. From one of these sheltered apartments in a railroad car, he can pass to pre-engaged parlours and chambers in the hotel, with his own separate table, and all his domestic manners and peculiarities unbroken. In fact, it is a little compact home travelling about.

"Now, all this is very charming to people who know already as much about a country as they want to know; but it follows from it that a stranger might travel all through England, from one end to the other, and not be on conversing terms with a person in it. He may be at the same hotel, in the same train, with

The open, spacious American cars were much more sociable and democratic than the compartments on British trains. They were "so lofty that the tallest man present could promenade up and down the aisle with his hat on," wrote Alexander Mackay in *The Western World*, published in 1849. (See page 152.) This drawing of a car on the Baltimore and Ohio Railroad was published by *The Illustrated London News*, April, 1861.

people able to give him all imaginable information, yet never touch them at any practicable point of communion. This is more especially the case if his party, as ours was, is just large enough to fill the whole apartment.

"As to the comforts of the cars, it is to be said, that for the same price you can get far more comfortable riding in America. Their first-class cars are beyond all praise, but also beyond all price; their second class are comfortless, cushionless, and uninviting. Agreeably with our theory of democratic equality, we have a general car, not so complete as the one, nor so bare as the other, where all ride together; and if the traveller in thus riding sees things that occasionally annoy him, when he remembers that the whole population, from the highest to the lowest, are accommodated here together, he will certainly see hopeful indications in the general comfort, order and respectability which

Interior of a Pullman sleeping car, showing the lower berths made up on the left of the aisle.
(See page 154.) From *The Illustrated London News*, October, 1869.

Pullman drawing-room car. From *The Illustrated London News*, October, 1869. (See pages 143, 155 and 156.)

prevail; all which we talked over most patriotically together, while we were lamenting that there was not a seventh in our party, to instruct us in the localities."

Very little escaped the eyes of the author of *Uncle Tom's Cabin*, and she was more complimentary than some English travellers were when they used American trains. "Everything upon the railroad proceeds with systematic accuracy," she said. "There is no chance for the most careless person to commit a blunder or make a mistake. At the proper time the conductor marches everybody into their place and locks them in, gives the word, 'All right,' and away we go. Somebody has remarked, very characteristically, that the starting word of the English is 'All right,' and that of the Americans 'Go ahead.' "(102)

Alexander Mackay, whose description of a Mississippi steamboat was quoted earlier, likened the typical American railroad car to "a small church upon wheels." He was impressed by the dimensions. "At either end was a door leading to a railed platform in the open air; from door to door stretched a narrow aisle, on either side of which was a row of seats, wanting only book-boards to make them look exactly like pews, each being capable of seating two reasonably sized persons. The car was so lofty that the tallest man present could promenade up and down the aisle with his hat on. In winter, two or three seats are removed from one side to make way for a small stove. . . ."(103) After mentioning that there were no "distinctions of class on American railways," and that to have them "would appear in this country to be an invidious distinction," he noted an inconsistency, for "they never carry that feeling into the regulation of their steamers, most of which have deck, as well as cabin, passengers."(104)

Dr. Thomas L. Nichols, in *Forty Years of American Life*, published in 1864, described the cars on the road from Cleveland to Cincinnati as "among the nicest I have ever seen." Even at that early date the luxury of air-conditioning was familiar. "They are not only brightly painted, gilded, and upholstered, and furnished with retiring rooms," he wrote, "but are warmed in winter, cooled in summer, and thoroughly ventilated always, in a manner that could scarcely fail to satisfy a *Times* correspondent. In the warmest days of an American summer, with the thermometer at a hundred and the train enveloped in clouds of dust, these cars are clean, airy, and cool. By ingenious machinery a constant current of air is cooled and washed clean from dust by being made to pass through showers of water. In winter these cars are warmed and ventilated with hot air, supplied in great abundance by a suitable apparatus." But he had some reservations. "These cars, it is true, are not very exclusive," he said. "They seat fifty or sixty passengers. The 'gentlemanly' conductor walks through the entire train to examine tickets, when it is in rapid motion; so the boy who sells newspapers, books and sugar-plums has free access, and the coloured gentleman who supplies the passengers with

Right: Mutton pies, buns and ginger beer were hawked by enterprising vendors at stations where there was no refreshment room. Twopence a pie and a penny for a bottle of "pop." Reproduced from *Little Mr. Bouncer and His Friend, Verdant Green*, page 165.

Juvenile. "DO YOU OBJECT TO MY SMOKING A CIGAR, SIR?"
Elderly Party. "OH NO, CERTAINLY NOT, IF IT DOESN'T MAKE YOU SICK!"

Left: The railway companies discouraged smoking, both in their trains and on their premises, and many passengers objected to the habit. As the Victorians had no tradition of respect for officials, the rules against it were consistently flouted. John Leech shows how lightly the rule was regarded by young and old. Reproduced by permission of *Punch* from the issue of . November 5th, 1859, page 183.

A FACT.

Three Gentlemen Smoking in a Railway Carriage—Guard puts in his head, and loquitur: *"There are two things not allowed on this Line, Gentlemen; Smoking, and the Servants of the Company receiving Money."* The result, a metallic pass from Gentlemen to Guard.

Reproduced by courtesy of *Punch* from the issue of October 23rd, 1858, page 170. (See opposite page.)

water, where that luxury is not kept in well-iced reservoirs in every car. But the lack of exclusiveness is compensated to the traveller who wishes to see the people of the country he is passing through."[105] On the New York Central railroad he found "the carriages much lighter, and to my taste handsomer in appearance than the English. There is no lack of paint, gilding, upholstery, and ornament. The seats are cushioned and backed with plush. There are stoves in winter and ice-water in summer." For night travel, "there are sleeping-cars, where, for a shilling extra, you can have a berth made up, and lie very comfortably under your blanket all night without disturbance. There is a wash-room in the corner of this car for your morning ablutions."[106]

The type of car invented by George Mortimer Pullman (1831–97), which bears his name and has since been identified with high standards of comfort and luxury, consolidated all the improvements in car design that had been made in a quarter of a century. The Pullman Palace Car Company was formed in 1867, and the comfort of travellers in America, already far in advance of anything British railways could provide, was raised to still higher levels of ease and luxury in the vehicles built at the Company's works at Pullman, Cook County, Illinois. "The first trip in one of these cars forms an epoch in a traveller's life," said W. F. Rae in *Westward by Rail*, published in 1870. "To one accustomed to English railway carriages they are specially welcome. The contrast between the waggon in which Roderick Random journeyed to London and a modern carriage is not much greater than the contrast between life on the rail in an English first-class carriage and in a Pullman's car. In order to form a fair notion of the character of the latter it

LEX TALIONIS.

Passenger (to Guard).   I SAY, LOOK HERE, YOU KNOW, HERE'S SOMEBODY NOT SMOKING!

Ten years later, *Judy* published a variation on the theme of the *Punch* drawing on the opposite page. The war between the public and the railway companies on smoking in trains and on railway premises was still raging; but the public was winning, and the arrogant railway magnates were beginning to realise, what shopkeepers had long recognised, that "the customer is always right." Reproduced on a slightly smaller scale from *Judy*, December 2nd, 1868, page 60.

is but necessary to recall the descriptions of those luxurious saloon carriages which the directors of our railways have had constructed for the use of the Queen. No Royal personage can be more comfortably housed than the occupant of a Pullman car, provided the car be an hotel one."[107]

Interior views of Pullman drawing-room and sleeping cars appeared in the *Illustrated London News* in October, 1869, and are reproduced on pages 150 and 151. They certainly confirm Rae's eulogy; so do other contemporary illustrations in English and American magazines; but praise of Pullman cars was not universal among travellers. In 1875 two volumes of assorted prejudices and observations were published by Thérèse Yelverton (Viscountess Avonmore), entitled *Teresina in America,* and the author who travelled in a Pullman Silver Palace Car concluded that "The name did the whole business. Once get a *name* to ring in the world's ears, and you need not trouble about the reality." She complained that she "met with *no silver whatever* in these cars; the fittings, lamps, bolts, hinges, door-handles, &c., were of the white metal called pinchbeck, or Britannia metal, and the palaces were fitted up in the ordinary hotel style, the floor carpeted and oil-clothed, the seat velvet-covered. Each passenger occupied just so many feet as would suffice to stow away his person in sitting during the day, or recumbent at night, for the bed is constructed by turning down the back of the seat; the iron stancheons, which may be considered silver bed-posts, being so fixed that they form another berth near the top of the car, so that the two persons who have sat *vis-à-vis* during the day, elongate themselves over and under each other at night, according to taste or agility in climbing, and irrespective of sex."

Her rather puerile complaints about the Silver Palace ran to over seven pages. There were no special cars for ladies, it was difficult to undress in a Pullman berth, there was no privacy in the lavatory, the cars were overheated, while "the insufferable tedium of sitting in one position, and even of staring at the same persons for so long a time, gives you a sort of nervous fidget." Amenities were rather grudgingly recorded, but were sneered at when they had unusual novelty. For example: "With your breakfast comes the morning paper, 'The Great Pacific Line Gazette,'—'The Overland Route'—printed on board each day, and narrating all the items of news of the preceding one, also a love story—editor, no doubt, the stoker. The passengers are allowed to contribute, and can advertise in the 'Gazette' for a lost slipper or a watch-key." There was "no stint of iced water," and there was a smoking carriage, and "you can breakfast and dine just as you would on a sea voyage." She admitted that "all this is very amusing for a day or two; but when it is prolonged for seven, eight, or even ten, all preconceived ideas of palatial accommodation have vanished."[108]

Even that touchy and critical Frenchman, Max O'Rell, writing in 1889, said that "Nothing can surpass the comfort and luxury of the Pullman cars, unless it be the perfected Pullman that is called the Vestibule Train. Six or

McCOUNTER JUMPER *repents of an Easter Trip in a Third-class Carriage.*

Reproduced on a slightly smaller scale from *Judy*, April 21st, 1869, page 266. The cattle truck is still the obvious and not very remote ancestor of the third-class coach. (See upper part of plate 3.)

seven carriages, connecting one with another, allow of your moving about freely over a length of some hundred yards. Dining-room, sleeping car, drawing-room car, smoking-room, library, bath-room, lavatory, the whole fitted up in the most luxurious style. What can one desire more? It is a hotel on wheels. It is your *appartement*, in which you whirl from New York to Chicago in twenty-four hours. Cook, barber, *valets de chambre*—you have all at hand. Yes, a barber! There is a barber's shop at the end of the train. . . . The platforms at the ends of the carriages are closed by a concertina-pleated arrangement having doors opening outwards. You pass from one carriage to the other without having to expose yourself to cold or rain; children may play about and run from carriage to carriage with perfect safety. Everything has been thought out, everything has been carried out that could conduce to the comfort of travellers. . . ."(109)

The novelty of American trains and their equipment and services had an irresistible attraction for English readers, who were unable to enjoy such refinements of comfort on their own railways. A lyrical account of a journey from London to Chicago, written by James Mortimer and published in *The Strand Magazine* in 1893, described an observation car, which was the latest attraction on the "Pennsylvania Limited," at that time "claimed to be the most perfect and luxurious railway train in the world." This car was "in reality a handsome sitting-room, with glass sides, and furnished with an abundance of wicker chairs and sofas. The rear platform is opened at the end, and is large enough to seat fifteen persons, protected by the sides of the car and a strong steel railing. In fine weather a seat in this open observatory, in full view of the rapidly-passing landscape, is a thing to be enjoyed, and is particularly appreciated by ladies and children. At the other end of the same car is fixed the desk of a stenographer and typewriter, employed by the Pennsylvania Railroad Company. His services to passengers are rendered free of expense, and letters or telegrams may be dictated to him, which he transcribes and dispatches at the next stopping-place.

"Forward of the sleepers is a smoking-car and library, containing lounges, couches, writing-decks, book-cases filled with standard and current literature, and the tables supplied with the daily newspapers and the periodicals of the times. In a corner of this snug retreat, which to the male passengers serves temporarily all the purposes of a club, is a refreshment buffet, with which one may instantly communicate by means of an electric button always at hand. Beyond this is a barber's shop, through which is obtained entrance to the gentleman's bath-room, and farther forward still is the passengers' luggage, carried from New York to Chicago without change, and delivered at the hotels immediately after the arrival of the train."[110]

Sleeping cars and Pullman cars were introduced by some British companies in the 1870's, but before making such additions to the comfort of travellers, the directors of the various lines were compelled to capitulate to smokers. A few rare concessions had been granted, notably by the Stockton and Darlington Railway, which introduced a smoking saloon, or cigar divan, in the middle of a composite carriage.[111] But apart from such exceptions, smoking was forbidden for nearly thirty years not only on trains but on railway premises. No sense of obligation to their customers was displayed by railway managements by this dictatorial prohibition: indeed, no sense of any kind. Until smoking carriages for all classes were made obligatory by Parliament in 1868, the railway companies behaved as if they were the masters and not the servants of the public. The only people who benefited from the non-smoking rule were the railway guards who allowed it to be broken for a consideration. Two phases of the tobacco war between the railways and the public are shown in pages 154 and 155, as recorded by *Punch* in 1858 and *Judy* ten years later. Eventually smoking compartments were provided for all classes.

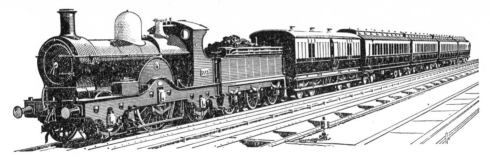

The first corridor train, put into service by the Great Western Railway between Paddington and Birkenhead in 1892. Although a new principle of design had been introduced, the stage-coach is still the obvious ancestor of the separate compartments. Drawn from a photograph supplied by the former Great Western Railway, and reproduced from *Industrial Art Explained* (1946 edition), by courtesy of George Allen & Unwin Ltd.

Improvements in the design of British carriages came slowly, at first in the form of expensive and exclusive luxuries. Family and saloon cars were built and operated on a few lines towards the end of the '60's. They had a spacious open main compartment, with seats round the sides and a couple of fixed arm-chairs, a second-class compartment for servants, and next to the main compartment, or between the two, a lavatory and a water closet.[112] The lack of this convenience on ordinary long-distance trains caused excessive discomfort, and although some rather odd appliances for the relief of travellers could be bought, it was impossible for ladies to ask for such things, even if they had known about them. When ladies travelled together in a compartment, as they generally preferred to, they were able to include in their luggage an innocent-looking circular basket, which contained a chamber pot. When sleeping cars were first put into service early in the '70's, on the North British and London and North Western long-distance trains, water closets were provided; but it was not until the Great Western built the first corridor coaches in 1892 that all classes of passengers had access to them. The first corridor train ran between Paddington and Birkenhead, and represented a new principle in coach design, though the stage coach was still the obvious ancestor of the separate compartments. (See above.) Long before that innovation, Sir James Joseph Allport (1811–92), the general manager of the Midland Railway, had introduced Pullman cars, following an extensive tour he made in the United States in 1873.[113] These cars were popular, and for a long time retained "news" value and an air of American luxury that captivated travellers. A typical advertisement issued by the Midland Railway in 1882 describes their merits. "The Pullman Cars are well Ventilated, fitted with Lavatory, &c., and accompanied by a Special Attendant. Charge for seat in Drawing Room Car, 5s., and for Berth in Sleeping Car 8s., in addition to the First Class Fare."[114]

Allport, an innovating man with an original mind, sometimes seemed to his more cautious contemporaries in railway management to be going too fast; but his belief in comfort was so soundly Victorian that they could not altogether distrust him, though they came near to doing so when in 1872 he backed his belief in the third-class traveller as a large potential source of revenue by introducing on the Midland system well-designed, comfortable third-class carriages with a uniform rate for their passengers of a penny a mile on all trains. The bleak crudity of third-class accommodation in the '60's is shown in the illustration reproduced from *Judy* on page 157. A roof and glazed windows had been added to the cattle truck prototype, but there were no other amenities: the lower orders were lucky to have seats at all. Allport changed all that, and when the revenue from second-class passengers fell as a result of improving the comfort and lowering the cost of third-class travel, he abolished second-class carriages on the Midland, and made a big cut in first-class fares. These changes, made in 1875, were proposed during the last months of the previous year, and a contemporary account of their reception by the shareholders of the Midland Railway and the opposition of some sections of the public reads as follows:

"A meeting held recently among the shareholders of the Midland Railway, to consider the proposed alteration in the style of travelling in the system which lies under the control of Mr. Allport, most effectually disposes of at least one of the principal objections to the movements which have been raised by those who regard anything novel with terror and affright, and who suffer from a double allowance of both when the novelty is really a step in the right direction. It is not so long since this same pioneer of improvement, this magnate who sits at Derby, and has iron arms reaching nearly all over the country, effected the greatest reform in the travelling of the poor that has been made since the institution of railways, and the benefaction has happily rewarded both giver and receivers alike. Those who have ever seen the poor third-class passengers shunted and thrust aside to allow the haughty express riders to pass, or have noticed the hungry and wistful aspect of weary Parliamentarians, as they waited their turn—which must have seemed as if it would never come, and, when it came, as though it would never end; or, what is still more to the purpose, have been third-class passengers themselves in the good old days— must be fully alive to the wisdom which has led to such all-round beneficial results. That the new arrangement is the outcome of the same mature thought, and will have an equally admirable result, we are quite certain—as certain as that the other companies will follow in the wake of Mr. Allport and the Midland, with regard to the new venture, in similar fashion to that adopted by them in connection with the old. To attempt to show the advantages of the change on paper would be almost as absurd as is the action of those who, because of interested reasons or crass stupidity, shake their heads and say the effort will result in failure; but we may say, with regard to the many pictures

The "Flying Scotsman" arriving at King's Cross, London, from Edinburgh. (Reproduced by permission of George Newnes Limited from *The Strand Magazine*, Volume III, page 201, 1892.) This crack train was claimed to be the fastest in the world, and between London and Edinburgh reached an average speed of 55½ miles per hour.

which have been drawn of the utter ruin of the Company and the misery of the travellers which are to accrue from the change, that we have not yet met one which did not in some way or other display meanness, selfishness, or utter ignorance of the principles on which railway business is transacted. Mr. Allport and his company, strange to say, do not look to second-class, or worse, writers for instruction in their business; and so we can only wish the adventurers all success in their courageous endeavours for the public good, though it would almost seem as if the public were the last to see the advantages offered them."[115]

Allport's policy for bettering and cheapening third-class travel was subsequently adopted by other companies; but for a long time the Midland kept the lead won by his enterprise, and "had the best stations in England and the most comfortable third class carriages in the world."[116] Allport was knighted in 1884. He was the pioneer of cheap, comfortable rail travel, and by his introduction of Pullman cars also the pioneer of standards of luxury that had long been available in America, though, apart from Pullman trains, British concessions to comfort were tentative and limited, even after the '70's. Few carriages were heated, and in winter first- and second-class passengers were (if they were lucky) provided with foot-warmers, long, flat rectangular metal containers, filled with hot water and thrust into the compartments by porters

London Bridge Station, exterior, after rebuilding in 1851. (Reproduced from *The Illustrated London News*, February 15th, 1851.) The paper made this critical comment: "The Buildings for the purposes of this line of Railway have, from the first, been distinguished for their taste and appropriateness; and, among these, the Terminus at London Bridge, or rather adjoining Tooley Street, was not the least remarkable for the neatness, artistic character, and reality of its *façade*. We regret, therefore, that this has disappeared, to make room, apparently, for one of less merit, with an addition of a row of unornamental houses and shops. Nevertheless, as change in the premises of a large metropolitan establishment, we have deemed it worthy of illustration." (See opposite page.)

a few minutes before a train started. They retained their heat for a surprisingly long time. A foot-warmer put in hot at Euston would still be warm and comforting to the feet at Rugby, nearly two hours later. Until gas lamps replaced them, carriages were dimly lit by pot lamps inserted in the roof of each compartment, burning rape oil,[117] and although American cars blazed with electric light during the last quarter of the century, British railway companies once converted to gas remained faithful to it until the Edwardian period. At night on some lines the ceiling light could be wholly or partly covered by a cloth pad on a brass swivel from which a cord hung down, but as the cord was often missing, only tall people were able to manipulate it easily: medium sized or short passengers had to stand on one of the seats.

The public had defeated the railway companies over smoking, but directors and managers were inclined to believe with Oliver Cromwell that people should have "Not what they want but what is good for them." For example, Sir Richard Moon (1814–99), Chairman of the London and North Western Railway, was a strict Sabbatarian, and able to impose his beliefs on thousands of people who did not share them. Possibly railway managers found it convenient to discourage travelling on Sunday. "Many roads are Sabbath-keeping," wrote H. C. Knight in his improving little work on the Stephensons, Father and Son, in the "Lessons from Noble Lives" series. "Some of those which do run on that day are poorly paid." No wonder, in view of the tardiness and discomfort deliberately contrived to deter those who wished to travel on Sunday. "Carrying the mail helps them out," he continued; "but is it *necessary* to keep up Sabbath violation on our great routes in order to forward the mail? Does not the Saturday telegraph do away with that necessity? Every important item of business can be put through on the wires in time. The side of the Sabbath is the side of God."[118] Slow and infrequent Sunday trains were grudgingly allowed by some companies; the ghost of Sir Richard Moon has never been laid, and to this day Britain has the worst Sunday train services in the world.

The construction of terminus stations in London had a stimulating effect on other forms of traffic. For instance, before the London and South Western

London Bridge Station, interior, the oldest terminus in London, opened in December, 1836, by the London and Greenwich Railway, rebuilt and extended later, but inferior in design and conception to the large terminal stations north of the Thames, like King's Cross, Paddington, and St. Pancras. Seventy-three years after it was built, John Davidson included some verses about its shortcomings in *Fleet Street and Other Poems* which summarised its defects in the first six lines:

> Inside the station, everything's so old,
> So inconvenient, of such manifold
> Perplexity, and, as a mole might see,
> So strictly what a station shouldn't be,
> That no idea minifies its crude
> And yet elaborate ineptitude. . . .

The illustration is reduced from a drawing in *Fun*, October 14th, 1865, page 50.

Railway opened Waterloo Station, the terminus was at Nine Elms, a semi-rural spot not far from Vauxhall Gardens, which was soon transformed, becoming "a place of great bustle, having occasioned the starting of a vast number of steam-boats from Hungerford market and London-bridge; together with omnibuses from all parts of town. Indeed the number of steamers have so increased above London-bridge that the very character of the Thames has become changed. Formerly the river was comparatively smooth and clear; but now the Thames is in perpetual agitation, and as thick as *pea-soup*. Once the river was covered with wherries, and sailing boats of every description; but now deserted by every thing, but steamers and the country craft."[119] Waterloo was opened in July, 1848, and Nine Elms became a goods station. (See Section VI of *A Balloon View of London*, on page 13.) North of the Thames, the main line stations, Paddington, Euston, St. Pancras, King's Cross, Liverpool Street, Cannon Street, Charing Cross and Victoria were ultimately linked up by the "Inner Circle" underground railway, operated by the Metropolitan and District companies: this project was not completed until 1884, but part of it, the first underground line in London, had been constructed by the Metropolitan Railway, from Paddington to Farringdon Street, and opened in 1863. (See opposite.) The trains were hauled by steam locomotives, and although they were not supposed to emit smoke or steam in the tunnels, a sulphurous atmosphere, as choking as a London fog, hung about the tunnels and stations, and ventilation holes, "blow holes" as they were called, had to be pierced in the tunnel roofs. Comfort on the underground trains was limited until the system was electrified after 1900.

New York had to wait until the next century for a subway, when the first line was opened in 1904. In the 1870's, there had been an abortive experiment with a pneumatic underground railroad. A trial section of tunnel was built below downtown Broadway, from Warren Street to Murray Street. The cars were driven along by a blast of air, ejected from a blowing machine, which was forced against the rear end of a car. It was not a success. Another plan for an underground shopping street under Broadway, with railroad tracks for steam trains running between the sidewalks, was killed by organised opposition. But soon New Yorkers had something far more spirited in the way of transport than anything that ran in a tunnel.

Five years after the first underground railway was opened in London, an experimental elevated railroad was built in New York, half a mile long, the cars being hauled by cable. The cable system never worked properly, so steam locomotives were used, which distributed soot and cinders generously over everything in the vicinity of the track. Despite these drawbacks, the elevated system was extended during the '70's, and lines constructed above Second, Third, Sixth and Ninth Avenues. (See plate 2.) An elevated, electrified line opened in Liverpool in 1893, ran beside the docks from Dingle to Seaforth, and was known as the "Overhead" railway. But New York endured its little

A trial trip on the Metropolitan Underground Railway, which was opened on January 10th, 1863. It was operated by the Great Western Railway at first, with broad gauge rolling stock, and ran from Paddington to Farringdon Street. The new coaches were superior in design and comfort to anything used on the main line railways: they were eight wheelers, lit by coal gas, with two lamps in each first-class compartment. The engineer was Sir John Fowler (1817–98), and working with him was Sir Benjamin Baker (1840–1907), then a young man of twenty-three: their most famous collaboration was the design of the Forth Bridge. The Metropolitan was the first underground railway line, and its opening naturally gave fresh substance to the Victorian faith in scientific and commercial progress. The illustration shows the sight-seeing train, thronged with V.I.P.s, passing Portland Road Station.

stubby, anthracite-burning steam locomotives until 1902, when the elevated system was electrified.[120] Both the New York "El" and the Liverpool "Overhead" have been demolished: now they belong to the history of transport.

The railway companies in Britain were subjected to unceasing criticism from the Press and the public. Alone of all the railway pundits, Allport understood public relations, though he would not have understood that term. He also served the public well, and the Midland was amply rewarded. Nearly all other representatives of management exhibited an arrogant complacency, and seemed to regard themselves as above criticism. Although they allowed the comfort of British trains to remain inferior to American standards, they achieved remarkable timing, and attained speeds that no other country could match. Trains like "The Flying Scotsman" were world famous. The permanent way on the main lines, particularly that of the London and North Western from Euston to Crewe, allowed trains to travel at a mile a minute or over without jolting or swaying, and so smoothly that it was possible for travellers to read and write in comfort, whether they travelled first, second or third class.

Periodically public exasperation with some aspect of railway management or cupidity sparked off discussions about the advantages of state ownership; but they were expressions of dissatisfaction rather than serious proposals. Escott's *Social Transformations of the Victorian Age*, published in 1897, touches heavily on this subject. The book, written with majestic pomposity, reveals the self-righteous benevolence of a mind inclined to reform, approving of progress, and unhampered by faith in any theoretical social system. Like all good Victorians, Escott was suspicious of state interference. "The issues between traders and framers of railway rates for the carriage of merchandise," he wrote, "are periodically expressed in the demand for the acquisition of the iron roads, like the telegraphic wires, by the State. The mighty sections of the Anglo-Saxon race on either side of the Atlantic present the two great exceptions to the State proprietorship or State control of the public locomotives. Seeing that half the railway mileage and capital of the world belongs to the United Kingdom and to the United States, these exceptions are themselves of considerable importance. The incorporation of the railway systems of the United Kingdom into the national service would, it has been calculated, involve the doubling of the annual Budget, and an addition to the permanent Civil Service of five per cent. of our male population. If this estimate be correct, it seems likely that a Minister of the Crown will think even more than thrice before he seriously proposes the assumption of such a responsibility by himself and his colleagues."[121]

ELEGANCE BEFORE COMFORT. VI.

Travelling dress with a "skirt of blue-grey summer cashmere, with twelve pleated flounces of the same material, edged with white Breton lace. Bodice of plaid cashmere, in two shades of blue-grey, fastened down in front with buttons, and draped below the waist in horizontal folds, which fall *en echarpe* at the back. Turned-down collar of plain grey-blue cashmere, with bow of grosgrain ribbon. Tight sleeves of plaid cashmere, with cuffs of plain material. Waistband of grey-blue corded silk." From *Sylvia's Home Journal*, 1881, pages 230 and 237.

(See next page, also pages 94 to 98.)

ELEGANCE BEFORE COMFORT. VII.

Travelling dress in beige, trimmed with ribbon and buttons, a winter outfit. From *Sylvia's Home Journal*, 1881, page 504. The article in which this illustration appears begins with a complaint about English lack of enterprise. "If only the manufacturers of woollen goods, at Bradford and other English towns, could learn to make such goods as are now being bought in such enormous quantities from France for the costumes of our winter season, there would be no reason for them to complain, or to seek help, as of late they have been doing."

(See **pages** 94 to 98 and 167.)

CHAPTER VII

COMFORT AND PLEASURE

Comfort and pleasure did not always coincide: the war between the sexes, never acknowledged but waged incessantly with fluctuating fortunes, determined from decade to decade whether men or women should be *more* or *less* comfortable. To compete with their husbands' external pleasures—dinners at Greenwich and the Star and Garter at Richmond and convivial evenings at clubs—women had to provide abundant home comforts. "Feed the brute!" said the widow to the young wife who complained that her husband was away from home a lot and cross and neglectful when he was there.[122] Inside and outside the home the war continued, sometimes bringing a male victory, sometimes a female; but often both men and women gained as a result of one of those victories, no matter who was the immediate and ostensible victor. Men won the long battle for liberty to smoke anywhere, even in the home, and women ultimately shared the pleasure of smoking when a young and adventurous generation in the late '80's broke down the idea that smoking was "fast." Men and women were often allies in that other and far more open war that was not peculiar to the Victorian age but has been going on since the stone age, the war between the young generation and the old, and it was the victories won by young people that encouraged and established many social changes.

To describe all the changes in social habits and manners that occurred between 1837 and 1901 would need a book ten times as long as this. Only the most conspicuous are briefly mentioned in this chapter. They include the institution of the summer holiday at the seaside; the metamorphosis of the ancient Christian feast of Christmas, which became a boisterously commercialised annual holiday; the advent of the safety bicycle, which increased outdoor life, improved health, and encouraged men and women to explore the deserted roads and little-known countryside and incidentally to neglect the duty of church-going; the introduction of the cigarette, which modified the views of the upper and middle classes about smoking; the extension of reading to all classes, and the appearance of cheap newspapers and magazines to cater for a new, literate but still uneducated public; the regulation by class of drinking in the public houses that had replaced the taverns and alehouses of former times; and the development of variety theatres or music halls, which finally put out of business the old singing rooms, like the "Cave of Harmony," described by Thackeray in the opening chapter of *The Newcomes*. All these changes were obvious: most of them came about gradually, though sufficiently fast for middle-aged people to say that the world was not what it was when they were young. But perhaps the most widespread and least recognised change was in the attitude of the upper and middle classes towards games, which ceased to be amusements and recreations, and became serious occupations, whether played on a muddy field, a lawn-smooth pitch, or a card table. Dickens may have foreseen this when he described whist as "a solemn observance, to which, as it appears to us, the title of 'game' has been very irreverently and ignominiously applied."[123]

Women were far less susceptible than men to attacks of solemnity about games; they retained a sense of proportion which men often surrendered in the spurious interests of "good form," and except for the horsey, hard-riding women of the aristocratic hunting class, the Victorian girl took her outdoor recreations, her croquet and tennis, without any of the earnestness that sobered her brothers, especially when they had been to a public school. Croquet was the favourite pastime for women after it was introduced from Ireland in the late '50's: before that athletic exercises were deemed unladylike, but croquet was a gentle game when it was played on the lawns of English country houses and parsonages, whatever it may have been in Ireland, where it was the sport of village teams using a primitive form of mallet made from a rugged chunk of oak with a broomstick socketed into it. These rustic tools were improved by a typical man of enterprise, John Jaques, who established a factory for making sets, wrote books about croquet, and made a fortune.[124] The game was popular all through the '60's, but declined after lawn tennis was introduced in 1874, which was played by both sexes with enthusiasm. Towards the end of the century golf was attracting increasing numbers of men, and even before special courses were laid out for them, ladies had played on the short links of some clubs, for the longer courses were exclusive to men: they were considered altogether too strenuous for women, and the Victorians were suspicious of strenuous women. There were transient fashions in recreation, like roller skating, which came from America, where the improved four-wheeled roller skate with rubber springs had been invented in 1863 by J. L. Plimpton, of New York; but skating rinks and "the rink girl" were unknown in England until about 1880.

While croquet could be played comfortably and gracefully in a crinoline, more energetic games like lawn tennis and golf could not; and the increasing interest of young women in outdoor games gradually led them to put a higher value on freedom of movement, although at first in the late '70's they appeared on the tennis court in tight gowns which swept the ground, and high-heeled black canvas shoes. Comfort still had to compete with elegance, and any concession to natural lines, giving play to the lithe figure of a young

Ramsgate Sands, a far less sympathetic study than Frith's painting, which is reproduced on plate 7, though both views show the overcrowding on pleasure beaches, and the immense amount of clothing worn by men, women and children when they visited the seaside. From *Fun*, August 19th, 1865, page 140.

woman, could very easily be condemned as indecent. But whatever they wore when playing, women never surrendered their basic common sense about the function of games. Women are and have always been secret deflators of male dignity; and by their insistence that games were amusements and not ends in themselves, Victorian women occasionally dared to puncture the integument of male conceit. When women abandoned this rational outlook about games, as they did early in the present century, they became almost as boring as men about their personal prowess, or, worse still, the prowess of their favourite champions.

The English may have had—may still have—the reputation for taking their pleasures sadly, but they certainly liked to take them comfortably. This was not always possible; and on some occasions comfort was knowingly sacrificed in the interests of pleasure, though only the young took that sacrifice lightly. The seaside holiday was one of these sacrificial occasions and a severe trial for the middle-aged, who were haled off to sit on packed beaches and listen to nigger minstrels and other less accomplished entertainers, while being importuned by hawkers selling everything from shrimps, winkles, peppermint bullseyes and oranges to cheap parasols, kites, toy trumpets, spades

Herne Bay, in Kent, was deliberately created as a seaside resort after 1830. On this page
and opposite the extent of its early development is shown, the view being reproduced from
a print issued after the completion of the pier, which was designed by Thomas Telford and
begun in 1831. A detailed record of the stages of the town's development exists in the pages
of a guide book entitled *A Picture of Herne Bay*, issued during the 1830's.

and buckets, returning after an exhausting day to empty the sand out of their
boots in furnished lodgings that were a poor substitute for orderly home
surroundings. What they had to endure on those congested acres is shown
by the two views of Ramsgate Sands on plate 7 and page 171. Men and
women of the middle classes began to feel and behave like elderly people in
their thirties; but if they were parents, duty to their children demanded an
annual visit to the seaside.

Until the early nineteenth century, watering and sea-bathing places were

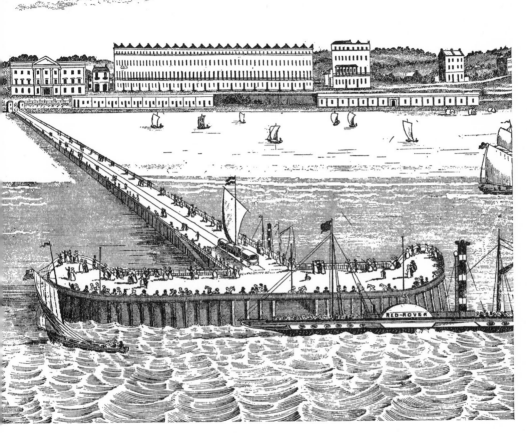

Continuation of the view of Herne Bay, showing the T-shaped pier and the terraces along the sea front. The elegance of Regency architecture has survived, and has affected the character of the buildings, which have classic graces; possibly because, in the words of the local guide book, the speculators who developed the place "were men of taste and skill." (See page 174.)

largely patronised by wealthy people, who went to take the waters, to dance, gamble, and enjoy congenial company: visitors also included designing mothers, husband-hunting for their daughters, and needy bachelors, fortune-hunting for themselves. A guide to such places in England and Wales, published in 1803, included well-known and established spas like Bath, Cheltenham, Buxton, Matlock, Malvern, Harrowgate (as it was then spelt), and Tunbridge Wells; also seaside resorts with good bathing, like Brighton—which had by then acquired a modish and wicked reputation—and Worthing,

Bognor, Eastbourne, Broadstairs, Margate, Ramsgate, Southend, Weymouth, Lyme Regis, and Tenby [125] Apart from bathing, these resorts catered for the taste of genteel Georgian society, and had theatres, assembly rooms, two or more good taverns, libraries, and a grand promenade. Nearly all such places had grown up from fishing villages or small, inconspicuous ports serving coastal trade; but during the 1830's, encouraged by the increase of steamboat traffic and before the railways really got into their stride, existing resorts were extended and entirely new ones developed, for the rising prosperity of the middle classes had created a huge demand for holidays by the sea.

Sometimes these new seaside towns were well planned. Brighton, Hove, and Tenby were Regency creations, enjoying the chaste architectural character of that period; and Herne Bay, one of the new towns of the '30's, inherited that character. The sea front and the pier, the latter designed by Thomas Telford and completed in 1831, are shown on pages 172 and 173. Piers, which became a familiar feature of such towns, had at first a purely maritime function. At Ramsgate, according to the guide book mentioned earlier, the pier, built of Portland and Purbeck stone, "extends about 800 feet into the sea before it forms an angle, and is twenty-six feet broad at the top, including the parapet."[126] It was begun in 1749 and cost some hundred thousand pounds. Under the heading of "Grand Promenade" the guide book continues: "When we have mentioned the vast length and breadth of the Pier, it is almost unnecessary to observe, that it forms the favourite walk for company; and certainly none can be more delightful, or more salubrious."[127] Telford's pier at Herne Bay extended 3,000 feet into the sea in the form of the letter T, the cross piece, 400 feet long, acting as a breakwater, so that vessels could lie east or west of the pier, protected from the prevailing wind; but although it was built primarily as a calling place for steamers, it provided a "grand promenade" for strollers. The first of all the promenade piers was the Chain Pier at Brighton, built in 1823, which lasted until 1896 when it was destroyed by a storm: by the middle of the century the pleasure pier had become an institution, like the promenade or esplanade, as it was sometimes called, along the sea front, and the sands and the deck chairs, the cast-iron band-stands, the glass and iron shelters, and the rows and rows of bathing machines, though these had been in use in a limited way since the 1730's. Georgian ladies and gentlemen had bathed in happy nudity, and contemporary records like Rowlandson's "Summer Amusements at Margate" supply evidence that the practice lasted as late as 1800; but the Victorians invented a uniform both for men and women, and what almost amounted to a ritual for the latter. In the section "Hints, Domestic and Personal," *The What-not; or Ladies Handy-Book*, for 1861, printed "A Few Words about Bathing," which gave details of this ritual. "Before bathing in the sea," said the writer, "it is wise, par-ticularly in the young and delicate, gradually to prepare themselves by having one or two tepid baths, and the first time a person bathes in the sea, they

The Zoological Gardens in Regent's Park, London, was not only a place where parents took their children, but was always crowded with sightseers, fashionable, and almost fashionable. Victorians of every class took pleasure in crowds. (See plates 6 and 7, and pages 171 and 172.) From *Fun*, June 24th, 1865, page 60.

should on no account, remain in the water longer than five minutes. Upon entering the machine the body should be wiped dry and the ordinary clothing being quickly resumed, a little exercise should be taken at once; remembering, however, that the replacing of the clothing is more important than that the surface of body should be completely dry.

"We hope our fair readers will not be shocked if we say a few words on swimming. No one can experience the real pleasure of bathing unless they possess this, to some persons, unfeminine accomplishment. Those, however, who have acquired this healthy art, should always practice it when in the water, as the muscular action required in swimming keeps the blood in motion, and by keeping up the temperature of the body causes the reaction to be more complete. The chief draw-back to ladies swimming is the bathing-dress used in this country. The most commodious, and at the same time the most pleasant to the wearer, is a garment, consisting of a dress and drawers in one, made of grey serge, and having a band to confine the waist. They are also far preferable, in all cases, to the common blue flannel, which when saturated with water, becomes very heavy and inconvenient."[128]

Children had a much better time at the seaside than their elders. Not that everybody approved of such holidays. Charles Kingsley objected on grounds of hygiene (though he did not use that word), when he condemned, in *The Water Babies*, Lady Harthover's visit to the seaside with her children, "in order to put herself and them into condition by mild applications of iodine. She might as well have stayed at home," he said, "and used Parry's liquid horse-blister, for there was plenty of it in the stables; and then she would have saved her money, and saved the chance, also, of making all the children ill instead of well (as hundreds are made), by taking them to some nasty smelling undrained lodging, and then wondering how they caught scarlatina and diphtheria: but people won't be wise enough to understand that till they are dead of bad smells, and then it will be too late. . . ."[129]

Comfort might be bleakly dissociated from pleasure for grown-ups at the seaside holiday; but the other annual holiday, at Christmas, was an occasion enjoyed by all except the congenitally grumpy. The now familiar trappings of Christmastime were unknown before the Victorian period, apart from holly, ivy and mistletoe, the yule log, mince pies and plum pudding. Those were almost as old as England, and mistletoe was linked with pagan magic, pre-Christian and pre-Roman; "an unholy plant," as the parson at Bracebridge Hall observed, "profaned by having been used by the Druids in their mystic ceremonies. . . ."[130] There was no Christmas tree at Bracebridge Hall or Dingley Dell; no grandfather clocks or grandfather chairs either: Squire Bracebridge sat in "his hereditary elbow chair,"[131] and old Mrs. Wardle used an easy-chair,[132] for fancy, cosy names for clocks and high-backed chairs had still to be invented. There were no Christmas cards or presents either, cluttering up the place, though there is a suggestion that the children at Bracebridge Hall may have had presents, because "a profusion of wooden horses, penny trumpets, and tattered dolls, about the floor, showed traces of a troop of little fairy beings, who, having frolicked through a happy day, had been carried off, to slumber through a peaceful night."[133] Washington Irving wrote about Christmas with the enthusiasm of an antiquary collecting and docketing ancient customs; Dickens gloried in it as a feast, in which he, both as author and man, was an eager participant, writing about food and drink with cheerful zest, and portraying Christmastime as the season for family gatherings. The Christmas tree was an idea imported from Germany by the Prince Consort, and Dickens called it "that pretty German toy," and heartily approved of its "multitude of little tapers" and the "motley collection of odd objects, clustering on the tree like magic fruit, and flashing back the bright looks directed towards it on every side. . . ." The tree gave enormous pleasure to children, and that was enough for Dickens; it gave additional lustre to the feast, and the toys and sweetmeats that bedecked it were presents for the young people, and, as the Christmas party was the one occasion in the year when relatives came from far and near to gather under one roof—and occasionally to stage a monumental row—there was a good excuse for giving

Even on such informal occasions as a regatta, costume for men, women and children was rigid, inflexible. In one of his early scientific romances, *When the Sleeper Wakes* (1899), H. G. Wells, looking ahead some two centuries, made one of his minor characters, a tailor, describe the Victorian period as "essentially cylindrical" sartorially. "With a tendency to the hemisphere in hats. Circular curves always." This sketch of Richmond regatta is reproduced from *Recollections of Richmond*, by Somers T. Gascoyne, published in 1898, page 163.

This "cylindrical" characteristic had become established in the 1820's and '30's, before the Victorian period began. The crowd on the left, drawn by George Cruikshank and described as "Sunday Ruralizing," is not very different in general appearance from the crowd sketched at Richmond some sixty-five years later. From *Sunday in London*, illustrated in fourteen cuts by George Cruikshank, and a few words by a friend of his. London: 1833.

presents all round. Long before the '90's when A. D. Godley wrote his *Pensées de Noel*, Christmas had been put on a paying commercial basis by shopkeepers everywhere, and his gently satirical poem expressed the feelings of many jaded people, particularly the third verse:

"When you roam from shop to shop,
Seeking, till you nearly drop
Christmas cards and small donations
For the maw of your relations,
Questing vainly 'mid the heap
For a thing that's nice and cheap:
Think, and check the rising tear,
Christmas comes but once a year."[134]

The designer of the first English Christmas card was probably William Charles Thomas Dobson (1817–98), a painter specialising in religious subjects, who produced a card in 1844; but the first card to receive a lot of publicity was by John Callcott Horsley (1817–1903), executed for Sir Henry Cole and published in 1846. It was a complicated design, with a tangled rustic framework, which linked a central scene showing a convivial family party with flanking sketches of the poor, receiving gifts of food and clothing. Sir Henry Cole (1808–82), who is generally named as the inventor of Christmas cards, was a most unusual civil servant—jovial, energetic and versatile—who shared with the Prince Consort the chief credit for the Great Exhibition. He wrote a number of topographical handbooks, using the pseudonym of Felix Summerly, edited a series of illustrated tales for children called *Felix Summerly's Home Treasury*, and was an artist and musician of some distinction.[135] With Christmas cards he released a torrent, which, as the years went by, almost swamped the post office, so that Christmastime became a period of nightmare activity, which the growing habit of posting presents made even more feverishly chaotic.

The Christmas tree gave a fresh wave of prosperity to the toy trade, and during the 1850's Tom Smith & Company, a London firm, created the Christmas cracker, and by the '90's they were making over eleven million crackers every season. The forerunner of the cracker was a sweetmeat with a love-motto wrapped in a piece of fancy paper and called a "Kiss Motto."[136] The cracker was really an elaboration of the very old custom of pulling the wish-bone of a chicken: but instead of the winner who held the biggest piece merely wishing, the winner of a pulled cracker got a tangible reward immediately, a sweet and a motto, then, as the idea was elaborated, some small toy, and, at a later stage, a mask or a paper hat as well. The noise and jollity of Christmas parties were increased by the cracker, paper hats diminished dignity, and only incurably stuffy people refused to unbend. After the passing of Sir John Lubbock's Act of 1871, December 26th became

The ghost of Pickwick haunted Victorian Christmas parties, Washington Irving's *Old Christmas* made a contribution to the games and festivities, and everybody felt that they were recapturing the spirit of the "good old times" on Christmas Eve and Christmas night. The first publicised Christmas card was designed in 1846 by J. C. Horsley, R.A., for Sir Henry Cole, but one was produced two years earlier by W. C. T. Dobson (see page 178). There was no Christmas tree, until the idea was imported from Germany by the Prince Consort. Dickens called it "that pretty German toy." *The Pickwick Papers* and Irving's *Sketch Book* were written before it was introduced. But the yule log was as old as England, and the magic of mistletoe many centuries older, one of the few surviving links with pre-Christian and pre-Roman Britain, and by no means the relaxing, innocent symbol it became in Victorian times. Reproduced from *Fun*, January 6th, 1866, page 170.

a bank-holiday, if it fell on a week-day, and the transformation of Christmas was complete: Christian observance, conviviality and comfort were happily associated: the alliance was recognised by the State, and there was no need for the Bob Cratchits of the world to be late for the office the morning after Christmas. The sponsor of that Act was known thereafter as Saint Lubbock, and in 1900 he became the first baron Avebury.

A smaller strain was put on the postal services in February. During the 1830's the printing of pictorial love-letters, sent by young men to reach their sweethearts on St. Valentine's day, grew in commercial importance, and though Valentines never rivalled Christmas cards in numbers, they certainly did in variety. Fifty years later, W. G. FitzGerald, writing in *The Strand*

Magazine, mourned the passing of the Valentine. He was not surprised. "At the present day," he said, "when ladies in bifurcated nether garments may be seen awheel in Piccadilly, or enjoying a cigarette in the smoking-room of their own club, it is no wonder that the pretty custom of sending valentines is fast falling into desuetude."[137]

That reference to "bifurcated nether garments" was typical of the circumlocutory style still used by some writers even as late as the '90's to avoid the word "bloomer," which continued to offend sensitive people although it had long been a generic term for any divided skirt or knickerbocker dress for women, thus immortalising the name of Amelia Jenks Bloomer (1818–94), the American dress reformer. Surtees, always frank, described Miss Grimes, the assistant editor of the *Swillingford Patriot*, as "an ardent Bloomer," and John Leech's portrait of her in *Mr. Sponge's Sporting Tour* (1853), wearing a pair of loose trousers, caught in at the angles, below a knee-length skirt, shows

JUDY—HER JOKE.

What! the Number wouldn't be complete without a picture of an old-fashioned Christmas party, and the happy family met together round the festive board Well, here you have the happy family having a few words before dinner.—It's horribly like real life, isn't it?

The Happy Family gathering. Reproduced from *Judy*, December 22nd, 1869, page 81.

THE BUSINESS OF MARRIAGE.

The family dinner on Sunday. The sixth of a series published by *Judy* in 1870, this scene being entitled "Omega," or as we might put it today "the Lot." Compare this scene, with its rumblings of discord, with Frith's painting, "Many Happy Returns of the Day" on plate 8. From *Judy*, June 1st, 1870, page 53.

an early example of this American innovation. The idea of a more rational form of dress for women, first thought of by Mrs. Elizabeth Smith Miller, was popularised when Mrs. Bloomer adopted it in 1849; but it never became a fashion until women took up cycling after the safety bicycle was perfected in the 1880's. Even then such obviously sensible garments were worn by very few women, and on bicycles made for ladies the horizontal bar between the saddle and the front frame was omitted and the back wheel protected on each side down to the level of the hub by a guard of stout strings, so there was no chance of a long skirt catching in the spokes.

The safety bicycle instigated the most revolutionary of all the social changes, for it took people away from home, as three-quarters of a century later, television brought them back. Muscular young men could ride long distances, but women could be kept to a safe range, a few miles at most, and the bicycle was soon accepted in the countryside, and even clergymen allowed their daughters to own (or more often share) a machine. The exercise was healthy and not violent. The roads were safe. Even the cycling clubs that sprang up in every sizable town, and the youths who rode so fast that they were called "scorchers," brought no serious hazards to country life, although they did

THE ROVER SAFETY
BICYCLE (PATENTED).

Safer than any Tricycle, faster and easier than any Bicycle ever made.
Fitted with handles to turn for convenience in storing or shipping. Far and
away the best hill-climber in the market.

Manufactured by

STARLEY & SUTTON,
METEOR WORKS, WEST ORCHARD, COVENTRY, ENGLAND.

Price Lists of "Meteor, "Rover," "Despatch," and "Sociable" Bicycles and
Tricycles, and the "Coventry Chair," Illustrated, free on application.

The advertisement relies wholly on the illustration for its attention power: the improved
safety bicycle was still "news," still enough of a novelty to command the interest of readers,
and still an outstanding item on a page crowded with competing announcements. From
The Graphic, January 31st, 1885, page 111.

No attempt is made to persuade anybody to adopt a new social habit, and makers of bicycles obviously thought that the picture spoke for itself. The advertisement for the Rover safety on the right appeared in *The Graphic* on October 17th, 1885, over eight months after the advertisement on the opposite page. One sentence refers to records, which were clearly still "news." *Below:* The "Salvo" still preserves the lines of the "penny-farthing" type, and already looks old-fashioned compared with the latest Rover. From *The Graphic*, April 25th, 1885.

THE ROVER SAFETY.

Now holds the 50 and 100 miles Road Records of the World.

Makers

STARLEY AND SUTTON, West Orchard, Coventry.

SEND FOR LISTS.

"SALVO" SAFETY.

NEW ILLUSTRATED CATALOGUES POST FREE.

STARLEY BROS.,
St. John's Works, Coventry.

kill a few chickens now and then; but the townsmen did not begin the serious invasion of the countryside until the bicycle became cheap as well as safe. What cheapened it was the growth of demand that enabled manufacturers to apply the economic laws of mass production, and demand was fostered by the use of the new powers of persuasion which were beginning to be used by organised industry and retail traders through the advertisement columns of newspapers and magazines.

Advertising was one of the most potent of the influences exerted by commerce on consumers, and the Victorian middle classes lived in a consumers' world, where shopkeepers on both sides of the Atlantic honoured the good trading maxim that "the customer is always right." Until the middle of the century newspaper circulations and the sale of space for advertisements were curbed by taxation, so newspaper proprietors could not take advantage of the mechanical improvements in printing which had cut production costs and made large circulations possible; but the tax on advertisements was abolished in 1853, then, two years later, the newspaper duty of 4d. a copy went, and in 1861 the duty of 3d. a pound on paper went too. Newspaper circulations then began to grow in response to a rising demand; the volume of advertising increased, and the dependence of industrial production on organised selling, and the effective use of advertising to stimulate sales, was recognised by enterprising manufacturers. The new possibilities of advertising were also recognised by importers and retailers; with the result that advertisements during the second half of the century were used to form and encourage new habits and create new demands, and to accelerate social changes by appealing to all classes, thus widening the market for new products and bringing down their individual cost. The safety bicycle could not have achieved its large and rapid popularity had it not been an excellent product; but consistent advertising expanded sales and lowered the price. The technique of persuasion was still elementary; advertisements were either baldly factual, relying on the established reputation of a firm, the novelty of a product like the bicycle, or, if they were concerned with health or the toilet, continuing the Georgian tradition of extravagant claims for cures and beauty treatments. The advertisements reproduced on the previous pages and opposite illustrate two extremes of Victorian copywriting. Seven other examples are given on pages 186 to 189, also 191 to 193 and 195.

The anonymous author of an essay on advertising, published in 1878 under the title of *Publicity*, in giving directions for writing an advertisement, said ". . . write out, no matter at what length, all that is needful to be said; next . . . examine critically what has been written, experiment carefully upon it, and ascertain how many words can be struck out without injury to the sense; and then submit the MS. to an experienced advertising agent, and procure a printed proof. It is rare to see a six-line advertisement which cannot be expressed in five. An advertisement should be plain and honest, not flowery—

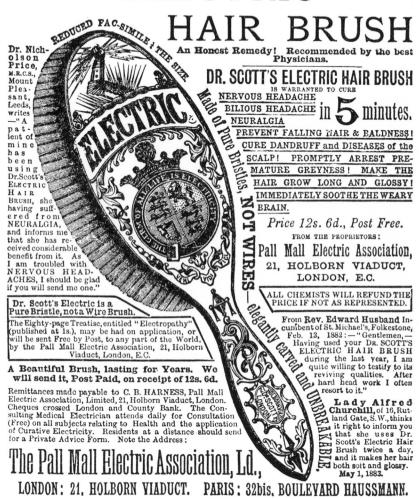

"The germ of all life is Electricity" is the slogan lettered round the belt that encircles the Royal arms on the back of the brush. Baldness had never troubled Georgian gentlemen who, decoratively bewigged, were indifferent about the abundance of their own hair, unless they wore it powdered: but Victorian gentlemen often resembled Mr. Spottletoe in *Martin Chuzzlewit*, "who was so bald and had such big whiskers, that he seemed to have stopped his hair, by the sudden application of some powerful remedy, in the very act of falling off his head, and to have fastened it irrevocably on his face." (Chapter IV.) From *The Graphic*, June 23rd, 1886, page 631.

G*

ROWLAND'S MACASSAR OIL

PRESERVES AND BEAUTIFIES THE HAIR.
It contains no lead nor mineral ingredients, and can now also be had in a golden colour for fair and golden haired people and children. Sold everywhere. Buy only ROWLAND'S MACASSAR OIL of 20, HATTON GARDEN, LONDON. Sizes 3s. 6d., 7s., 10s. 6d., and 21s. Sent by post for 3d. extra.

"**BRIGHT'S DISEASE and LIVER** COMPLAINT.—'The Holman Pad' has stood the severest and most thorough test for years. It has a national reputation established through its wonderful efficacy in all ailments that have their origin in a torpid liver, diseased kidneys, or stomach ailment. Endorsed by thousands of earnest, intelligent, living witnesses, who will tell you that the 'Holman Pad' is a cure for these diseases. Read the pamphlet entitled 'Nature's Laws,' sent free to any address. HOLMAN PAD CO., 92, Great Russell Street, London."

"**GET A BOTTLE TO-DAY OF** 'PERRY DAVIS's' PAIN KILLER.' It instantly relieves and cures severe scalds, burns, sprains, bruises, toothache, headache, pains in the side, joints, and limbs, all neuralgic and rheumatic pains. Taken internally cures at once coughs, sudden colds, cramp in stomach, colic, diarrhœa, and cholera infantum. PAIN KILLER is the great household medicine, and has stood the test of fifty years. Any chemist can supply it at 1s. 1½d. and 2s. 9d.

"**WHAT I KNOW ABOUT INDI-**GESTION.—AN AUTOBIOGRAPHY.— "It appeals forcibly to those who have allowed the palate to decide everything for them, and have paid the inevitable penalty of their folly."—Globe. Send for a copy to-day, it costs but 2d., including postage.—J. M RICHARDS, publisher, 92, Gt. Russell Street, London

THOSE WHO DON'T   [USE]   THOSE WHO DO
WARDE'S CAPILLARE. SOLD EVERYWHERE.

Above: A column of advertisements from *The Graphic*, November 24th, 1883, page 527. The first explains the extensive use of the Anti-Macassar. The others (except the cure for baldness) are in the eighteenth-century tradition of advertising, though the language is not so frank as that used by Georgian copywriters.

Below: The safety-razor was advertised in the 1880's, but it was regarded as dandified, even a trifle unmanly. Several decades passed before it ceased to be a relatively expensive luxury. From *The Graphic*, October 17th, 1885.

THE STAR SAFETY RAZOR

PERFECT SAFETY. NO EXPERIENCE REQUIRED. IMPOSSIBLE TO CUT ONE'S SELF!

DR. OLIVER WENDELL HOLMES, in his new book, "Our Hundred Days in Europe," in closing a very strong endorsement of this Razor, says:—"It is pure good will to my race which leads me to commend the Star Safety Razor to all who travel by land or by sea, as well as to all who stay at home."

TEDDY WICK, the Champion Barber, who shaved at the Royal Aquarium ten men with it in one minute and fifty-eight seconds, says:—I am more than pleased with the little Razor, and think it a marvellous invention. No Barber or private gentleman who shaves himself should be without it.'

PRICE OF RAZORS.

	s.	d.
In Enamelled Box.	7	6
In Leather Case	10	0
„ with extra blade.	15	0
„ „ 2 extra blades.	20	0
„ „ 3 extra blades.	25	0
„ „ 4 extra blades.	30	0
„ „ 6 extra blades.	40	0
Price of Strop.	1	6

A. J. JORDAN,
Sole European Agent.
6, 8, and 10, BAKER'S HILL,
SHEFFIELD
(And St. Louis. U.S.A.)
Send Money Orders.

This cut is just half size of the Razor when put up in Enamelled Box.

TO FOREIGNERS AND VISITORS

TO THE
GREAT EXHIBITION.

Among the number of objects of interest besides the Exhibition which will engage the attention of the Visitors to the "World's Fair," London shops and their decorations are certain to challenge their notice when perambulating the metropolis. Pre-eminent among these, and in a direct line from the Crystal Palace, stands the extremely elegant Establishment lately opened by

H. P. TRUEFITT,

AT 114, PICCADILLY;

being a branch of his far-famed Establishment at Nos. 20 and 21, Burlington-arcade (established upwards of thirty years). The Front, unequalled, it is believed, in any capital of Europe, is elaborately carved in Caen stone; whilst the spacious saloons for Hair-cutting, and private rooms for Hair-dressing, dyeing the Hair, and washing the head, are arranged with exquisite taste, and replete with every convenience. None but Assistants of first-rate talent are engaged; and in the shop will be found a splendid selection of every requisite for the toilet. The prices are in strict conformity with the economical spirit of the times. The charge for Hair-cutting is One Shilling. Everything in the same proportion.

LADIES' HAIR-DRESSING.—In this department H. P. TRUEFITT can now challenge the world, having secured the assistance of artists who are allowed to be unequalled; whilst his frequent visits to Paris secure every novelty in style, without the enormous prices charged by foreigners in this country. Lessons in Hair-dressing, without any extra charge for court hair-dressing. A splendid assortment of Ladies' fancy Twist Combs.—20, 21, *Arcade*; 114, *Piccadilly*.

CERTAINTY IN DYEING THE HAIR has at last been thoroughly effected by the "TINCTURA," a fragrant extract, by which any shade in brown or black is produced instantly and permanently. Those who have been deceived by any of the dyes at present will appreciate the value of this important discovery. Private rooms, replete with every convenience, are reserved expressly for its application.—114, *Piccadilly*.

PERFECTION IN WIG-MAKING is accomplished by the introduction of H. P. TRUEFITT's NEW DIVISION, which combines the durability of the skin with the transparency of the net parting, and perfectly avoids that great objection to ornamental hair, the DARK LINE ON THE FOREHEAD, it being now impossible to discover where the wig commences. This valuable discovery is applicable to ladies' bands, fronts, &c.—114, *Piccadilly*; *and* 20, 21, *Arcade*. [1 195

Haircutting, even behind a shop front elaborately carved in Caen stone, only cost one shilling. From *The Official Catalogue of the Great Exhibition of* 1851, Volume I, page 37, advertisement section.

nothing need be said in it for mere ornament. It should claim nothing which is not strictly true, but should be sure to claim AS MUCH as is true." [138] The advertisements for the Salvo and Rover safety bicycles on pages 182 and 183 are certainly plain and honest and innocent of flowery language, innocent too of any attempt at persuasion, apart from carefully drawn illustrations of the machines. Not that novelty was regarded as an all-sufficient recommendation, for when safety razors were advertised in the 1880's, testimonials from eminent men were included, though several decades passed before this time-saving device became a cheap, universal convenience. (See opposite.) A very old habit had to be changed, and the use of a safety razor was for a long time considered a trifle unmanly, a confession of nervousness. But the safety

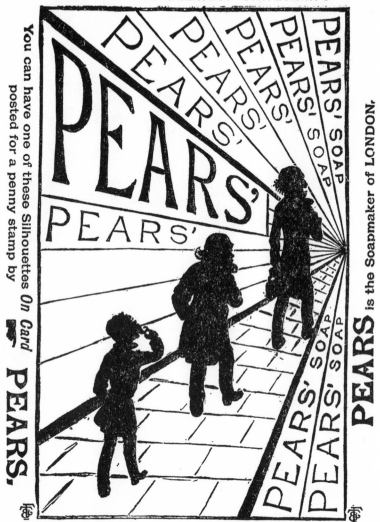

CURIOUS OPTICAL ILLUSION !
WHICH IS THE GREATEST STATESMAN ?

In the above Silhouette Churchill does not appear so tall as Salisbury, nor Salisbury so tall as Gladstone, but if measured they will all be found of equal height.

N.B.—No other equality is to be inferred.

An advertisement that compelled attention by taking liberties with public men. Nothing whatever is said about the product that is being advertised, though the name is repeated eleven times. It is purely reminder advertising, and there was a great deal of it during the second half of the nineteenth century. From *The Graphic*, February 6th, 1886, page 167.

Illustrated advertisements for Virginian cigarettes,
Richmond Straight Cut, No. 1.

MR. GLADSTONE has given up
cutting trees, and has taken to the
best cut of all, which is

ALLEN & GINTER'S'
RICHMOND STRAIGHT CUT
No. I CIGARETTE.

Cigarette Smokers who are willing to pay a little
more than the price charged for the ordinary trade
Cigarettes will find the Richmond Straight Cut No. 1
superior to all others. They are made from the
Brightest, most Delicately Flavoured, and Highest
Cost Gold Leaf grown in Virginia, and are absolutely
without adulteration or drugs. ALLEN & GINTER,
Manufacturers, Richmond, Va.
CAUTION.—Avoid imitations of this brand. The
genuine have the signature of ALLEN and GINTER
on each package.—H. K. TERRY and CO., Sole
Importers, 55, Holborn Viaduct. Price list post free.

Above: The use of a famous public man, like Mr.
Gladstone, always attracted attention. (He figures
in the Pears' soap advertisement opposite.)
From *The Graphic*, November 13th, 1884. *Right:*
From the same paper, August 16th, 1884. Both
examples represent a very elementary use of
persuasion.

THE LARGELY - INCREASED
demand from all parts of the world for the absolutely pure and high-grade RICHMOND STRAIGHT-
CUT No. 1 CIGARETTE is a guarantee of their great
superiority over the goods manufactured in sections
where the IMPERIAL leaf used by us is not obtainable : like the Havana segars, the leaf from which
they are made is only procurable by the manufacturer at the point of production.
The genuine bears the signature of
ALLEN & GINTER, RICHMOND, VIRGINIA,
HENRY K. TERRY & CO., Sole Consignees,
55, HOLBORN VIADUCT, LONDON, E.C.
Price List Free. Please mention this paper.

bicycle was new and comfortable, and ended the era of the penny-farthing and
other rather clumsy machines, which had made their riders figures of fun, and
often victims of humiliating accidents.

Cigarettes had to compete with cigars and pipes, and it is doubtful whether
women as potential consumers were even thought of by the original makers
and distributors. Tobacco was strong stuff: smokers had to be segregated: all
traces of its scent and flavour had to be obliterated, and gentlemen wore a
smoking cap, like a truncated tarboosh, to protect their hair, and a smoking
jacket, which could be removed after they had indulged. Both are worn by
the irate old gentleman seated by the fire in the drawing from *Judy* on page 180.
"The pitiable resources to which gentlemen are driven, even in their own

houses, in order to be able to enjoy the pestiferous luxury of a cigar, have given rise to the occasional introduction of an apartment specially dedicated to the use of Tobacco," said Robert Kerr, in *The Gentleman's House* when he described the smoking-room.[139] Most married men took their cigars or pipes to the kitchen or stables. But these restrictions melted away during the last quarter of the century, after the cigarette became everybody's smoke. Robert Peacock Gloag (1825–91) was the first British cigarette manufacturer, and although he had started his business in 1854, using Turkish tobacco, there was not much competition from other makes until the 1860's. His Scottish origin prompted him to give such names to his brands as "Standfast 92nd," after the Second Battalion of the Gordon Highlanders, and "Cantilever," as a tribute to the construction of the Forth Bridge.[140] By the '80's Virginian cigarettes were being imported from America and heavily advertised, and such advertising went far beyond factual statements, and used all kinds of attention-catching devices and arguments, not always plausible, and took the most astonishing liberties with the names and faces of public men, like Mr. Gladstone. (See pages 188 and 189.) By the turn of the century the cautious lower strata of the middle class grudgingly modified their belief that women who smoked were "fast." When Miss Posh startled Mrs. Pooter by saying "Don't you smoke, dear?" her husband replied: "Mrs. Charles Pooter has not arrived at it yet."[141]

The day-to-day life of the Pooter family, described by George and Weedon Grossmith in *The Diary of a Nobody*, covered a total period of fifteen months, and originally ran as a serial in *Punch* during 1888–89, being issued in book form in 1892. (It has sold steadily ever since.) This picture of the respectable, innocent and happy life of the poorer middle classes in a London suburb shows how social changes that were only beginning sixty years earlier had by the late '80's become time-honoured customs, like the annual seaside holiday at Margate or Broadstairs, and the magnification of Christmas with cards and present-giving. Cycling was still new enough to make the enthusiasm of Pooter's friend Cummings seem a trifle eccentric—he was a constant reader of the *Bicycle News*—and, as we have just seen, cigarette smoking by women could still shock the staid but by no means censorious Pooter. Those new habits were increasing the independence of young women: cycling very obviously, while an occasional cigarette could gently assert a tentative equality with men. Other changes were on the way, destined to accelerate the emancipation of women in Britain and America far more than the efforts of political reformers who wanted them to have votes, and two of the most far-reaching instruments of change were the typewriter and the telephone. The former brought economic independence and a professional career to many girls, the latter released them from a narrow social life, which could be closely supervised by their mothers and fathers. Both were slow starters in England, and in America the professional woman typist was well-established in the '80's,

From *The Graphic*, May 24th, 1884, page 515. See Elegance before Comfort, pages 94 to 98.

HANDSOME BRASS AND IRON BEDSTEADS.

HEAL and SON'S SHOW ROOMS contain a large assortment of Brass Bedsteads, suitable both for Home use and for Tropical Climates; handsome Iron Bedsteads with Brass Mountings and elegantly Japanned; plain Iron Bedsteads for Servants; every description of Wood Bedstead that is manufactured, in Mahogany, Birch, Walnut Tree Woods, Polished Deal and Japanned; all fitted with Bedding and Furniture complete, as well as every description of Bedroom Furniture.

HEAL AND SON'S NEW ILLUSTRATED CATALOGUE

CONTAINS DESIGNS AND PRICES OF **150** DIFFERENT ARTICLES OF BEDROOM FURNITURE, AS WELL AS OF 100 BEDSTEADS, AND PRICES OF EVERY DESCRIPTION OF BEDDING,

SENT FREE BY POST.

HEAL AND SON,

BEDSTEAD, BEDDING, AND BEDROOM FURNITURE MANUFACTURERS,

196, TOTTENHAM COURT ROAD,

LONDON.

MATTRESSES, WARRANTED NOT TO WEAR HOLLOW IN THE MIDDLE.

HEAL and SON have Patented an improvement in the manufacture of Mattresses, which prevents the material felting into a mass, as it does in all Mattresses made in the ordinary way. The Patent Mattresses are made of the very best Horsehair only, are rather thicker than usual, and the Prices are but a trifle higher than other good Mattresses.

Above: Many advertisements were straightforwardly factual, relying on typographical presentation and making no attempt to use persuasion, like this example issued in 1858 by Heal and Son. From *Murray's English Handbook Advertiser*, page 15, included as a supplement to *A Handbook for Travellers in Kent and Sussex*. (London: John Murray, 1858.)

Opposite: A picture of a factory or even a portrait of the founder of a business often confused the message of an advertisement. It was many years before advertisers realised that advertisements had to sell goods to the public, not industrial architecture or the whiskers of the founder. From the Advertisement section of *The Official Catalogue* of the Great Exhibition of 1851, Volume I, page 41.

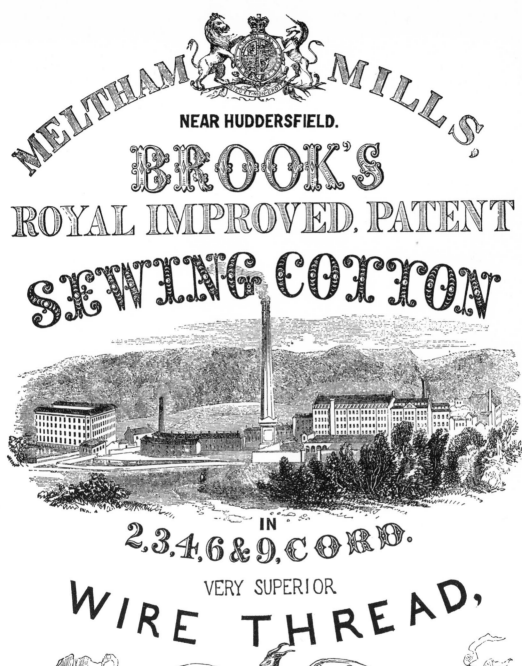

MELTHAM MILLS,

NEAR HUDDERSFIELD.

BROOK'S
ROYAL IMPROVED, PATENT
SEWING COTTON

IN
2, 3, 4, 6 & 9, CORD.

VERY SUPERIOR
WIRE THREAD,

AND CROCHET COTTON.

In 1880 the Bell and Edison Telephone Companies amalgamated, and became the United Telephone Company Ltd. In 1883 the Post Office proposed to set up a system in competition, but was opposed by the Treasury, which in those days believed that the State should do no more than supplement private enterprise and not attempt to replace it. By the end of the 1880's the telephone in England had become an accepted, though still rare, method of communication in business, and, to a much lesser extent, in private life. From *The Graphic*, September 1st, 1883, page 233.

while the telephone was still a joke with the comic papers in England long after it was installed in thousands of American offices and homes. (See page 20, opposite and above.)

The pleasure of reading was enjoyed by nearly all respectable people, though mothers and fathers were unremittingly vigilant about the books they allowed their sons and daughters to open. In many nonconformist homes, novels were rejected with the same abhorrence as the theatre and dancing and music, other than the unmelodious sacred music of which the more savagely puritanical sects approved. The English and Scots were serious Bible-readers; a habit which provided a moral structure that supported them in spirit and behaviour throughout life, and implanted a love and understanding of the splendid language of the Authorised Version. This spiritual and literary heritage encouraged standards of criticism that tended to exclude innovations, unconventional thoughts and ideas, and any approach to nature that might have revealed the coarseness or crudity of life. The facts of sex were rigorously debarred from fiction. Du Maurier's *Trilby*, published in 1895, was considered daring and almost as unsuitable for ladies to read as a French novel, although the hero, "Little Billee," was very properly horrified when he discovered that Trilby posed in "the altogether." What was really shocking was that the author obviously thought "Little Billee" should have followed his own inclinations by marrying Trilby instead of being restrained by the conventional objections of his relations. There was also the encounter between Little Billee and the vicar, "a very nice-looking vicar—fresh, clean, alert, well tanned by sun and wind and weather—a youngish vicar still; tall, stout, gentlemanlike, shrewd, kindly, worldly, a trifle pompous, and authoritative more than a trifle. . . ." The description was distasteful to a reading public that had been fed on a diet of heroes who were either soldiers or churchmen, with sailors—notoriously loose in their morals and therefore less favoured— as an occasional change. But clean-limbed gallant colonels, of the type illustrated on page 67, and manly curates who became even more manly vicars and rectors when they married and had enormous families, were favourite

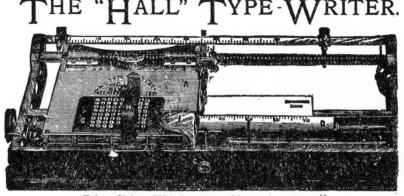

Typewriters were still novelties in the 1880's: few offices in Britain were equipped with them, though they were common enough in American cities. When he visited the United States in 1889, Kipling had met "the typewriter girl" in San Francisco, and observed that "Only a woman can manage a type-writing machine, because she has served apprenticeship to the sewing-machine." (*From Sea to Sea*, by Rudyard Kipling. Volume II, No. XXV, page 15. London: Macmillan & Co.) He basically disapproved of girl typists while admitting the convenience of their services. They had not yet become recognised in Victorian England. The early machines were complicated, inconveniently designed, and not very easy to operate.

This advertisement is reproduced from *The Graphic*, January 23rd, 1886, page 91.

figures in the works of women novelists. When Little Billee admitted to that "very nice-looking vicar," who was also a prospective father-in-law, that he no longer attended any place of worship and enjoyed reading Darwin, the vicar after calling him a *thief*, said: "You're trying to *rob me* of my Saviour! Never you dare to darken *my* door-step again!"[142] The facts of science were almost as shocking as the facts of life.

The language of many popular Victorian writers might seem stilted, when they described tender scenes between men and women, and at other times impossibly melodramatic. But it was an age when melodrama was appreciated; when ordinary people made speeches and pronouncements to each other in the home; when flowery compliments and thunderous denunciations did not seem ill-placed or out of character in novels and novelettes, though writers had to be careful of the words they put into the mouths of their characters. It had long been a convention to disguise expletives with a dash, or, which made them seem far more potent, to use the letters at the beginning and end. D——n and b——t looked much worse printed that way, but until the end of the period the convention remained. It was always disregarded by some writers, and finally broken down by story-tellers·like W. W. Jacobs in the '90's. Even so, magazines safeguarded the sensitivity of their readers. For instance, in a story by W. W. Jacobs called *A Safety Match*, one of the characters says: "I won't do nothing so damned silly." The story is included in *Sea Urchins*, which was published in 1898. When it first appeared in *The Strand Magazine* in February of that year, the editor altered "damned" to "darned."[143] In *Treasure Island*, Stevenson side-stepped the problem in describing Ben Gunn's imitation of Flint's last words, when he wailed "Darby M'Graw" over and over again, "and then, with an oath that I leave out, 'Fetch aft the rum, Darby!' "[144]

The delicacy of Victorian ladies was such that they seldom if ever acknowledged the true sex of cats and dogs: cats were always referred to as *she*, dogs as *he*: a tomcat was a lustful and disreputable animal: the word *bitch* was *never* heard and rarely printed. There were some robust exceptions, like the description of Lord Scamperdale inspecting farmer Springwheat's family, when he said to Jack Spraggon: "Now, that's what I call a good entry . . . all dogs, all boys, I mean?" At which Mrs. Springwheat laughed, and identified the two girls for him.[145] But Surtees was writing about country people and fox-hunters, and in *Handley Cross* allowed Mr. Jorrocks to indulge in some coarse repartee.[146] There could be no pleasure for respectable readers if they were made uncomfortable by some loose expression or uneasy by some original idea. The fury that new voices aroused was not caused by what they said or how they said it, but by the implied threat to mental and moral comfort, which was identified with respectability, and protected by hypocrisy. Even so, the first edition of Samuel Butler's *Erewhon* sold out in three weeks, and that new and unusual voice puzzled everybody, including

M. ELLEN STAPLES.   R. TAYLOR.

"OH, GERTRUDE! DON'T SAY ME NAY AGAIN!"

The language might seem stilted and austere, even a little unnatural; but there was elegance in the carefully controlled tenderness of the scene. From an illustration to "Lady Grace," by Mrs. Henry Wood, published in *The Argosy*, September, 1887.

M. ELLEN STAPLES.   R. TAYLOR

SHE WAVED HIM ASIDE IN HER WILFUL MANNER.

An illustration from "Lady Grace," by Mrs. Henry Wood, from *The Argosy*, May, 1887. This instalment of the story was followed by an obituary notice of the novelist by her son, Charles W. Wood, editor of *The Argosy*. Of her work, he said: "Her purpose was to interest and amuse her readers. At the same time, she always endeavoured, as far as possible, to elevate them; to raise the standard of morality; to set forth the doctrine of good and evil; to point out the two paths of life, and the consequences that must follow the adoption of either."

FRANK DADD.   R. TAYLOR.

"IT IS NOT POSSIBLE THAT YOU MEAN TO KILL ME!"

Melodramatic scenes, generally associated with foreigners, enlivened the decorous relation of
novels and novelettes. This scene, from "The Missing Rubies," by Sarah Doudney, is where
John Wouriski is threatening Madame Valerot, formerly Pauline Lorenski, who followed
the remark quoted in the caption by saying: "The murder will be discovered; you will lose
your own lives." From *The Argosy*, October, 1887.

George Cruikshank's *Sunday in London*, published in 1833, showed the sordid side of life in the metropolis, and attacked the fashionable follies, for it was a tract, aimed at the falling off of church attendance. In the text that accompanied Cruikshank's savage illustrations—for he had all the anger of Hogarth—it was said that "wherever we of this age of intellect, have 'a Christian church,' there you are sure to find the most conspicuous temples of the Great Spirit of the age—that is, of Gin." The illustration reproduced here is entitled: "Gin-temple turn-out at Church-time."

The "Public Bar" of the public house, depicted by Du Maurier. This is reduced from an illustration in *Punch*, October 11th, 1879, which has the following caption:

"CATCH 'EM ALIVE, OH!"

Costermonger. "I call yours a *SIGHNOCURE*, Jim. You claps that 'ere Paper round yer 'at, and there you are—a penny each!"

Fly-Catcher. "Ah, but look at the labour of catchin' 'em, and stickin' of 'em on at the outset, Bill!"

Reproduced by permission of *Punch*.

The Spread Eagle, in High Street, Wandsworth, typical of the spacious public houses built in prosperous and busy suburbs during the last decades of the nineteenth century. A canopy of cast-iron and glass protects the entrance. Built in 1898. *Drawn by David Owen.*

many of the most progressive people who, unaware that he was laughing at mankind, thought he was laughing at Darwin. The most popular fiction was pervaded by a vaguely pious optimism, and the villains were generally foreigners.

Comfort had to be preserved, and the desire to keep it intact with all its cosy associations was illustrated by the deliberate segregation of classes in public houses. The old taverns and ale-houses disappeared; the unlicensed boozing kens, hush-cribs and whistling shops and the slightly more respectable drinking dives of the eighteenth century were raised in architectural status, and changed into glittering gin-palaces, and gin, as one habitual drunkard said, was "the shortest way out of Whitechapel," or any other dismal slum. The gin-temple or gin-palace at first catered almost exclusively for the lower orders; and later the less ostentatious and far cosier public house was designed to cater for everybody—the labourer who wanted a pot of beer, the middle-class householder or young clerk like Lupin Pooter who wanted beer or spirits and a comfortable bar to sit in, or the swell who wanted hock and seltzer or a brandy and soda. To make all classes of customers feel comfortable and to charge them according to their pockets, there were three bars: public, private, and saloon. These class divisions applied also to many refreshment rooms at large railway stations. By the '90's spacious public houses were built in the principal streets of every town, with ample room for the three bars, and such attractions as billiard rooms and snack counters. (See page 201.) Only the small pubs in country villages and market towns kept to one democratic bar, though there was nearly always a bar parlour for exclusive drinking or a snuggery, which was virtually a club for regular customers: some of the less pretentious suburban pubs had only public and private bars. There was nothing like the long, spacious, unsegregated American saloon, as democratic in conception as a railroad car, with its free-lunch counter, its cocktails and mixed drinks and silver ice-buckets, and muscular, white-coated bouncers to heave drunks on to the sidewalk. The later and more ornate gin-palaces had a multiplicity of mirrors, decorated with brilliant-cutting, which sparkled and glittered cheerfully. The whole atmosphere differed from the American saloon. In the English pub the bars always had a cosy intimacy; whether it was the gin-palace type, respectably suburban, or unpretentiously rural.

The "One Man Band," who "began life with a Punch and Judy show, and then played the drum and pan-pipes," adding to these basic instruments, the tambourine, triangle, cymbals, concertina, and hurdy-gurdy. From an article on "Street Musicians," by Gilbert Guerdon, published in *The Strand Magazine*, 1892, Volume III, page 70. (See opposite and page 207.) Reproduced by permission of George Newnes Limited.

German bands were a familiar sight in the streets of London and other cities in the second half of the nineteenth century. From an article on "Street Musicians," by Gilbert Guerdon, published in *The Strand Magazine*, 1892, Volume III, page 71. (See opposite page.) Reproduced by permission of George Newnes Limited.

The music hall had developed from the old saloon theatres of the 1830's, and from the regular "sing-songs" and "harmonic meetings" in the bar-parlours of public houses; and the halls kept up the tradition of catering for comfort and pleasure by allowing the audience to be served with refreshments during performances. The rise and prosperity of the music hall and variety theatre in the second half of the century was spectacular; in active and often bitter competition with the regular theatres, the halls developed a form of entertainment that no theatre could supply—intimate, informal, and jovial. By the '90's their progress "from pothouse to palace" was complete and, although many respectable people decried them as "common" and "vulgar," middle-class couples visited them surreptitiously when they thought there was no risk of being seen by their friends. (See illustration from *Judy* on page 58.) The performers were topical, lively, and without reverence for eminent and pompous statesmen, whose pronouncements they parodied, and whose private lives often prompted some caustic comment. The halls and the songs they popularised were a virile element in national life, as typically Victorian as the operas of Gilbert and Sullivan, gay, light-hearted, and appealing to the mass of people who were not apologetic about enjoying themselves and who loved life without any of the critical hesitancies of the more rigid sections of the middle class or the inhibitions of the loveless puritans.

The Victorians were fond of music. Every young lady was taught to read music and to play the piano, and to sing, whether she had a good voice or not.

"MOST MUSICAL, MOST MELANCHOLY!"

Mrs. Gushington Parvenu :—"Very nice. What is the name of that piece, dear?"

Niece :—"It's a sonata, Aunt."

Mrs. G. P. (who imagines she detects something of the Italian in the title) :—"Ah, yes, delightful. It's considered a very fine opera too, is it not, dear?"

The upright cottage piano, with its fretwork panel backed with pleated coloured silk above the keyboard, was an essential part of the furnishing of the small suburban drawing-room. The drawing-rooms of large town and country houses would have a grand piano, and a cottage piano in the nursery or schoolroom for the children to practise their scales and five finger exercises. Reproduced on a slightly reduced scale from *Fun*, August 1st, 1874, page 54.

Every young lady was taught to read music and to play the piano. Both sexes had a social obligation to contribute personally to entertainment at a party, either by singing or playing some instrument. Good manners demanded that the performance should be at least plausible, and this meant hours of practice at home. From *The Young Lady's Book*, edited by Mrs. Henry Mackarness (London: George Routledge & Sons, 1876). Page 297.

At home and at parties, both sexes honoured a social obligation by contributing personally to the entertainment, either by playing some instrument, singing or reciting. Itinerant musicians haunted the streets, performing on a variety of instruments—flute, bassoon, cornet, fiddle and bagpipes, and one of the most favoured was the penny tin whistle. Nobody could explain that name. "I think no one ever bought one for a penny," said Robert Louis Stevenson. "Why should the alternative name be tin whistle? I am grossly deceived if it be made of tin. Lastly, in what deaf catacomb, in what earless desert, does the beginner pass the excruciating interval of his apprenticeship? We have all heard people learning the piano, the fiddle, and the cornet; but the young of the penny whistler (like that of the salmon) is occult from observation; he is

DISSOLVING VIEWS.

AMUSEMENT AND INSTRUCTION BY MEANS OF

CARPENTER & WESTLEY'S

IMPROVED

PHANTASMAGORIA LANTERNS,

WITH THE

CHROMATROPE AND DISSOLVING VIEWS,

AND EVERY POSSIBLE VARIETY OF SLIDERS,

INCLUDING

Natural History, Comic, Lever, Moveable and Plain,

Astronomical, Views in the Holy Land,

Scriptural, Portraits, &c.

No. 1 Lantern, with Argand-Lamp, in a Box, 2*l*. 12*s*. 6*d*.
No. 2 ditto, of a larger size, 4*l*. 14*s*. 6*d*.
A pair of Dissolving-View Lanterns, No. 2, with Apparatus,
11*l*. 11*s*.

The Lamp for the No. 2 Lanterns is very superior. (*The price of
the Lanterns is without Sliders.*)

Public attention is called to the superiority of the Paintings executed for the Lanterns. A pair of the most
IMPROVED LANTERNS, with Specimens of the Paintings, may be seen in the GREAT EXHIBITION.

Paintings of any size or subject painted to order.

Lists of the Sliders and Prices upon application to the Manufacturers, Messrs. CARPENTER & WESTLEY,
Opticians, 24, Regent-street, Waterloo-place, London.

The magic lantern was the forerunner of the cinematograph, and "dissolving views," were
a succession of pictures, projected on a screen and melting into each other without the abrupt
change from one picture to another when ordinary slides were used. From the *Official
Catalogue of the Great Exhibition*, Volume I, page 24, advertisement section.

never heard until proficient. . . ."[147] Another name for it was the American
flageolet. Among street musicians were the One Man Band; German bands,
composed of highly skilled performers on brass instruments, who wore uniform
and raised the standard of street music (see pages 202 and 203); and organ-
grinders, usually Italians, who, accompanied by a small monkey on a chain,
squeaked out popular tunes on a hurdy-gurdy, a barrel-organ, or the larger
and more melodious piano-organ.

Innumerable singers took up their stand at street corners or wandered up
and down, until paid to go away, and when the summer holiday season was
over troupes of nigger minstrels left the sands for the suburbs, and entertained
or irritated householders. Some of the more unscrupulous performers would
pick out a street where straw was laid down, which was done to deaden the

"Miss Fanny Bouncer was both good-humoured and clever, and, besides being mistress of the usual young-lady accomplishments, was a clever proficient in the fascinating art of photography, and had brought her camera and chemicals, and had not only calotyped Mr. Verdant Green, but had made no end of duplicates of him. . . ." *The Adventures of Mr. Verdant Green*, Part II, Chapter VIII, page 160 (1853–56).

noise of traffic when there was illness in a house: this ensured immediate payment for stopping whatever sounds they were making. (Carts and horse-drawn traffic using cobbled streets or surfaces formed from granite blocks made far more noise with their iron-bound wheels and clip-clopping horses than modern traffic with its rubber tyres.) On the whole, street musicians were tolerated and encouraged, otherwise such considerable numbers of them could not possibly have made a living.

Music in the home not only gave pleasure, but informed and sharpened the critical faculties, so poor performers were occasionally deterred from facing an audience, even in the home circle. They could always fall back on recitations. Children were trained from an early age to learn off by heart various pieces of

A Game of Draughts.

Draughts, "though strictly a scientific game," according to *The Young Ladies' Treasure Book*, was regarded as a sedate and proper pastime for girls from the age of Alice upwards.

A DOMESTIC EXTRAVAGANZA.

Mamma. "WHY, GOOD GRACIOUS, NURSE! WHAT'S THE MATTER WITH ADOLPHUS? HE LOOKS VERY ODD!"

Nurse. "AND WELL HE MAY, MUM! FOR HE THOUGHT THE COLOURED BALLS IN MISS CHARLOTTE'S NEW GAME OF SOLITAIRE WAS BULL'S EYES, AND HE'S SWALLOWED EVER SO MANY OF 'EM!"

May 22nd, 1858. Reproduced by permission of *Punch*.

Right: The solitaire board, pierced with thirty-seven holes, in each of which a marble or a peg was placed. From *The Young Ladies' Treasure Book.*

verse and prose. Tennyson was a great favourite, and "The Charge of the Light Brigade" was considered particularly suitable for boys, "The Brook" for girls, and "Locksley Hall" for either sex. Nobody was allowed the luxury of idleness, either at home or at a party: only the old and infirm were permitted to be non-participants in entertainments and games. Young people were always expected to be busy and helpful. There were many polite accomplishments for young ladies, needlework and fancy work, water-colour painting, and photography; and there were home entertainments, including that forerunner of the cinematograph, the magic lantern, which was popular at Christmas parties, particularly when the appliance could produce dissolving views, which gave jerky animation to the pictures on the screen. There were charades, to challenge dramatic talent; guessing games, word games like Dumb Crambo, amateur theatricals, and variations of young Burwin-Fosselton, who entertained the Pooters with his imitations of Irving, performing in hundreds of suburban homes. Games included chess, draughts, back-gammon, solitaire, and dominoes, while whist was the principal card game until bridge came in about 1894, though there was a craze for bézique in the '70's and '80's. There were innumerable round games, Muggins, Old Maid, Lives and Snip-Snap-Snorem, in which any number of players could take part, though sixteen was the limit in Lives. To the vast majority of people, games still gave innocent pleasure: enjoyment was more important than skill, and in the home games were played without restraints, and even strict Sabbatarians saw nothing odd or remotely sinful in playing cards up to midnight on Saturday. The ability of the Victorians to keep their ideas in separate compartments allowed pleasure to be compatible with comfort most of the time. For the middle classes and the rich it was a happy age.

H

Hospital Saturday, September 1st, 1883, the tenth annual collection for the Hospital Saturday Fund. *Top left:* Lady Constance Howard at Apsley House. *Top right:* Mrs. Grylls at Clarence House. "Of all the lady collectors whom he saw," reported *The Graphic*, "our artist seems to have been chiefly attracted by Mrs. Grylls, who, he says, was charmingly dressed in mourning, and asked every passer-by in so fascinating a fashion that it was impossible to refuse her." *Bottom left:* At the East End: corner of Commercial Road and White Horse Street. *Bottom right:* Corner of Oxford Street and Regent Street, where the observant artist "was pleased with the self-possession of a young lady of fourteen . . . who was placed so close to the kerb as to be in danger of passing vehicles, but nevertheless bravely distributed her appeals to the wayfarers." Reproduced, with a slight reduction, from *The Graphic*, September 8th, 1883, page 241.

CHAPTER VIII

COMFORT AND CONSCIENCE

THE philosophy of comfort could not stifle an active conscience, and every Victorian possessed one that was by turns clamorous or quiescent and always unpredictable. Women were far more susceptible to its awkward and often inconvenient promptings than men, whose devotion to business and pleasure had stiffened their ability to ignore what they did not want to see or acknowledge. But nobody could be sure that his or her conscience would not suddenly awaken and, without warning, start working overtime. The structure of sentimentality and class snobbery was as ornate as Victorian ornament, and the exercise of charity which could partly allay the prods of conscience was sometimes an unconscious form of snobbery, though none the less effective because of that or less welcome to the recipients. Throughout their lives the upper and middle classes were constantly reminded of the needs of less fortunate people, and from childhood were encouraged to cultivate a form of pious self-congratulation. An early lesson in such Christian complacency is conveyed by a piece of tea-time dialogue from *Happy Hours; at Wynford Grange*, one of those improving stories for children that maintained the moral tone of the nursery. The characters are a brother and sister and their governess.

" 'How nice this bread-and-milk is,' said Harry.

" 'I wish,' said Eleanor, 'that we could give some of it to the poor little girl that we saw when we were walking this morning; she looked so hungry and tired, and was crying so sadly.'

" 'Poor child,' said Miss Maberley, 'her mother is very ill indeed. I fear she is dying, and that they have scarcely sufficient food to eat, or fire to warm them. You ought to be very thankful that God has given you these, and many other comforts.' "(148)

The voice of conscience, whether clear or muffled, made prosperous people intermittently uncomfortable and induced fits of spiritual disquiet which often generated an irrational eagerness to redress wrongs, almost any wrongs—preferably wrongs a long way off. Dickens satirised this tendency when he described Muggleton as "an ancient and loyal borough, mingling a zealous advocacy of Christian principles with a devoted attachment to commercial rights; in demonstration whereof, the mayor, corporation, and other inhabitants, have presented at divers times, no fewer than one thousand four hundred and twenty petitions, against the continuance of negro slavery abroad, and an equal number against any interference with the factory system at home. . . ."[149] Slavery was abolished in British colonies by Act of Parliament in 1833, and thereafter moral indignation could be indulged over the retention of the system in America. The idea of redressing wrongs nearer home was far more uncomfortable. There was an easy way out for wealthy people, and they took it by subscribing generously to charities. "The English think that a cheque-book can solve every problem in life," said Mrs. Cheveley in *An Ideal Husband*; but that was one of Oscar Wilde's slick half-truths. Only insensitive people really believed that. Mere donations to charities were not enough to buy off a really virile conscience. Gifts to the churches were apt to be diverted to missionary enterprises, and although there was a moderate glow of enthusiasm among orthodox Christians for converting the heathen, there was a fairly widespread feeling that charity begins at home, and should perhaps stay there. The Victorians liked to see something for their money, and welcomed schemes of practical philanthropy which gave tangible evidence, preferably in bricks and mortar, that their donations had been well spent. Hospitals were enlarged and improved, new hospitals were built, and in rural districts cottage hospitals were established, the first in 1859 at Cranleigh in Surrey. The whole system of caring for the sick was overhauled; the income of hospitals was derived almost entirely from gifts and bequests, and by the '70's thousands of voluntary helpers were devoting a large part of their leisure to collecting money. Hospital Saturday in London became an annual event, when members of the nobility and gentry and scores of humbler people stood in every thoroughfare with collecting boxes. (See page 210.)

Housing for old people, pensioners no longer capable of work, had been provided in a piecemeal fashion in the form of almshouses since the early sixteenth century; and many more were built during the Victorian age, also homes for impoverished widows and spinsters of the middle classes, who were officially described as "decayed gentlewomen." Such provision only touched a tiny part of the huge and growing problem of housing, for in every city slums darkened life and destroyed any hope of decency or happiness for thousands of people, and housing was the chief item on the agenda of the Society for Improving the Condition of the Labouring Classes. The philanthropic housing movement spread beyond London, attracting gifts from the rich in many cities; but no comprehensive plan of slum-clearance and rehousing could be sponsored by any Society. One of the most constructive contributions to housing the London poor came from an American philanthropist, George Peabody (1795–1869), who had settled in London in 1837 and built up a large business as a merchant and money-broker. Apart from his gift of half a million pounds for building working-class homes in London, there was something about his character that appealed to the public; he was

HOW TO TAKE A HINT.

John Bull:—"WELL, MR. PEABODY, AFTER YOUR SECOND SPLENDID DONATION, DON'T YOU THINK IT'S MY TURN TO DO SOMETHING FOR THE POOR?"

George Peabody (1795–1869), an American philanthropist, built up in his own country one of the largest mercantile concerns in the world, established himself in London as a merchant in 1837, and relinquished his American interests in 1843. His generous gifts to educational and scientific bodies in the United States amounted to over a million pounds, and his donation of £500,000 for building working-class homes in London gave fresh impetus to the study of large-scale housing. Tall, utilitarian tenement blocks in various parts of London have perpetuated his name, and there is a statue of him behind the Royal Exchange (see plate 5), by an American sculptor and poet, William Wetmore Storey (1819–95), of which there is a bronze replica at Baltimore, Maryland. It was unveiled on June 25th, 1869, a few months before his death. His popularity in England was great, and, as this cartoon from *Fun* suggests, he supplied an example to home-grown philanthropists which stimulated the great movement for slum-clearance which has continued ever since. He was offered a baronetcy by Queen Victoria, but declined it.

immensely popular; his example stimulated native philanthropists and injected fresh vitality into the movement for slum-clearance and housing. A statue was erected to him during his lifetime; it was unveiled on June 25th, 1869, a few months before his death, and was an exceptional work, for nearly all statues of famous people portray them standing or astride a horse, but George Peabody in bronze sits at ease with his legs crossed in a clumsy elbow chair, intended to suggest the Greek style of the early part of the century, sedately regarding the back of the Royal Exchange. (See plate 5, also page 213.) Tall, rather bleak blocks of tenement dwellings still perpetuate his name.

When philanthropists turned their attention to improving the conditions of the poor by suggesting and sponsoring legislation that regulated hours of work in factories, they incurred the hostility of the industrialists and economists who belonged to the Manchester school of individualists, the exponents of *laissez faire* who made greed seem respectable by calling it enlightened self-interest. These people, who believed sincerely that God helps those who help themselves, approved of charity dispensed by individuals, and regarded it as one of the Christian obligations of the rich; but they attacked any individual or collective suggestions for reform which might disturb the delicate balance of a complex society, halt progress and diminish prosperity. Periodic unemployment, incurable poverty, and sweated labour were items of the economic price that had to be paid to keep the country prosperous and progressive. To accept such conclusions was not always comfortable, and they came under a running fire of scathing comment in *Punch*, which gave a platform to conscience-rousers like Thomas Hood (1799–1845), whose "Song of the Shirt" appeared anonymously in the Christmas number of 1843. This denouncement of sweated labour shocked many people: it was not easily forgotten, but the conditions it condemned were not redressed. Articles, poems and cartoons in *Punch* constantly reminded readers of the poverty and distress that surrounded them. A full-page cartoon, entitled "The Homeless Poor," published on January 22nd, 1859, showed two shivering, half-clad men sheltering in a doorway, one saying to the other: "Ah! We're badly off—but just think of the poor middle classes, who are obliged to eat roast mutton and boiled fowl every day!" Du Maurier's drawing of a portly dean talking to a starving beggar on a bitter day with snow on the ground was published twenty-five years later, on January 23rd, 1886. Under the title of "Consolation," Mr. Dean said (sympathetically): "Ah, my poor fellow, your case is very sad, no doubt! But remember that the rich have their troubles too. I dare say, now, *you* can scarcely *realise* what it is not to know where to find an investment which will combine *Adequate Security* with a *Decent Interest on one's Money!*"

Beggars haunted every city and suburban street; some had regular pitches, and made a pretence of selling matches or bootlaces, but all relied on their ragged clothes and broken boots to arouse the compassion and charity of passers-by. After *Trilby* was published in 1895, and Du Maurier's description of her exquisite feet had captivated the public, *Scraps* published a drawing of a barefoot beggar saying to a companion: "Got a pair of old boots you can give me?" The other was surprised, and said: "Why, I thought yer bare feet was good for trade." "Yus they are," was the reply, "but all the kids are saying, ''Ullo Trilby!' "

The English conscience was reinforced and activated by the increasing influence of the Scots, who in their private and public lives exemplified the stern idealism, the devotion to duty, the rejection of frivolities and the rationing of enjoyment which easy-going Southerners admired, but were usually content to admire theoretically or at a distance. ("Industry, regularity, respectability, and a preference for the four per cents. are understood to be the very foundations of a green old age," Stevenson had written in the opening chapter of *The Wrong Box*.) The Scots in the nineteenth century were even more puritanical than the English nonconformists, but far more intelligent. They had apparently adopted William Prynne's view, expressed two hundred years earlier, that pleasures could form "no part, no particle of a Christian's comfort; he can live a most happy joyful life without them; yea, he can hardly live happily or safely with them."[150] Those two Scottish engineers, George Stephenson and his son Robert, had all the limiting virtues of the puritan mind; elevating anecdotes about them multiplied; and they were praised unreservedly by Samuel Smiles in his account of their lives, for they represented everything Smiles most admired: energy, industry, inventive genius and a long, successful climb from a humble origin. George Stephenson was not averse to reminding people that he began life as a poor ploughboy.[151] He was always ready to help and advise young men, but unless they were soberly clad they could expect a preliminary rap over the knuckles. One youngster who called on him carried a gold-headed cane. " 'Put by that stick, my man,' said Stephenson, 'and I will talk with you.' " He was not foolishly modest about his own abilities; but always ready, like a good puritan, to attribute his success to his incapacity for gaiety.

" 'You will, sir, I hope, excuse me,' he said, on another occasion, to a gaily dressed youth; 'I am plain-spoken, and am sorry to see a clever young man like you disfigured by that fine-patterned waistcoat and all those chains and fangdangs. If I, sir, had bothered my head with these things when I was of your age, I would not have been where I am now.' "[152] Had he entered

AN UNTYPICAL VICTORIAN HERO

On the two pages that follow, illustrations are reproduced from the second of two articles in *The Graphic*, on General Gordon, by A. Egmont Hake, published on March 15th, 1884 (pages 265–68). Charles George Gordon (1833–85) was the antithesis of everything that was cosy, comfortable, conventional and formal in Victorian life. (See pages 219 and 220.)

GORDON AT GRAVESEND, 1867: TEACHING THE RAGGED BOYS—HIS "KINGS"

"He called them his 'kings,' and for them he got berths on board ship. One day a friend asked him why there were so many pins stuck into the map of the world over his mantelpiece, and he was told that they marked and followed the course of the boys on their voyages—that they were moved from point to point as his youngsters advanced, and that he prayed for them as they went, day by day."

THE PRESENT MISSION TO THE SOUDAN—"GOOD-BYE" AT CHARING CROSS STATION

Duke of Cambridge   General Gordon
Lord Wolseley   Colonel Stewart

"The same day that saw him arrive at Charing Cross from Brussels, saw him depart on his present mission to the Soudan."

Parliament like his son Robert he would have been pained by the sight of "chains and fangdangs" adorning the decorative form of young Disraeli, and incredulous and outraged if anybody had predicted that such a foppish creature could rise to be Prime Minister.

Francis Bacon had said of the puritans: "Let them take heed that it be not true which one of their adversaries said, *that they have but two small wants, knowledge and love.*" One of the most powerful adversaries of puritanism was Dickens who unknowingly expounded the philosophy of comfort, but never hesitated to make everybody feel uncomfortable when he denounced injustice, misery, suffering, and stupidity. Sydney Smith once wrote: "What passes in the mind of one mean blockhead is the general history of all persecution."[153] Dickens exposed mean blockheads mercilessly, and believed that all persecution would end, all injustice and misery and poverty vanish, if only there were more good men: that was the outstanding need of the times, better people, who by their personal goodness could make any system work for the benefit of all. He returned to this basic solution for social ills in every book he wrote, and in this he was in agreement with orthodox religion though completely out of sympathy with introspective people who withdrew themselves from the world in order to cosset their own souls. Dickens thoroughly approved of the middle-class civilisation with its comfort, conviviality and good intentions; it was his own class, and although he had a generously indignant compassion for the predicament of the working class, he knew as little about them as, say, Dr. Thomas Arnold, Thackeray or Trollope.

Charles Kingsley, who like Dickens thought that the world would be a better place for everybody if there were more good people in it, advocated a hearty, manly, courageous outlook, and was pardonably irritated when his brand of moral tonic was described as "muscular Christianity." The label was appropriate enough for members of such athletic professions as the Army; it was suitable, too, for cricket-playing country parsons, and in the second half of the century its application was broadened as fresh generations were inculcated with games worship at the public schools and the head prefect type with an art-proof mind became the symbol of the English round the world—at least of the ruling classes. Such men took their responsibilities heavily: they were brave, self-disciplined, incapable of shirking an unpleasant task, and usually behaved exactly as Kingsley believed hearty, manly fellows should. They did their duty, sustained by an innate sense of moral and racial superiority, which always kept their conscience on an even keel. This convenient stability was the subject of a drawing in *Fun*, on December 12th, 1874, the week after the Queen had distributed medals for conspicuous gallantry during the Ashanti War, which showed a small girl talking to her soldier uncle, with this caption:

Not Half so Painful. *Miss Mary:* "But, Uncley, Dear, you didn't think it fun to kill all those black Negro men?" *Uncle:* "No, dear, not fun. We regarded it as a sacred though disagreeable duty; like—like—er . . ." *Miss Mary:* "I know, like saying your catechism!"

The Church of England continued to attract and advance the most impressive-looking clergymen who maintained ecclesiastical dignity. Orthodox Anglicanism discouraged any form of dramatic intensity, for the unregulated voice of conscience could lead to ungentlemanly excesses, which were quite out of place in the Church. Religious fervour found other outlets. For example, the Salvation Army, which grew out of a Christian Mission founded by William Booth in 1865, and was from its inception a philanthropic as well as a religious body; also the American evangalising missions of Moody and Sankey which visited England during the '70's, '80's and '90's, and introduced in a modified form the collective hysteria of the camp meeting. Mark Twain had described that brand of revivalism in *Huckleberry Finn*, which was published in 1884,[154] and the gospel campaigns of Dwight Lyman Moody and Ira David Sankey were more successful in their own country, though English nonconformists eagerly adopted their book of Gospel Hymns.

Occasionally one individual could by his actions and beliefs make people of all classes feel uncomfortable, particularly when he was a conspicuous public figure and insisted on acting out of character. Eccentric men have always been tolerated and even admired and respected in England; but people were perplexed when a man was a spectacular hero, world-famous, unconventional, outspoken, and reproached by the frugality of his private life all those who were happy in their enjoyment of "easy circumstances," "a competence," or "a genteel sufficiency." A man like that was anathema to those in authority; he made nonsense of polite usages and conventional lies; and was as unstable—by ordinary, comfortable standards—as a volcano: nobody knew when he would erupt and scorch with fire things he believed to be wrong or unjust or dishonest. Such a man was General Charles George Gordon (1833—85), a turbulent mixture of saintliness, ambition, courage and fortitude, with an appetite for power that he was able to gratify, a capacity for compassion that he was able to indulge, and a habit of telling the truth with tactless and embarrassing insistence, which infuriated his superiors and contemporaries, but seldom diminished their respect for his integrity. He was an officer of the Royal Engineers who had won distinction in the Crimean War, had commanded an army for the Chinese Imperial government and successfully crushed the Taiping Rebellion, was thereafter known as "Chinese" Gordon, and when the Egyptian government appointed him Governor of the Equatorial Provinces of the Sudan, voluntarily reduced his salary from £10,000 to £2,000 a year. After his return from China and before his Egyptian appointment. he was made Commander of the Royal Engineers at Gravesend, to supervise the building of forts for the defence of the Thames, and although society was ready to acclaim him as a hero and he was already a popular figure with the public, he "lived a life of charity and peace, giving to the poor, attending the bedsides of the sick and dying; and when in 1871 he was called away to . . . new duties . . . the gratitude and sorrow that followed him were heartfelt and universal."[155] He had spent much of his leisure at Gravesend teaching street arabs and sailor boys; he found them employment, corresponded with them in after life, and called them his "kings." (See page 216.) Such activities did not commend him to fashionable people; no smart hostess could exhibit him as the "lion" of the moment; his monastic seclusion and his large but unadvertised charity made even men who had well-controlled consciences feel a little uneasy; and when he did occasionally emerge, nobody knew what this strong but by no means silent man was going to do or say next. Time and again he cracked the imposing carapace of officialdom, exposing that amorphous compound of cowardice and confusion, the official mind.

When he was killed at Khartum on his last mission to the Soudan, sacrificed, as many believed, to the evasive, ill-defined political policy of Gladstone, the whole nation was horrified. Gordon, by his heroic death, gave a severe jolt to the Victorian conscience. In a telegram, which was not in cipher and could therefore be read by any clerk, the Queen put into words what thousands of her subjects thought. "Mr. Gladstone and the Government have, the Queen *feels it dreadfully*, Gordon's innocent, noble, heroic blood on their consciences." People said that no longer should Gladstone be called the G.O.M. (Grand Old Man) but M.O.G. (Murderer of Gordon).[156]

Gladstone himself possessed a highly sensitive conscience, and a passion for righting wrongs, redressing injustices, and safeguarding the liberties of oppressed minorities. "You cannot fight against the future," he had said in his speech on the Reform Bill in 1866. "Time is on our side." Twenty years later, in a speech at Liverpool, he said: "All the world over I will back the masses against the classes." (June 28th, 1886.) He had one of those fine Victorian faces, resembling like so many of his eminent contemporaries, the confident and accomplished statesmen and adventurers of the first Elizabethan period. Like other great public men, he was sustained by Christian principles, and many people then supposed that they were compatible with political principles—a supposition that was at least plausible in a world governed by generally accepted codes of honour which gave validity to political undertakings and international treaties.

Conscience could make non-Christians, agnostics and others, just as uncomfortable as orthodox believers; perhaps more so, for many of the ardent reformers were recruited from enlightened and progressive sections of the middle classes, men and women who accepted a personal obligation to improve social and economic conditions, and dedicated their lives to that end. They had no patience with sporadic visits to slum-dwellers, known to the fashionable world as "slumming," or with the rural lady bountiful, distributing soup and blankets to deserving cottagers: such activities, and indeed most forms of charity, they dismissed as mere palliatives. They wanted reform, not revolution, and like all good Victorians they believed in the inevitability of progress: it was something that would keep on and on with bigger and more beneficial results.

There were a few dissident voices: Samuel Butler's *Erewhon* seemed almost blasphemous, for it doubted the sanctity of science and suggested that the machine might one day become a master instead of a servant. In the chapters quoted from "The Book of the Machines" he even made the prescient suggestion that there was "no security against the ultimate development of mechanical consciousness, in the fact of machines possessing little consciousness now."[157] Butler was intellectually isolated from his age: his appraisal of the preoccupations of his contemporaries had the cool, unemotional detachment of an anthropologist observing tribal habits, an attitude of mind that ensured the maximum amount of irritation for everybody. "People must and will go to church to be a little better," he said, "to the theatre to be a little naughtier, to the Royal Institution to be a little more scientific, than they are in actual life." He wrote that in *Alps and Sanctuaries*, nine years after *Erewhon* was published, and had said earlier in the same paragraph: "I would persuade all Jews, Mohammedans, Comtists, and free-thinkers to turn high Anglicans, or better still, downright Catholics for a week in every year, and I would send people like Mr. Gladstone to attend Mr. Bradlaugh's lectures in the forenoon, and the Grecian pantomime in the evening, two or three times every winter. I should perhaps tell them that the Grecian pantomime has nothing to do with Greek plays. They little know how much more keenly they would relish their normal opinions during the rest of the year for the little spiritual outing which I would prescribe for them . . ."[158]

No matter what they believed or doubted, very few Victorian intellectuals and reformers had the inclination or capacity to take spiritual outings. Tennyson underlined one of the most perplexing truths about his own age when he wrote:

"There lives more faith in honest doubt,
Believe me, than in half the creeds."

Doubters and freethinkers could be as hidebound and easily shocked as Anglicans or nonconformists, particularly when the Mission of Science was questioned or ignored as unimportant, as it was by so many supporters of the "Aesthetic Movement." Faith in Progress seldom wavered; it was constantly strengthened by fresh applications of science, new inventions, and revelations of hitherto unsuspected natural forces, all welcomed by the innocently receptive faithful, who compared such stupendous achievements with the manifest degeneration of the aesthetes as they sank more or less gracefully into decadence, captivated by the macabre art of Aubrey Beardsley and the smooth epigrams of Wilde—the oily, voluptuous Oscar whose ultimate fall seemed to discredit for all time "Art for Art's Sake." By comparison, science was so clean and decent, though perhaps not always safe. Apprehensive predictions were made occasionally. "War balloons will no doubt figure largely in the coming European war," said William G. Fitzgerald, in an article on photography that appeared during 1895 in *The Strand Magazine*.[159] In the same year H. G. Wells published *The Time Machine*, whose hero, the Time Traveller, "thought but cheerlessly of the Advancement of Mankind, and saw in the growing pile of civilisation only a foolish heaping that must inevitably fall back upon and destroy its makers in the end."

As early as 1892 push-button war was envisaged by James F. Sullivan, who wrote and illustrated a monthly feature for *The Strand Magazine* called "The Queer Side of Things," in which he often burlesqued the promised benefits of science. This particular article was entitled "The End of War," and some of the text and one of the illustrations from it are reproduced on the opposite page. It included this sentence: "Well, war seemed to grow ever more terrible; until it came to such a pass that a single human being could destroy a whole nation by simply pressing a small button with his finger."[160] But such imaginative flights were far too fantastic to trouble the conscience or upset the comfort of any reader in the last decade of the progressive and pre-eminently civilian century.

PUSH-BUTTON WAR—1892

Opposite: A page from an article entitled "The End of War," by J. F. Sullivan, which appeared in *The Strand Magazine* in June, 1892, Volume III, page 646. This late Victorian prediction of push-button war was included in the regular feature which Sullivan wrote in the early issues of the *Strand*, called "The Queer Side of Things." (Reproduced by permission of George Newnes Limited.)

have not spoken of their having that before."

"No; I was not quite sure what it was. You see, I seemed to hear them continually talking about it as something very valuable —something that ought to fetch a long price; and I fancy it must be an article of commerce. In fact, from what I can glean, it seems that, when the competition between, for instance, the manufacturers of any given nation has become very keen, they begin to part with their 'consciences' —to put them up in the parcels of goods; give them away with a pound of tea, as it were. And I dreamed that certain of the nations—for example, one called 'Great Britain,' and others named 'Germany,' and 'America'—did a very large export trade in these articles. From this I conclude that the article must be a something to fall back upon when the natural resources of a nation—produce and industry—have given out. Let us take it, then, that 'conscience' is a highly prized article of commerce. Well, I say, I dreamed that they were always ready to sacrifice even this article to the soil: every one of them seemed eager to exchange the commodity for the smallest slice of earth; and nations would do *anything* to obtain an extra bit of the latter. In fact, there seemed to be a fairly definite standard of relative market value between blood, and earth, and conscience— perhaps a quart of the two former, mixed, for a square foot of the latter; or something of that kind.

"But about war. Gradually, I dreamed, the firearms became more and more destructive, while all the elements, and everything in existence, were pressed into the service of war; and so absorbed were my human beings in the perfecting of war that they invented a subsidiary state of affairs called 'Peace,' which, on referring to these creatures' dictionaries, I found to be 'An interval necessary to the effective preparation of war.' The nations were never altogether in their element during these intervals; and, of course, any protracted peace meant the gradual impoverishment of the soil for want of the fertiliser

"Well, war seemed to grow ever more terrible; until it came to such a pass that a single human being could destroy a whole nation by simply pressing a small button with his finger. This rendered the

thing *too* wholesale, for it was found that the supply of the fertiliser—(let us speak of it in future under this name, as it is so much less unpleasant)—began to exceed the requirements of the soil, and thus to be rather detrimental to production than otherwise. Then I fancied that all the nations—that is, all that was left of them— solemnly consulted about the matter; and I heard talk of a mighty power not long discovered, and then being gradually brought to perfection; and I saw all the nations devote the ensuing interval of peace to destroying their great and com-

"A SINGLE HUMAN BEING COULD DESTROY A WHOLE NATION.

plicated machineries of war, which had required so much thought and labour to produce. The enormous guns, with the great cracks in them which had resulted from firing them once to try them, were placed in museums, never more to be used; the great ships which had all, in the course of their regular business, run upon rocks, began to be visited by curious sightseers, who travelled to them on the flying machines which had been constructed as engines of war.

"Then I seemed to perceive, from the

Pugin's skit on the conventional classical monument, published in his *Contrasts*, second edition, 1841.

CHAPTER IX

MEMORIALS AND MONUMENTS

O F all Victorian monuments, the best known and the most criticised is the Albert Memorial. Sir George Gilbert Scott's first idea was to erect a monolithic obelisk, 150 feet high, with the apex capped by a large cross; but he abandoned it for an edifice that should give large-scale expression to a mediaeval metal-work shrine. "Those exquisite productions of the goldsmith and the jeweller profess," he said, "in nearly every instance to be models of architectural structures, yet no such structures exist, nor, so far as we know, ever did exist. Like the charming architectural visions of the older poets, they are only in their primary idea founded upon actual architecture, and owe all their more gorgeous clothing to the inspiration of another art. They are architecture as elaborated by the mind and the hand of the jeweller; an exquisite phantasy realised only to the small scale of a model. My notion, whether good or bad, was for once to realize this jeweller's architecture in a structure of full size, and this has furnished the key-note of my design and of its execution."[161]

Half a dozen architects had been invited to enter a competition for the Memorial, and Scott's design was accepted. Before work was begun on it, he noted that "This was an idea so new, as to provoke much opposition. Cost and all kinds of circumstances aid this opposition, and I have no idea how it may end; I trust to be directed aright."[162] The idea of using the form of a mediaeval shrine, enlarged to protect a statue of the Prince, had also occurred to Thomas Locke Worthington (1826–1909), who published the first design for an Albert Memorial in *The Builder*, September 27th, 1862, and Scott's design certainly owes something to this forerunner.[163] (Worthington's design, on a much smaller scale than Scott's, was erected in Albert Square, Manchester.)

Although this exaggerated shrine was admired by many, some contemporary critics attacked the design, and of these John T. Emmett was the most pungent. He made his attack in *The British Quarterly Review* for April, 1880, and after complaining that the monument "has had as much explanatory notice as would fill a 'Times' newspaper, and the unenlightened public has been left to wonder why a work so perseveringly and highly praised should seem so unimpressive and ungainly,"[164] described and dissected the structure,

ICTINUS   MNESIKLES   CHERSIPHRON   METAGENES   PUGIN   COOKERELL   BARRY

Sculptures on the podium of the Albert Memorial, illustrated in *Six Essays* by J. T. Emmett, and described by him as "Ideal Architects," on the left, and "Architects in the Modern Sense," on the right.

the sculpture, and the ornament in detail. It was fortunate that Scott, a kindly though conceited man, had died two years before this article was printed, for he would have been wounded and distressed by such blistering comment.

Emmett objected to the long flights of steps leading up to the monument, observing that "when an architectural student totally without ideas starts in design, such piles of steps and piers are his immediate resource. The monument is thus founded, in a way quite *un*monumental, on a vast conglomerate of coal cellars and street kerbs." He proceeded to examine the sculpture. "As 'steps' are the first refuge for the architectural destitute," he wrote, "so the 'Four Quarters of the Globe' assist the monumental sculptor. They admit of any nonsense; no one can tell assuredly what all the figures mean, or why they came together. Thus they are used unmeaningly, to make a show and catch the eye, with no attempt to satisfy the understanding. Next is the podium, covered with figures just as irrelevant as the 'Four Quarters of the Globe.' In one corner is a group of fancy portraits, named after celebrated ancient master workmen; somewhat interesting, as they represent the carvers, and thus probably the best and most refined idea of the style and manner of the classic architect. These figures are not shown in workmen's dress, nor in heroic fashion without clothes, nor are they actively engaged in handicraft, nor yet 'assigning to the individual workmen their appropriate tasks'; they are a set of weak-limbed, semi-idiotic and half-naked loungers, wrapped in sheets, engaged and much perplexed in watching one who, specially insane, is busy in a bungling way with compasses and paper and will surely make a painful puncture in his knee. These ideal architects have nothing of the workman in their figure, muscle, implements, or swaddling clothes. The carver evidently thought, with most of his contemporaries, that Greek master workmen were in some way superhuman, beings of pure thought, not working men at all, but absolute creators, who evoked the Parthenon complete from their superior intellects, just as Minerva sprang, all armoured, from the brain of Jove. Another corner has a group of modern 'architects of eminence.' The shrewd, successful, speculating draughtsman, 'clever at a plan,' and the pedantic scholar are appropriately distinguished, while the enthusiastic architectural reformer turns his back upon the pair."

Both groups are reproduced at the top of the opposite page, and the modern "architects of eminence" are Cockerell, Barry and Pugin, the latter portrayed in his mediaeval robes.

Armstead and Philip were the sculptors nominated by Scott for the figures on the podium; the others, with the exception of Redfern "who modelled the greater part of the figures in the flèche," were chosen by the Queen.[165] "Being men of less established fame than the older sculptors," Scott observed, "they undertook the work at a far lower price than these would have done, and, as it proved, to their own cost. In my own opinion the result places them on quite as good an artistic footing as most of their more academic companions. . . ."[166] Much as he disliked the figures on the podium, Emmett disliked the other sculptures even more.

"Above the podium," he continued, "the groups of odds and ends called 'Agriculture,' 'Commerce,' 'Manufacture' and 'Engineering' serve, very needfully, to make up something of an outline for the monument. Then the large granite columns, polished by machinery, support a canopy with arches, and an elaborate deformity of spire which, by some occult contrivance in the nature of a juggler's trick, is hung up in mid air. The ornamental work is a dull manufacture; the coarse jewellery merely serves to give a sense of costliness and of extravagant, unlimited expense, and the small bantam angels that, below the cross, are clawing upwards to the sky, supply the fashionable, sanctimonious element. The shrine, constructively, is but a four-legged table; and the real architect or master was the man who wrought the heavy girders that tie in the columns and support the spire. In the whole structure art is wanting, and instead we have a 'trophy' or advertisement composed of manufactured goods, a model for a pastrycook's pagoda. But this is no discredit to the nominal designer of the work; small blame is due to him, if little praise. He was an 'architect as we now understand the term,' and his production is, according to the present system, in the 'Imitation Style.' . . ."

Nothing else ever written about the Albert Memorial reached the high temperature of Emmett's invective: no other monument, before or since, has inflamed so many critics. But if the Albert Memorial resembles "a pastry-cook's pagoda," then the Wellington monument in St. Paul's Cathedral is more like a gloomy wedding cake. Designed by the sculptor, Alfred Stevens (1818–75), and usually regarded as his most important work, it has a podium, which supports the sarcophagus and the recumbent bronze figure of the Duke, and is surrounded by Corinthian columns. Above this is an arched marble canopy, with bronze groups at each end, representing Truth and Valour. Four malformed Ionic columns adorn this upper part, and their distorted shape and ornamental treatment might be the work of an Elizabethan architect, misguided by some Flemish copy-book. The shafts of the twelve Corinthian columns appear to be wrapped round with some dingy lace curtain material, an effect created by a mechanical pattern lightly incised on the dirty white marble: their arborescent capitals lack the crisp clarity of execution that gives ornamental vitality to formalised acanthus leaves; while the enrichment of the moulded detail on the podium seems to have been carved upside down. Alfred Stevens may have been an accomplished sculptor, but he was as incapable of producing an inspired composition in the classic idiom as the Elizabethan and early Jacobean architects.

Classical monuments, tombstones and memorial tablets in churches were used throughout the nineteenth century, though the graciousness and grandeur of the Georgian tradition expired early in Victoria's reign, and Pugin's gibe at the conventional classic type of monument was not wholly unjustified. (See page 224.) Nobody regretted the demolition of King's Cross, Battlebridge, in 1845, which was ridiculous in design, while the robed figure of George IV, uneasily clutching the sceptre and orb, commemorated a monarch whose figure was as deplorable as his private life: both were best forgotten in an age when the Court was well-conducted and morally irreproachable. The most impressive and familiar of the classical monuments in London is Nelson's, in Trafalgar Square, a Corinthian column with a bronze capital, designed by William Railton (1803–77) and erected in 1839–42. The four lions by Landseer that guard the base were added several years later.

The first of the large Gothic monuments was erected in Prince's Street Gardens, Edinburgh, and completed over a quarter of a century before the Albert Memorial. (They are shown together on plate 16.) It was different in design and conception from the latter, representing Romantic rather than Revivalist Gothic, which was most appropriate as it commemorated the genius of Sir Walter Scott. The classic orders could not, of course, be permitted to dignify such a structure, notwithstanding the precedents of the Burns Monument, which imitated a Greek temple, and the National Monument with its Doric columns on Calton Hill: no statue to the author of the Waverley novels could with literary and artistic propriety be sheltered by anything

DESIGN FOR A MONUMENT

"Mr. Baker, a young artist, of Southampton, exhibited a new design for a monument, intended as an improvement upon the ordinary run of tombstones and mural tablets so much in vogue. It is a Gothic composition, intended to stand some 20 feet high, though the model is only 4 feet 3 inches high, and is of Caen stone. In form it is triangular, and at the corners are figures of the cardinal virtues—Faith, Hope, and Charity; with appropriate texts from Scripture underneath each. On the principal panel the usual formulary—'In memory of'— is already inscribed, leaving only the name of the party to be inserted. Mr. Baker, will, we have no doubt, find some patrons amongst those who have a taste for this sort of posthumous display: but, for our own part, we confess we think that art has been already too much misapplied in these matters; whilst nature, with a few simple everlastings and flowers, would afford a tribute from the living to the dead much more pleasing in effect, and much more congenial in sentiment.

In a sanitary point of view, also, such a change would not be unimportant, it being now well ascertained that the planting of trees and flowers in burying-grounds is of positive service to the health of the neighbourhood." *The Crystal Palace and its Contents* (London: 1852), page 359.

except a Gothic canopy. A competition was held four years after his death, and an architect named George Meikle Kemp (1795–1844) won the third prize; but two years later, when the entries were scrutinised again, Kemp, who had made some improvements to his design during this interval, was chosen for the work. (He did not live to see it finished, for he was drowned in 1844.) He created a tall, picturesque example of late Georgian Gothic, opulent in ornamental detail, with a succession of pinnacles marking the ascent of the slender, fretted spire that streamed up from the canopy. The niches were occupied by various characters from the novels. Below the canopy was a seated statue of Sir Walter with his dog, Maida, beside him; the work of Sir John Steell (1804–91).

At the inauguration in 1846, Adam Black, Provost of Edinburgh, received the monument on behalf of the city, and in language that Scott might well have used informed the assembly that "The forked lightning may dash these turrets to the ground, the tooth of time will corrode these marble features, but over the monuments of his mental creation the elements have no power. Continents as yet unexplored will be taught by the wisdom of Scott, and rivers unknown to song will resound to the lays of his minstrelsy." Adam Black was the founder of the publishing house, and five years later he acquired the Waverley copyrights, so he "had the benefit as well as the satisfaction of the fulfilment of his prophecy."[167] Thirty years later a statue of Adam Black was set up next to the Scott Memorial, and is shown in the foreground on plate 16.

Monuments to famous men were nearly always associated with a statue, and unless the subject was a soldier or a sailor, who appeared in uniform, the formal dress of the period was used, which did not always lend dignity to the wearer when represented in bronze or marble. The figures of Cockerell and Barry on the Albert Memorial (page 226) and the statue of George Peabody behind the Royal Exchange (plate 5) have a stuffed look, a rigidity of line that makes them seem slightly absurd; and this is attributable largely to their clothes, which, unlike those of the previous century, were devoid of decorative exuberance. Even Stuart and Georgian sculptors had doubts about the use of contemporary dress, and often used classical costume for their statues of the great. There were comparatively few memorials that dispensed with a statue, and when this convention was ignored something symbolic, and occasionally eccentric, was erected, like the memorial to Sir Richard Francis Burton, the explorer and translator of the *Arabian Nights*, which stands in the Roman Catholic cemetery at Mortlake in south-west London. (See plate 5.) It represents an Arab tent, and the following verse by Justin Huntly McCarthy is inscribed on a tablet at the base:

> Farewell, dear friend, dead hero! The great life
> Is ended, the great perils, the great joys
> And he to whom adventures were as toys,
> Who seemed to bear a charm 'gainst spear or knife
> Or bullet, now lies silent from all strife
> Out yonder where the Austrian eagles poise
> On Istrian hills. But England, at the noise
> Of that dread fall, weeps with the hero's wife.

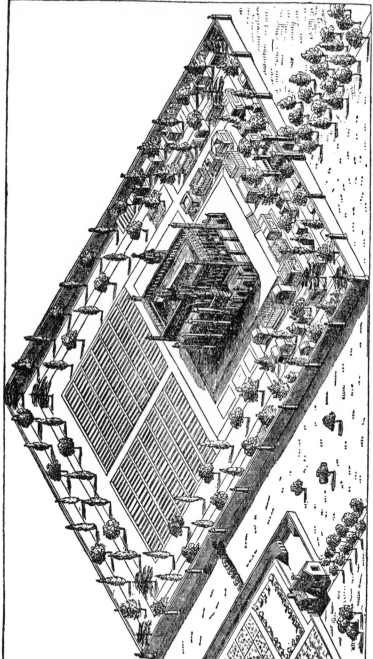

An isometrical view of a small churchyard, "adapted for an agricultural parish, where the majority of the inhabitants are in moderately good circumstances, and whence it is supposed that the superfluous population will migrate to the towns, and leave the number of permanent inhabitants comparatively stationary." This design was included, rather inappropriately, in the section on "Second-Rate Gardens," in *The Suburban Gardener and Villa Companion*, which John Claudius Loudon published in 1838 (pages 602–6). The church shown is adapted from a design published in *The Architectural Magazine*, which Loudon edited, in December, 1837 (pages 566–72) by an architect who concealed his identity under the letter "F." This may have been Charles Fowler (1791–1867), a contributor to the Magazine, who on this occasion preferred to remain anonymous.

Oh, last and noblest of the errant knights,
The English soldier and the Arab sheik,
Oh, singer of the East who loved so well,
The deathless wonder of the Arabian nights,
Who touched Camoens lute and still would seek
Ever new deeds until the end, farewell.

Epitaphs were generally short and pointedly pious on Victorian monuments. The dignified loquaciousness of the Georgian period which enumerated virtues, real or tenderly invented, was reduced to some almost abrupt statement, little more than an ejaculation, such as: "Cut off in the prime of Life," or "Not Lost, but Gone Before." The winged angel of indeterminate sex sparkled in white marble in hundreds of the new cemeteries that served the growing suburbs: broken columns, an occasional urn, or some Gothic extravaganza relieved the monotony of inscribed headstones and crosses, like the design on page 229 which was intended to stand 20 feet high, and was ornamented with the figures of Faith, Hope and Charity, with suitable texts engraved below each. The monumental marble mason worked in commercial alliance with the undertaker, and the cost of death and burial and the headstone or more ambitious monument, put up when the earth of the grave had settled, was adjusted on a class basis. You could travel to the hereafter First, Second or Third, according to your means and social standing. Cremation was regarded with abhorrence by the majority of people, and was illegal until the mid-1880's. No undertaker encouraged it, for small urns and memorial tablets could never be as profitable as coffins and headstones.

The prescribed ritual for a bereavement was laid down, and in an article on "Death in the Household," published in *Cassell's Household Guide*, these directions were given: "The blinds of the windows of the house should be drawn directly the death occurs," said the writer, "and they should remain down until after the funeral has left the house, when they are at once to be pulled up. As a rule, the females of the family do not pay any visits until after the funeral. Neither would it be considered in good taste for any friends or acquaintances to visit at the house during that time, unless they were relatives of the family, when of course it would be only proper for them to do so."(168)

Some warnings were included about allowing women to attend funerals, and the treatment of the undertakers' staff.

"It sometimes happens among the poorer classes that the female relatives attend the funeral; but this custom is by no means to be recommended, since in these cases it but too frequently happens that, being unable to restrain their emotions, they interrupt and destroy the solemnity of the ceremony with their sobs, and even by fainting. As soon as the funeral is over it is usual for the mourners to separate, each one taking his departure home.

"While on the subject, we would caution our readers against, out of a

ABERDEEN POLISHED GRANITE MONUMENTS,
FROM £5.
LETTER-CUTTING ACCURATE AND BEAUTIFUL.
BEST QUALITY GRANITE AND MARBLE WORK OF ALL KINDS.
IRON RAILINGS AND TOMB FURNISHINGS FITTED COMPLETE.,
PLANS, PRICES, AND CARRIAGE-FREE TERMS TO ALL PARTS OF THE WORLD, FROM

J. W. LEGGE, Sculptor,
ABERDEEN, SCOTLAND.

Advertisement included among other commercial announcements at the end of *The Old and New Churches of London*, by Alfred and J. M. Capes. London, 1880.

mistaken and thoughtless kindness, offering, and even forcing wines, spirits, and other liquors upon the undertaker's men. If they were given instead a cup of tea or coffee and a sandwich, it would, in the generality of cases, be both more acceptable to them, and also keep them in the condition necessary for the proper performance of their duties."

The Victorians seldom improvised their conduct: they had precise codes of behaviour and knew what to do on nearly every occasion that arose in life, or death. In the eighteenth century people would say that they liked to have everything pleasant about them: it was a common expression, and had the Victorians used a comparable phrase they would have said that they liked to have everything cosy about them. They succeeded: even the trappings of death gave an illusion of comfort in the tomb —for a well-made coffin of oak, with an inner shell, and ornamental handles of polished

---

ECONOMIC

FUNERAL COMPANY,
29, *New Bridge-street, Blackfriars,*
ESTABLISHED JANUARY, 1843.
UNDER DISTINGUISHED PATRONAGE.

The object of this establishment is to offer every means of economy, combined with respectability, in FUNERALS, to any magnitude, at stated charges; and the public is respectfully invited to strictly examine the plans of this office, the first established in England for the observance of Funeral economy.

Artisan's Carriage Funeral, 3*l*. 18*s*. 6*d*. and 5*l*. 10*s*. 6*d*.

The deceased and mourners conveyed in separate carriages.

Tradesmen's ditto, with Hearse and Pair, and Coach and Pair, 7*l*. 12*s*. 6*d*.

First Class Funeral, including a Shell, Lead Coffin, and Outside Case, Hearse and Four Horses, Two Coaches and Pairs, with Plumes and full equipments of superior description, 29*l*. 12*s*. 6*d*.

The cortège and style adopted will be found unexceptionable.

" Those who have ever required the employment of an Undertaker in their family must feel the necessity of such an Establishment, and its great pecuniary advantages over the old system of conducting this business."—*Court Journal*. [1 179

Economy, respectability, and class distinction. From the advertisement section, *The Official Catalogue of the Great Exhibition of* 1851, Volume I, page 11.

brass or gilded metal was a final example of good, substantial furnishing with the best materials.

What epitaph would be most suitable for the Victorians? *They made money, and little else?* That applied only to one section of society. *They believed in the mission of Science and the glory of Progress?* That merely indicates a climate of opinion. Perhaps the most just and generous would be this: *They were Confident, Comfortable, and Good.*

The clumsy lettering
of a graceless age on
the tomb of the classic
tradition.

SOURCES OF REFERENCES IN THE TEXT

CHAPTER I. THE VICTORIAN SCENE

(1) *2000 Years of England*, by John Gloag. (London: Cassell & Company Ltd., 1952.) Chapter IX, pages 85–86.

(2) *Anticipations*, by H. G. Wells. (London: Chapman & Hall Ltd., 1902.) Section II, page 45.

(3) *The American Nation*, by John and Julian Gloag. (London: Cassell & Company Ltd. Revised and enlarged edition, 1955.) Chapter XI, pages 112–13.

(4) *Ibid.*, Chapter XI, page 111.

CHAPTER II. HOME

(5) *Catalogue of Hurst House Estate, the Lancashire Residence of the late Joseph Evans, Esq., J.P., D.L.* Issued by J. B. & B. Leach, for the sale to be held on October 25th, 1889, at the Public Sale Room of the Law Association, Cook Street, Liverpool. The Catalogue is in the possession of Huyton Urban District Council.

(6) *Hints on Household Taste, in Furniture, Upholstery and other Details*, by Charles L. Eastlake, F.R.I.B.A. (London: Longmans, Green & Co. Second edition, 1869.) Introduction, pages 7 and 8.

(7) *The Young Ladies' Treasure Book.* (London: Ward, Lock & Co. Undated but probably 1881–82.) Introduction, page 3.

(8) *Op. cit.*, Chapter XIX, pages 187–88.

(9) *Op. cit.*, Chapter VI, pages 67–69.

(10) *Op. cit.*, Chapter XIX, page 193.

(11) *Mr. Sponge's Sporting Tour*, Chapter XXXVII.

(12) *The Young Ladies' Treasure Book*, Chapter XVII, pages 160–61.

(13) *Op. cit.*, Chapter XIX, page 195.

(14) *The Cabinet-Maker's Guide; or Rules and Instructions in the Art of Varnishing, Dying, Staining, Japanning, Polishing, Lackering, and Beautifying Wood, Ivory, Tortoiseshell, & Metal*, by G. A. Siddons. (London: Sherwood, Gilbert & Piper, Paternoster Row. Fifth edition, 1830.) Pages 5–6.

(15) *Vice Versa*, by F. Anstey. Included in the omnibus volume of his works, *Humour & Fantasy*. (London: John Murray, 1931.)

(16) *The Young Ladies' Treasure Book*, Chapter XIX, page 192.

(17) "Edward Simpson, *alias* 'Flint Jack,'" by John Blacking. *Antiquity*, Volume XXVII, No. 108 (December, 1953), pages 207–11.

(18) *Hints on Household Taste*, by Charles L. Eastlake, F.R.I.B.A. (Second edition, 1869.) Chapter II, pages 57–58.

(19) *Op. cit.*, pages 58–59.

(20) *The Collected Ghost Stories of M. R. James.* (London: Edward Arnold & Co., 1931.)

(21) *Encyclopaedia of Cottage, Farm, and Villa Architecture and Furniture,* by J. C. Loudon. (London: Longman, 1833.) Chapter III, Section IV, page 353.

(22) *Op. cit.,* page 353.

(23) *Op. cit.,* page 301.

(24) *Op. cit.,* page 319.

(25) "The Windsor Chair," by R. W. Symonds. First of two articles. *Apollo,* Volume XXII, No. 128, August, 1935, page 69. The catalogue he quotes was for the furniture of Thomas Coke, for sale on February 12th, 1728, in the Great Piazza, Covent Garden.

(26) *The Architecture of Country Houses,* by A. J. Downing. (New York: D. Appleton & Co., 1850.) Section XII. The chairs on page 442 are reproduced from page 323 of Loudon's *Encyclopaedia.*

(27) *The Architecture of Country Houses,* by A. J. Downing. Section XII, pages 409–10.

(28) *Hints on Household Taste,* by Charles L. Eastlake, F.R.I.B.A. (London: Longmans. Second edition, 1869.) Chapter VI, pages 163–64.

(29) *Decoration and Furniture of Town Houses,* by Robert W. Edis, F.S.A., F.R.I.B.A. (London: Kegan Paul & Co., 1881.) Lecture I, pages 27–29. Lecture IV, pages 156–57.

CHAPTER III.   COMFORT AND ELEGANCE

(30) *Cassell's Household Guide to Every Department of Practical Life: being a Complete Encyclopaedia of Domestic and Social Economy.* (London: Cassell & Company Limited. New and Revised Edition, prepared for subscription only, 1875.) Volume I, page 126.

(31) Catalogues of Heal & Son Limited, London. 1858–60.

(32) *Encyclopaedia of Cottage, Farm and Villa Architecture and Furniture,* by J. C. Loudon. (London: Longman, 1833.) Pages 1048–49.

(33) " 'Grandfather' Clocks." *Furniture and Decoration and the Furniture Gazette,* Volume XXXIV, No. 767, May, 1897, page 93.

(34) "A Chapter on Easy Chairs." *Furniture and Decoration and the Furniture Gazette,* Volume XXXIV, No. 772, October, 1897, page 201.

(35) *The Architecture of Country Houses,* by A. J. Downing. (New York: D. Appleton & Co., 1850.) Section XII, page 414.

(36) *The Art of the House,* by Rosamund Mariott Watson. (London: George Bell & Sons, 1897.) Chapter V, page 75.

(37) "Sketches of Couches." *Furniture and Decoration and the Furniture Gazette,* Volume XXXIV, No. 770, August, 1897, page 153.

(38) *The Autobiography of an Idea,* by Louis H. Sullivan. (New York: W. W. Norton & Company Inc., 1926.) *Pioneers of Modern Design, from William Morris to Walter Gropius,* by Nikolaus Pevsner. (New York: The Museum of Modern Art, 1949.)

(39) *The Universal System of Household Furniture,* by William Ince and John Mayhew. (This work was first published in London in parts, issued between 1759 and 1762.) "Back stools" are shown on plates LV and LVI.

(40) U.S. Patent, April 23rd, 1831. D. Harrington. Quoted and illustrated in *Mechanization Takes Command*, by Siegfried Giedion. (New York: Oxford University Press, 1948.) Page 402, fig. 236.

(41) *Official Catalogue of the Great Exhibition* (1851). Volume II, Class 22, page 639.

(42) *Ibid.*, Volume II, Class 26, page 746.

(43) *Furniture and Decoration and the Furniture Gazette*, Volume XXXIV, No. 766, April, 1897, page 72.

(44) *Life on the Mississippi*, by Mark Twain. (First published in 1883.) Chapter VI.

(45) *The What-Not; or Ladies' Handy-Book*. (London: Kent & Co., Paternoster Row, 1861.) "The Wreck of the Tartar," page 25.

(46) *Furniture and Decoration and the Furniture Gazette*, Volume XXXIV, No. 764, February, 1897, pages 26–27.

(47) *Hints on Household Taste*, by Charles L. Eastlake, F.R.I.B.A. (Second edition, 1869.) Chapter VI, pages 157–58.

(48) "Scenario for a Human Drama," by P. Morton Shand. *The Architectural Review*, January, 1935, page 26.

(49) *Edward Johnston*, by Priscilla Johnston. (London: Faber & Faber Ltd., 1959.) Chapter IV, page 74.

(50) *The Gillow Records* at Lancaster, where whatnots are described and illustrated as early as 1790. (E. & S. Book, No. 579.)

(51) *The Dictionary of English Furniture*, by Percy Macquoid and Ralph Edwards. (London: Country Life Ltd. Second, revised edition, 1954.) Volume II, entry DAVENPORT, page 202. *A Short Dictionary of Furniture*, by John Gloag. (London: George Allen & Unwin Ltd. New York: The Studio Publications Inc., 1952.) Entry DAVENPORT, page 225, also Section I, page 33.

(52) "Writing Tables." *Furniture and Decoration and the Furniture Gazette*, Volume XXXIV, No. 773, November, 1897, page 222.

(53) "New Designs of Cabinets." *Furniture and Decoration*, Volume XXXIV, No. 771, September, 1897.

(54) *The Adventures of Mr. Verdant Green*, by Cuthbert Bede (Edward Bradley). (London: James Blackwood & Co., 1853–56.) Chapter X, page 77.

CHAPTER IV.   THE COSY HEARTH

(55) *The Elements of Architecture*, by Sir Henry Wotton. The First Part. *Reliquiae Wottonianae*. (London: 1672. Third edition.) Page 39.

(56) *Domestic Life in England, from the Earliest Period to the Present Time*. (London: Thomas Tegg & Son, 1835.) Page 154.

(57) *The Pickwick Papers*, by Charles Dickens. Chapter XXVIII.

(58) *The Gentleman's House, or How to Plan English Residences, from the Parsonage to the Palace*, by Robert Kerr, F.R.I.B.A. (London: John Murray, 1864.) Section II, Chapter I, page 113.

(59) *Op. cit.*, pages 105–6.

(60) *Decoration and Furniture of Town Houses*, by Robert W. Edis, F.S.A., F.R.I.B.A. (London: Kegan Paul & Co., 1881.) Lecture III, page 122.

(61) *Mr. Sponge's Sporting Tour*, by Robert Smith Surtees. Chapter XXXIX.

(62) *The Gentleman and Cabinet-Maker's Director*, by Thomas Chippendale. (London: First edition, 1754.) Thomas Johnson, a contemporary of Chippendale's, published three books of designs: *Twelve Girandoles*, 1755; *The Book of the Carver*, 1758; and *One Hundred and Fifty New Designs*, issued in monthly parts between 1756–58.

(63) *English Furniture and Furniture Makers of the Eighteenth Century*, by R. S. Clouston. (London: Hurst & Blackett Ltd., 1906.) A full account of Weale's forgeries is given in Chapter III, pages 38–42.

(64) *The Young Ladies' Treasure Book*, Chapter I, page 7.

(65) *The Englishman's House from a Cottage to a Mansion*, by C. J. Richardson. (London: 1870.) Introduction, page 44.

(66) *The Young Ladies' Treasure Book*, Chapter XIX, pages 192–93.

(67) *Decoration and Furniture of Town Houses*, by Robert W. Edis, F.S.A., F.R.I.B.A. (London: Kegan Paul & Co., 1881.) Lecture III, pages 126–27.

(68) *The Englishman's House*, by C. J. Richardson. (London: 1870.) "The Fireplace," page 404.

(69) *Ibid.*, page 405.

(70) *Ibid.*, pages 405–6.

(71) *The Englishman's House*, by C. J. Richardson. (London: 1870.) Pages 120–23.

(72) "Sundry Sanitary Building Appliances." A paper read at the Ordinary General Meeting of the Royal Institute of British Architects, January 12th, 1863, by John Taylor, Junior, M.A., F.S.A. Printed in the *Papers read at the R.I.B.A. Session, 1862–63*, pages 91–93.

(73) *Hints on Household Taste*, by Charles L. Eastlake. (London: Second edition, 1869.) Chapter V, pages 127–28.

(74) *Ibid.*, page 129.

(75) *Punch*, June 4th, 1859, page 228. Caption to a drawing of a fire-place: "An Ornament for the Fire Stove—Crinoline Useful at Last."

(76) *Cassell's Household Guide*. (London: 1875.) "Household Decorative Art—XXIII," Volume II, page 167.

(77) *Ibid.*, page 166.

(78) *Ibid.*, pages 166–67.

(79) *Decoration and Furniture of Town Houses*, by Robert W. Edis, F.S.A., F.R.I.B.A. (London: Kegan Paul & Co., 1881.) Lecture III, page 129.

CHAPTER V. COMFORT IN TRAVEL: THE ROAD

(80) *Personal and Professional Recollections*, by the late Sir George Gilbert Scott, R.A. Edited by his son, G. Gilbert Scott, F.S.A. (London: Sampson Low, Marston, Searle & Rivington, 1879.) Chapter II, pages 83–84.

(81) *Tom Brown's Schooldays*, by Thomas Hughes. (First published in 1857.) Chapter IV.

(82) *Personal and Professional Recollections*, by Sir George Gilbert Scott. Chapter II, page 84.

(83) *The England of Nimrod and Surtees*, by E. W. Bovill. (Oxford University Press, 1959.) Section XV, page 129.

(84) *Lives of the Engineers*, by Samuel Smiles. (London: John Murray, 1862 edition.) Volume II, Part VIII, Chapter XI, page 427.

(85) *Op. cit.*, page 429.

(86) *Op. cit.*, page 430, note on McAdam.

(87) *The Sketch Book of Geoffrey Crayon, Gent.* [Washington Irving]. (London: John Murray. New edition, in two volumes, 1824.) Volume II, "The Stage Coach," page 18.

(88) *David Copperfield*, by Charles Dickens. Chapter XIX.

(89) *Personal and Professional Recollections*, by Sir George Gilbert Scott. Chapter II, page 83.

(90) *Rides on Railways*, by Samuel Sidney. (London: William S. Orr & Co., 1851.) Pages 151–55.

(91) *Locomotion in Victorian London*, by G. A. Sekon. (Oxford University Press, 1938.) Section V. Train's invitation card is reproduced on the plate facing page 94.

(92) *London, the Unique City*, by Steen Eiler Rasmussen. (London: Jonathan Cape. English edition, 1937.) Chapter VII, pages 138–40.

(93) *Ibid.*, pages 139–40.

(94) *The Pickwick Papers*, Chapter XXII.

CHAPTER VI.   COMFORT IN TRAVEL: THE RAILWAY

(95) *Samuel Kelly: An Eighteenth Century Seaman*, edited by Crosbie Garstin. (London: Jonathan Cape, 1925.) Part II, Section 13, page 183.

(96) *Life on the Mississippi*, by Mark Twain. Chapter XVI. "Fast Time on the Western Waters."

(97) *Ibid.*, Chapter VI.

(98) *The Western World; or Travels in the United States in 1846–47*, by Alex. Mackay. (London: Richard Bentley, 1849.) Volume III, Chapter I, pages 8–9.

(99) "The Man who Drove the 'Rocket.' " *The Strand Magazine*, Volume XXIV, December, 1902, pages 786–87.

(100) *The Railroad Passenger Car*, by August Mencken. (Baltimore: The Johns Hopkins Press, 1957.) Part I, Chapter II, page 11.

(101) *Handley Cross*, by Robert Smith Surtees. (First published in 1843.) Chapter IX.

(102) *Sunny Memories of Foreign Lands*, by Harriet Beecher Stowe. (London: Sampson Low, Son & Co., 1854.) Letter III (April 16th, 1853), pages 31–32.

(103) *The Western World; or Travels in the United States in 1846–47*, by Alex. Mackay. (London: Richard Bentley, 1849.) Volume I, Chapter III, page 31.

(104) *Op. cit.*, Volume II, Chapter VIII, page 249.

(105) *Forty Years of American Life*, by Dr. Thomas L. Nichols. (London: John Maxwell & Company, 1864.) Volume I, Chapter XX, pages 241–42.

(106) *Op. cit.*, Volume II, Chapter I, pages 8–9.

(107) *Westward by Rail*, by W. F. Rae (London: Longmans, Green & Co., 1870.) Chapter II, pages 28–29.

(108) *Teresina in America*, by Thérèse Yelverton [Viscountess Avonmore]. (London: Richard Bentley & Son, 1875.) Volume II, Chapter II, pages 4–10.

(109) *Jonathan and His Continent*, by Max O'Rell and Jack Allyn. Translated by Madame Paul Blouët. (Bristol: J. W. Arrowsmith, 1889.) Chapter XXXVI, pages 252–53.

(110) "From London to Chicago," by James Mortimer. *The Strand Magazine*, Volume VI, August, 1893, pages 210–12.

(111) *British Railway History, 1830–1876*, by Hamilton Ellis. (London: George Allen & Unwin Ltd., 1954.) Part II, Chapter IV, pages 280–81.

(112) *Op. cit.*, Part III, Chapter III, pages 372–73.

(113) *Ibid.*, page 374.

(114) *The Graphic*, August 19th, 1882. Classified advertisement, page 171, column 2.

(115) *Fun*, November 28th, 1874, page 218.

(116) *The Trains we Loved*, by Hamilton Ellis. (London: George Allen & Unwin Ltd., 1947.) Chapter II, page 31.

(117) *British Railway History, 1830–1876*, by Hamilton Ellis. Part II, Chapter IV, page 280.

(118) *The Rocket; or the Story of the Stephensons, Father and Son*, by H. C. Knight. (London: Thomas Nelson & Sons, 1880.) Chapter IX, page 113.

(119) *Illustrated London, or a Series of Views in the British Metropolis and its Vicinity*, engraved by Albert Henry Payne. The Historical, Topographical and Miscellaneous Notices, by W. I. Bicknell. (London: E. T. Brain, 1847–48.) Page 269.

(120) *New York City Guide*. (London: Constable, 1939.) Page 404.

(121) *Social Transformations of the Victorian Age*, by T. H. S. Escott. (London: Seeley & Co. Ltd., 1897.) Chapter III, pages 37–38.

CHAPTER VII.   COMFORT AND PLEASURE

(122) *Punch*, October 31st, 1885, page 206.

(123) *The Pickwick Papers*, by Charles Dickens, Chapter VI.

(124) "A Century of Croquet," by Amoret and Christopher Scott. *Country Life*, Volume CXXVI, No. 3286, February 25th, 1960, page 386. Also, article on CROQUET in *Encyclopaedia Britannica*. Eleventh edition.

(125) *A Guide to all the Watering and Sea-Bathing Places; with a Description of the Lakes; A Sketch of a Tour in Wales, and Itineraries*. (London: Printed for Richard Phillips, 71, St. Paul's Churchyard, 1803.)

(126) *Op. cit.*, "Ramsgate," page 282.

(127) *Ibid.*, page 283.

(128) *The What-not; or Ladies' Handy-Book*. (London: Kent & Co., 1861.) Page 266.

(129) *The Water Babies*, by Charles Kingsley. (First published 1863.) Chapter IV.

(130) *The Sketch Book of Geoffrey Crayon, Gent*. (London: 1824.) Volume II, page 58.

(131) *Ibid.*, page 35.

(132) *The Pickwick Papers*. Chapter V.

(133) *The Sketch Book*, Volume II.

(134) *Lyra Frivola*, by A. D. Godley (London: Methuen & Co., 1899.) Pages 9–10.

(135) *The Royal Society of Arts, 1754–1954*, by Derek Hudson and Kenneth W. Luckhurst. (London: John Murray, 1954.) Part II, Chapter XI, page 191.

(136) "Christmas Crackers." *The Strand Magazine*, Volume II, December, 1891, pages 616–22.

(137) "Vanishing Valentines," by W. G. FitzGerald. *The Strand Magazine*, Volume IX, February, 1895, pages 127–33.

(138) *Publicity: An Essay on Advertising*, by An Adept of 35 Years' Experience. (London: G. S. Brown, 1878.) Chapter VIII, page 244.

(139) *The Gentleman's House*, by Robert Kerr, F.R.I.B.A. (London: John Murray, 1864.) Part II, Division I, Section II, Chapter XIV.

(140) *Prologue to Cigarettes—The Story of Robert Peacock Gloag, England's First Cigarette Maker*, with annotations by Eric Gurd. (Issued by the Cartophilic Society of Great Britain, 1942.) Section I, page 6.

(141) *The Diary of a Nobody*, by George and Weedon Grossmith. (This appeared as a serial in *Punch*, during 1888 and 1889, and was published in book form in 1892.) Chapter XXIII, entry July 4th.

(142) *Trilby*, by George du Maurier. (London: Osgood, McIlvaine & Co., 1895.) Part V, pages 274–75.

(143) "Sea Urchins," by W. W. Jacobs. (London: Lawrence & Bullen Ltd., 1898.) Page 30. *The Strand Magazine*, Volume XV, No. 86, February, 1898, page 203.

(144) *Treasure Island*, by Robert Louis Stevenson. (First published in book form, 1883.) Part VI, Chapter XXXII.

(145) *Mr. Sponge's Sporting Tour*, by Robert Smith Surtees. Chapter XXVII.

(146) *Handley Cross*. The concluding sentences of Chapter XIII.

(147) *The Wrong Box*, by Robert Louis Stevenson and Lloyd Osbourne. Chapter XII.

CHAPTER VIII. COMFORT AND CONSCIENCE

(148) *Happy Hours; at Wynford Grange*, by Cuthbert Bede [Edward Bradley]. (London: James Blackwood, 1859.) Chapter IV, pages 56–57.

(149) *The Pickwick Papers*, by Charles Dickens. Chapter VII.

(150) *Histriomastix*, by William Prynne. An attack on stage plays, published in 1633.

(151) *The Life of George Stephenson and of his son Robert Stephenson*, by Samuel Smiles. (London: John Murray, 1868 edition.) Part II, Chapter XV, page 397.

(152) *The Rocket; or the Story of the Stephensons*, Father and Son, by H. C. Knight. (London: Thomas Nelson & Sons. Lessons from Noble Lives series, 1880.) Chapter IX, page 115.

(153) *Essays, Social and Political*, by Sydney Smith. (London: Ward, Lock & Co.) Essay on America.

(154) *Huckleberry Finn*, by Mark Twain. Chapter XX.

(155) "General Gordon, Who he is and What he has done," by A. Egmont Hake. *The Graphic*, Volume XXIX, No. 746. March 15th, 1884. Page 266.

(156) *The Grand Old Man*, by George Edinger and E. J. C. Neep. (London: Methuen & Co., 1936.) Part II, Section VII, page 221.

(157) *Erewhon*, by Samuel Butler. (First published 1872.) Chapter XXIII.

(158) *Alps and Sanctuaries*, by Samuel Butler. (First published 1881.) Chapter V.

(159) "Some Curiosities of Modern Photography," by William G. Fitzgerald. *The Strand Magazine*, Volume IX, February, 1895, page 194.

(160) "The End of War," by James F. Sullivan. The Queer Side of Things. *The Strand Magazine*, Volume III, June, 1892, page 646. This article was included in a book by Sullivan entitled *Queer Side Stories*, published in 1900 by Downey & Company. (London.)

CHAPTER IX. MEMORIALS AND MONUMENTS

(161) *Personal and Professional Recollections*, by the late Sir George Gilbert Scott. (London: Sampson Low, Marston, Searle & Rivington, 1879.) Chapter VII, pages 263–64.

(162) *Ibid.*, Chapter V, page 225.

(163) "The Battlefield: A Pictorial Review of Victorian Manchester," by Cecil Stewart, M.A.(Manchester), D.A.(Edinburgh), F.R.I.B.A. *Journal of the Royal Institute of British Architects*, May, 1960, page 240.

(164) "The Profession of an 'Architect,' " reprinted from *The British Quarterly Review*, April, 1880, and included in *Six Essays*, by John T. Emmett. (London: Unwin Brothers, 1881.)

(165) Scott, *op. cit.*, Chapter VII, page 265.

(166) *Ibid.*, Chapter VII, pages 265–66.

(167) *Adam and Charles Black, 1807–1957. Some Chapters in the History of a Publishing House.* (London: A. & C. Black, 1957.) Section I, page 18.

(168) *Cassell's Household Guide.* (London: New and Revised edition, 1875.) Volume III, pages 344–46.

THE PLATES

The sixteen plates that follow have been selected to supplement and enlarge the scope of the drawings and engravings in the text, and to illustrate the subjects of the nine chapters. The architectural background of the Victorian scene in London and New York is suggested by the first two plates, thereafter various aspects of social life are shown, the components of cosiness and comfort in the home, the concessions to elegance, and monuments to the good and great. Beauty, gaiety and good design certainly existed in the Victorian period, also a great deal of happiness. The brightness of the picture was dimmed by the fact that there was far more ugliness than beauty, an immense amount of bad design, and far-reaching social misery.

Plate 1. THE VICTORIAN SCENE AND THE ARCHITECTURAL BACKGROUND

The Pentonville Road, with St. Pancras Station and Hotel in the distance, designed by Sir George Gilbert Scott (1866–70). The London mist has softened the harsh texture and abrupt angularities of this product of the Gothic Revival—one of the largest Victorian Gothic buildings in the world. *Reproduced by courtesy of the Trustees of the London Museum*, from an oil painting by John O'Connor, dated 1881.

NEW YORK CITY IN THE 1870's AND 1880's

Left: Wall Street.   *Right:* Trinity Church, fronting on Broadway and facing into Wall Street. Designed by Richard Upjohn, and completed in 1846.   *From a pictorial souvenir of New York, published about 1880.   In the author's possession.*

GRAND CENTRAL DEPOT.

Plate 2. The Grand Central Depôt, New York, erected at Forty-second Street in 1871.

Above and left: The New York Elevated Railroad, operated by steam.

From a pictorial souvenir of New York, published about 1880. In the author's possession.

Railway stations were used as sites for posters and permanent enamelled iron plates, advertising practically everything that could be bought and used. Reproduced from the frontispiece of *A History of Advertising*, by Henry Sampson (1874).

Plate 3. Third-class travel in the '50's. Brighton and Back for 3/6, painted by Charles Rossiter in 1859. *Reproduced by permission of the Museum and Art Gallery, Birmingham.*

Third-class travel in the '90's. Interior of a third-class dining saloon on the Great Northern Railway, *circa* 1898. *From a contemporary photograph, reproduced by courtesy of British Railways.* (See pages 157, 159 and 160.)

Plate 4. PUBLIC DRINKING FOUNTAINS

Above: The first public drinking fountain erected by the Metropolitan Drinking Fountain Association, 1859, at St. Sepulchre Church, Holborn Viaduct. *From a contemporary lithograph, in the author's possession.*

Above: Granite drinking fountain in Kensington Gardens; a standard design used in London parks and commons.

Right: Horse-trough and drinking fountain, Roehampton Gate, Richmond Park. Late nineteenth century. *Photographs by Richard C. Grierson, A.R.I.B.A.*

Plate 5. *Above and to the right:* The statue of George Peabody, the American philanthropist, behind the Royal Exchange, London. (See page 213.) One of the few seated statues.

Left: The memorial to Sir Richard Francis Burton, explorer, traveller and translator of the *Arabian Nights*. This stone and marble monument, representing an Arab tent, was erected by his widow in the Roman Catholic cemetery at Mortlake, in south-west London. (See pages 230 and 232.) *Photographs by Richard C. Grierson, A.R.I.B.A.*

Plate 6. PLEASURES OF THE PEOPLE

Derby Day, by William Powell Frith, painted in 1857. *Reproduced by courtesy of the Trustees of the Tate Gallery.*

Plate 7. PLEASURES OF THE PEOPLE

Ramsgate Sands, by William Powell Frith, exhibited at the Royal Academy in 1854 under the title of "Life at the Seaside."
Reproduced by gracious permission of Her Majesty the Queen. (See pages 171 and 172.)

"Many Happy Returns of the day," from the painting by William Powell Frith, dated 1856, now in the Corporation
Art Gallery, Harrogate, and reproduced here by their courtesy. The order, comfort, and quiet happiness of the
Victorian home are depicted by a master of realistic painting.

Plate 9.   VICTORIAN ELEGANCE
A Ball at Chiswick House, 1889, from a painting by Percy Charles Edward Bovill. The artist's father is portrayed, sitting in the foreground. *Reproduced by courtesy of the late P. J. Bovill, Esq., son of the artist.*

Left: Elegance before comfort. Papier-mâché chair in black, with painted decoration and mother of pearl inlay.

Right: Compromise with comfort. The frame is japanned black, the upholstery has a red Berlin wool background with multi-coloured bead embroidery, shading into grey and dark green. *Circa* 1850–60. *In the possession of Mrs. Grace Lovat Fraser.*

Plate 10

Above: A Shadow Box, dated 1851. The doll is surrounded by artificial flowers of cloth and painted paper. *In the possession of Mrs. Grace Lovat Fraser.*

Right: Cottage ornament, in white glazed pottery. The mantel-shelf of any cottage or small house in the west country would be thronged with ornaments of this kind: some crude, some comic, but all designed and made with gusto.

Plate 11. Two groups of Staffordshire ornaments. The Prince and Princess below on the right are obviously intended to represent the Prince of Wales and Princess Alexandra, whose marriage took place in 1863. The formal clothes of the period could be made as decorative as the more fanciful costumes of earlier times in the hands of the potters, who preserved throughout the nineteenth century a traditional convention of ornamental treatment.
In the possession of Mrs. Grace Lovat Fraser.

Plate 12

ON THE TABLE OR MANTEL-SHELF

Artificial flowers and leaves, some cut from coloured cloth, but mostly of knitting wool stitched over wire frames, and protected from dust by glass domes. (See page 40.) *In the possession of Mrs. Grace Lovat Fraser.*

ON THE SIDEBOARD

Cut glass mid-Victorian decanters: full-bellied, long-necked types, decorated with shallow oval cuts below and a small diaper pattern on the necks. *In the author's possession.*

ON THE DESK

Glass ink bottle, *circa* 1850, and spirit container with dipper for lighting cigars. *In the author's possession.*

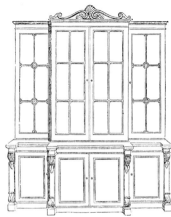

Plate 13. *Above:* A library bookcase in mahogany, with broken front, and attached Doric columns at angles of lower part. *Circa* 1835–45. (*In the possession of Bayliss, Jones & Bayliss Ltd., Wolverhampton.*)

Left and right: Designs for bookcases from Loudon's *Encyclopaedia of Cottage, Farm and Villa Architecture and Furniture* (1833).

Plate 14. A davenport in walnut with carved, cabriole legs supporting the desk: a restrained example of early Victorian cabinet-making. *Circa* 1845–50. The view above shows the rising nest of drawers flanked by pigeon-holes, and the sliding desk. The drawer fronts are of satinwood. In the base are four drawers, running the whole width of the piece, with dummy fronts on one side. On the left the detail of the carving shows a bold, precise interpretation of acanthus, floral and scroll motifs. (*In the possession of Stanley Pollitt, Esq.*) (See page 81.)

Plate 15. *Left:* A small mahogany sideboard with a shaped back, sparingly carved, showing the persistence of classical motifs. *Circa* 1845–50. (See page 87.)

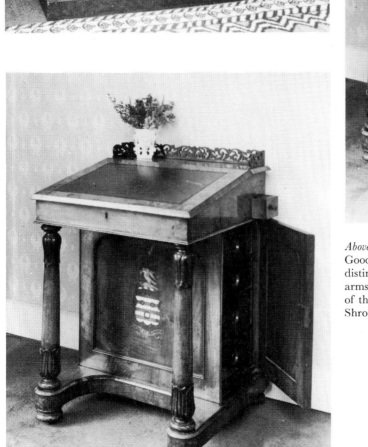

Above and left: Two views of a walnut davenport. Good proportions and a memory of classical elegance distinguished the columns supporting the desk. The arms and crest depicted on the panel below are those of the family of Harris of Cructon (or Cruckton) in Shropshire. *Circa* 1835–45. (*In the possession of Mrs. Alan Deller.*) (See page 81.)

Plate 16. TWO MONUMENTS TO THE
GOTHIC REVIVAL

Above: The Albert Memorial, designed by Sir George
Gilbert Scott (1810–77), and built in Kensington
Gardens between 1863 and 1872 at a cost of £120,000.
(See page 226.) *Photograph by Richard C. Grierson.*

Right: The Memorial to Sir Walter Scott in Prince's
Street Gardens, Edinburgh, designed by George Meikle
Kemp (1795–1844), and inaugurated by Adam Black,
the Provost, in 1846. (See page 228.) *Reproduced by
courtesy of the British Travel and Holidays Association.*

INDEX

Figures in italics refer to captions of illustrations
in the text.

I